5-20-76

REFUGEES FROM MILITARISM

Draft-Age Americans in Canada

by

Renée G. Kasinsky

Transaction Books
New Brunswick, New Jersey

Library of Congress Catalog Number: 75-46232.
ISBN: 0-87855-133-1.
Printed in the United States of America.

Library of Congress Cataloging in Publication Data

Kasinsky, Renée G.
    Refugees from militarism.

    Includes bibliographical references and index.
    1. Vietnamese Conflict, 1961—1975 —— Draft resisters.
2. Vietnamese Conflict, 1961—1975 —— Desertions. 3. Americans in Canada. I. Title.
DS559.8.D7K37   959.704'38   75-46232
ISBN 0-87855-113-1.

1924149

For Harold and my son, Yuri Benjamin, who hopefully will never have to make the painful choices these American refugees were forced to make

This study of American war refugees in Canada focuses on draft dodgers and deserters who emigrated or fled to Canada between 1965 and 1970. In 1970 there was an estimated 70,000 draft-age refugees in Canada, mostly draft dodgers, although beginning in 1969 the number of deserters began to surpass the dodgers. These men are "forgotten Americans" who have become profoundly disillusioned with the American dream and have come to Canada as pioneers seeking a new life. This book describes how these men made the decision to leave their home country and the consequences of that decision for their careers, identities, and "patriotism." It explores the impact they have made on Canadian life and the implications of their flight to Canada for the American government's handling of dissent to the Vietnam War.

From the point of view of the United States government, these refugees are felons who are in violation of the Selective Service Act but are permitted to utilize the escape hatch to Canada in order to diffuse their political protest. In Canada these men are officially recognized as persons eligible to apply for immigrant status. The men view themselves as political refugees.

In this book Dr. Kasinsky has utilized the interactionist approach. Direct observation across Canada and participation in Canadian groups aiding these refugees provided the largest source of data. She also made use of detailed questionnaires, taped in-depth interviews of diverse "social types," and utilized historical documentation to study more than 800 refugees with considerable cross-checking of data and conclusions.

The first section of the book focuses on the career routes of middle-class draft dodgers and working-class deserters, tracing the crucial episodes in their lives within the Armed Forces as well as their decision to leave the country. Canadian authorities' treatment of them is discussed in relation to Canada's economic and cultural dependency upon the United States. The second section explores the economic and social assimilation of Americans into Canadian life. As a result of forced emigration, many exiles are found to be more politicized and open to exploration of new life-styles. Dr. Kasinsky concludes that the large majority of refugees have successfully resettled in Canada, and, although they do want the right to travel freely to visit their families and friends, are not interested in securing amnesty to return to the United States.

Contents

Acknowledgments

I owe many thanks to all the American refugees who have shared their experiences with me over the years, most of whom have become new Canadians; and to the Vietnamese people, who, in their struggle for liberation, encouraged these Americans to begin their lives anew.

I have had no research assistants to lean on during the seven years it has taken to write this book. But thanks to my husband, Harold, who encouraged me throughout, I have had continual help in the form of intellectual stimulation, domestic assistance, child care and first-class editorial assistance. (The latter, he threatens, will have to last a lifetime!)

I have received helpful suggestions on an earlier draft from professors Anthony Platt and Jerome Skolnick, University of California, School of Criminology; Dorothy Smith, University of British Columbia; and Anthony Richmond, York University. An unidentified reviewer, M. Québecois, suggested the usefulness of the "marginal man" concept.

Invaluable assistance was given to me at various stages of the research by my good friends, Mary Sanchez, Michael Wong, Richard Sullivan, Darryl and Sheila Adams. I am thankful to Patricia Waldron for her careful typing of my manuscript, and to Irving Louis Horowitz, Susan Ferris, Scott Bramson, and Barbara Ciletti of Transaction Books for their help. My special thanks to Ken Nygaard for his imaginative diagram on the channeling of American youth and to Joyce Kasinsky who, among other things, corrected the proofs.

The research was supported by a grant from the Center for the Study of Law and Society, University of California, for which I thank Professor Sheldon Messinger. This book has been published with the help of a grant from the Social Science Research Council of Canada using funds provided by the Canada Council.

REFUGEES FROM MILITARISM

I

NEW CANADIANS AND THEIR AID GROUPS

1

Fugitives from Injustice

It was a typically wet January day in Vancouver, British Columbia, when three American deserters set out together to hitchhike to parts of eastern Canada in early 1970. They had heard from the rumor mill that there it was easier to get jobs in order to qualify for permanent residence status. Little did they suspect that that very evening they would find themselves in the custody of Royal Canadian Mounted Police (RCMP) officers who would deliver them across the American border at the Sumas crossing into the hands of the United States Shore Patrol. In short order their world had been turned upside down again. They were very far from their original destinations and no longer in the free zone north of the 49th parallel. In the course of a 48-hour period they had been illegally deported from Canada, placed in a Navy patrol van and sent to the military stockade at Ford Ord, California.

Of all the allegations of deserters being "shanghaied" across the border by Canadian officials cooperating with their American counterparts, this case alone has been publicly documented. It resulted in a federal judicial inquiry in Canada.

The three protagonists in this case were Army deserters who had enlisted under the pressure of the draft. None had completed high school and no one was over 22 years old. In almost all ways they were typical of the backgrounds of most deserters in Canada. John Kreeger came from Chico, California, an affluent community, although his family lived on welfare allotments. He had to hide this fact from his teachers in high school, who would have disapproved of his poverty. "My mother's a poor person living in a rich person's world," John said. In high school John's teachers and counselors made it clear to him that he was "wasting their time and that he could be serving his time in the Army and saving the taxpayer's money." Despite his protests, he was dropped from the school rolls and subsequently channeled into the military. He did not enlist, however, until he received his notice of induction. Upon enlisting in the Army, he made it clear that he would do "anything but the infantry." From the outset John never wanted to be a soldier, hoping he would receive a discharge for being excessively AWOL. During the time he was AWOL, he traveled in underground circles where he met many other AWOL GI's who were also trying to get out of the service. He survived by getting odd jobs and living off charity. John eventually met some people from the resistance in the San Francisco area and obtained access to the *Manual for Draft-Age Immigrants to Canada*. His attitude regarding desertion began to undergo a change. The first times he went AWOL he was told by those around him that it was a crime to desert from the Army; then he was being commended for his actions. John said of the resistance people:

> They were strong leftists, and they felt that you were doing your part for the country when you go AWOL and desert. I found this very strange. I had felt like it was bad, before, and after being with these people, it made me feel I was doing something good. I felt like it depends on how you look at it — it depends on which end you look at. It began to occur to me that it's really a crime to kill people in Vietnam. The government's been committing a crime in Vietnam.

Since John had been AWOL so long, he was convinced he would go to Leavenworth Federal Penitentiary if he returned to the Army. So he made the decision to "split" to Canada. He made use of the contacts of the underground railroad, staying in various homes of sympathizers along the western seaboard. He crossed the Canadian border legally as a visitor on January 16, 1970.

In Vancouver, John received immigration counseling at the Vancouver Committee to Aid American War Objectors and was referred to the hostel run by the American Deserters Committee. There he met two other deserters, also from California, who had been AWOL only a couple of weeks. He had been in Canada only three days when they made plans to leave Vancouver together.

Before the actual deportation occurred, John Kreeger, while still in custody, contacted a Unitarian minister, who contacted a lawyer, and together they made public their knowledge of the illegal deportation on CBC's *Weekend* national show. David Lewis, leader of the New Democratic Party (Canada's Labor party) in 1970, raised the issue in Parliament and stated that "it seems clear that whoever is responsible for the deportation has acted entirely illegally and reprehensibly." The public pressure by the NDP as well as citizens' groups like the British Columbia Civil Liberties Association resulted in a government judicial inquiry into the incident.[1] Meanwhile, the deserters escaped from military custody. Two were recaptured and the third, John Kreeger, managed to evade law enforcement authorities in the United States with support from friends and the underground. A month later he was helped to return to Canada legally in order to testify at the inquiry.

Judge Stewart, who conducted the inquiry, came to the conclusion that the three deserters had been unlawfully returned to the United States by RCMP constables in the presence of an immigration officer. However, he exonerated both the constables and the immigration officer. He argued that misunderstanding, confusion and coincidence were the reasons for the deportation and that it "was an isolated and unplanned incident." This became a contentious issue.

The outcome of the inquiry made a "special case" of John Kreeger. Although he was not given landed immigrant status because he did not qualify under the immigration point system that favored the educated, skilled immigrant, he received a special work permit unlike other deserters at the time. He became known to a number of professional people, including his lawyer, who helped him with legal problems, housing and references when he needed them. Most deserters did not have these kinds of contacts. Yet this did not help John to find a job and live an easy life. He was still a transient, unskilled youth and had a difficult time securing employment. It took six months of hard times before John located his first job at a Vancouver warehouse, beginning at the bottom of the pay scale with no union benefits. And there have been many lean days and short-term monotonous jobs since then.

In the fall of 1973 John began to feel more secure in Canada. A multicolored information center bus rolled up to John's corner in Vancouver, a working-class section where many immigrants lived. It carried the word of a 60-day amnesty for all those illegal immigrants and visitors who would be given the opportunity to become landed immigrants, regardless of their poor education and training. The glut of deportation appeals facing the appeals board made it impossible to obtain an appeal hearing for as long as a decade, necessitating a more lenient approach toward those illegal immigrants and visitors who came to Canada before November 30, 1972. John had read an advertisement concerning this Adjustment of Status Program. However, his prior experience made him mistrustful of the Department of Manpower and Immigration's intentions. It was only when the word came from the Canadian Coalition of War Resisters' information bus, sponsored as part of Immigration's $ 1.4 million advertising campaign, that John went down to the Vancouver immigration office to register and obtain landed immigrant status.[2]

Three years had passed since John was welcomed into Canada by the Vancouver Committee to Aid American War Objectors, only to be illegally deported. The activity of the aid groups had come full circle. They had begun as an informal assistance network for American war objectors and were officially regarded by Ottawa officials as antiestablishment protest groups. The aid groups had become so effective in their immigration counseling that the Canadian Immigration Department was forced to solicit their assistance and fund them for uncovering the thousands of illegal immigrants to whom the Canadian government offered amnesty. Thus within a seven-year period an oppositional movement had become part of established Canadian life.

The Vietnam War and Exile

The Vietnam War may well have been the most unpopular war in American history. In order to conduct it, it became necessary for the government to appeal to law and order and apply illegal measures to stifle ever-growing dissent and resistance.

The government found it necessary to end the draft, to offer conditional clemency for war resisters in order to placate hostile public opinion and eventually to extricate itself entirely from a direct military role in the conflict in Southeast Asia. The unpopularity of the war toppled two presidents from their high office; Lyndon Johnson by his refusal to run for another term and Richard Nixon by resignation upon exposure of his involvement in the Watergate scandal. Resistance to it was expressed by the opposition of young draft-age American men like John Kreeger who personally suffered the consequences of the war and its unpopularity. The resistance movement in the United States estimated that by 1974 approximately 200,000 men in America were either fugitives from the draft or the military, were awaiting trial or were in prison.[3]

Official government statistics from August 4, 1964, the date of the Tonkin Gulf resolution in the Senate, to December 29, 1972, the last day on which a registrant entered involuntarily into the Armed Forces, indicate that approximately 1.8 million men had been inducted.[4] By June 1973 the draft was nonexistent and in its place was a volunteer army. Approximately 8,000 men had been convicted for refusal to accept induction. Half of them had received probationary sentences, the other half served jail time.[5] As of January 1, 1974, official figures cited a total of 4,400 fugitives from the Selective Service System, of which an estimated 3,000 were in Canada.[6]

The number of desertions during the Vietnam War was even more indicative of the unpopularity of the war. Approximately half a million men deserted from all services for varying lengths of time. The high number of long term AWOLs far exceeded that of the Korean War and rose with the increasing public dissatisfaction of the Vietnam War.[7] At the end of 1973, official statistics reported almost 29,000 deserters at large, with some 2,000 believed to be in foreign areas.[8]

In summary, the government estimated in 1974 that between 5,000 and 6,000 Americans, both dodgers and deserters, were in exile in Canada. My own estimated figures of American refugees from both the Selective Service System and the military are at variance with the official government figures cited above. Using Canadian immigration statistics of draft-age American males during the Vietnam War years, I estimate that there are between 30,000 to 40,000 American exiles in Canada alone. The specific data that this estimate is based on will be examined in chapter 4. The official statistics for those men who had been fugitives from the draft and the military have been greatly deflated and do not properly present the widespread nature of dissent to the Vietnam War that existed among draft-age American youth during this period.

American war refugees in Canada fall into two distinct groups: draft dodgers and deserters. These were the descriptive terms used by Canadians to refer to these men, with no perjorative meaning intended. Between 1964 and 1974, they fled the United States and immigrated to Canada as an expression of their opposition to the Vietnam War.

How did these Americans view themselves in relation to the United States government and how did their refugee status affect their lives in Canada? To what extent did class and social background factors affect America's treatment of resisters and influence their careers in Canada? What sustained the successful refugee in exile in psychological and material terms and what kinds of aid did he receive? What impact have these men made on Canadian life? Did these political refugees successfully assimilate into Canadian life or did they try to return to the United States?

These men perceived themselves as persons who were caught in the dilemma of having to choose between obeying their consciences or obeying the rules of the state. The sons of the middle class who had a college education became draft dodgers when they were no longer favored by the deferrals of the Selective Service System. The sons of the lower income and working classes were inducted into the armed service directly from high school, or else they volunteered in the hope of obtaining a skill and traveling beyond their narrow life circumstances, and they became the deserters. The careers of both the draft dodgers and the deserters who made the lonely decision to leave for Canada will first be discussed. For the dodger this occurred when the Selective Service System interfered with his life and career aspirations; for the deserter, the break came when he was incorporated into the Vietnam War machine. Their personal confrontation with the draft and the Vietnam War helped these young men to define their beliefs and forced them into bold, assertive action in which they sought refuge in the "North Country Fair."

Once in Canada, however, these men had to apply for landed immigrant status and permanent residence. The draft dodgers were successful for the most part in obtaining such status, whereas the door was closed to the majority of deserters. These men began to realize that the channeling of the Selective Service System, which in the words of Lauter and Howe had "succeeded in drawing ever more sharply the lines of class in the United States,"[9] was being continued in Canada via the Canadian Immigration Act. The immigration system, heavily biased towards an individual's education, occupational training and skills, discriminated in favor of the educated, skilled draft dodger and against the working-class, unskilled, uneducated deserter.

The Canadian groups that helped these Americans resettle in Canada were initially organized as apolitical charitable organizations whose major objective was to obtain landed immigrant status (permanent residence) for all refugees seeking their help. However, when a large number of deserters who sought their aid were unsuccessful in obtaining immigrant status, these organizations were forced to become political pressure groups struggling against the continental channeling of draft dodgers and deserters.

The draft dodgers, then, for the most part, were able to start their new lives where they had left off, continuing their education, finding skilled and professional work or maintaining themselves as small entrepreneurs in the counterculture. The deserters continued to be fugitives, without landed immigrant status, with its consequences of living underground, unemployed and without roots, until an amendment of the Immigration Appeal Board Act in 1973 permitted all illegal visitors to obtain such status under relaxed criteria.

These American refugees became disillusioned and increasingly estranged from the mainstream of American society. As new pioneers they attempted to transplant the American dream onto their Canadian lives. Although most of the draft dodgers were successful in beginning their lives anew, most of the deserters were not able to get a foothold in Canada. Thus the question of amnesty and returning to the United States, for most of these refugees, was seen as a political question. They resisted any conditional amnesty, including President Ford's terms for 1975. Most draft dodgers indicated that they would not return to America to live, as they had already transplanted their lives. Only deserters who had not assimilated into Canadian life were tempted to return, although most did not because the terms did not accept the justice of their position in opposition to the Vietnam War. Those politically articulate refugees like Roger Williams, who wrote *The New Exiles* and who eventually succeeded in returning to the United States, explained that repatriation rather than amnesty was the issue at hand. "The question, really, is not whether or not anyone, or any government, has the right to prevent them from returning when they have done nothing in light of the Vietnam War, which can remotely be called a crime. They have the inalienable right to return."[10]

These young men stood at a unique moment in history. To comprehend their reasons for going into exile is to understand one of the major sociopolitical forces that shaped the lives of all draft-age American males in the Vietnam War period: the continental youth channeling system of North American capitalism. This system had a political, social and economic component. It was a system designed by the state (political) which manipulated the career patterns and life chances of draft-age youths (social) in order to integrate them into North American capitalism and to maximize its productive capacity (economic).

The channeling began with the Selective Service System exerting control over the career patterns and life chances of all draft-age American youth. It was designed to subordinate these youth to the interests of the American economy, an economy dominated by multinational corporations.[11] It then guided the dissidents of the Selective Service System into exile, creating both the middle-class draft dodger and the working-class deserter. It favored the dodger since his education and skills were of most use to the economy. This selection process based upon distinctions of class (education and occupation skills) was continued in Canada vis-à-vis the Immigration Act and Canada's branch plant economy. United States-based multinational corporations were able to channel dissident youth from the motherland and reintegrate the middle-class dodger into the branch plant economy of Canada, which was under their economic control. Thus the story of America's refugees from militarism represents the intersection of personal biography with social history. The experiences of these Americans stand witness to one of the central conflicts of our time in the West: the struggle between individual conscience and the political aspirations of the state.

An Observer's View

I spent six years in Canada as a participant observer, from the summer of 1969 through 1975, interviewing and meeting with American refugees. Research on those who were fugitives was a very sensitive area; the importance of trust and rapport was critical in obtaining the most minimal personal information. Due to their suspicion of outsiders, survey techniques proved to be an ill-suited method of obtaining information about political refugees. Many had extremely distrustful feelings regarding their exile status and could not afford to reveal information about themselves to an anonymous researcher whose motives they suspected and whose use of the data obtained was unknown. Therefore, an important aspect of my observation method was to establish a trusting relationship with individuals and groups over a sustained period of time so that I could observe representative and uncensored behavior. For this study, being a woman was a distinct advantage in establishing the necessary rapport with these American refugees. I was not subjected to as much questioning, especially with regard to the possibility of my being an undercover FBI agent or spy for the American government, as were male observers. It was also less embarrassing to those men who felt uncertain or ashamed of their actions to disclose their feelings to a woman who was not perceived as a competitor, or as someone who would pass judgment on their choice because he might have acted differently himself with regard to his own military status.

My home base was Vancouver, British Columbia, the major port city in western Canada, where American refugees flocked by the thousands due to the relatively mild climate and the spectacular countryside. More than two-thirds of my direct observation was done in Vancouver, although I spent much time during these years in the major cities of Toronto, Ottawa and Montreal, where the major American refugee aid groups were located. Since

I was an American citizen who had immigrated to Canada around the same time as the start of my study, I experienced many of the same problems these young Americans faced in getting settled in a new country. I had to find a place to live, obtain landed immigrant status, get a job, begin making new friends and reorient myself to a different country. But since I was not a fugitive from justice, I did not have to use underground contacts in coming to Canada as some of these Americans did. Neither was my choice in coming to Canada forced on me by the lack of any viable alternatives in the United States other than jail or the military. I was not cut off from my friends and relatives and could easily cross the border and return freely to the States — a simple act that most of these men could not do without risking arrest.

My methodology consisted of observing the total process whereby these Americans first became political refugees to their eventual assimilation in varying degrees into Canadian life. To observe the first part of this process, I became a volunteer worker at the Vancouver Committee to Aid American War Objectors, doing a variety of routine tasks such as sending out replies to incoming correspondence from Americans inquiring about Canada and answering phone calls. This gave me the opportunity to casually chat with newcomers, observe their interaction with the aid of counselors, and generally learn about the functioning of the aid group. The aid group was often the first contact with their newly adopted country and helped place these newcomers in private homes or refugee hostels for the first few weeks. In addition to direct observation, I used a historical approach to describe the refugee aid organizations in Canada since their inception in 1966.

During 1969 and 1970, at the height of the emigration, I systematically spent time at some of the refugee hostels in Vancouver, chatting with the occupants and observing some of their activities. I regularly attended house meetings, gatherings and public places where many of these Americans congregated. I also attended special meetings and conferences for American refugees and their supporters. As a sympathetic party, I had a number of American refugees living in my home for their first weeks in Canada during the duration of my research. I made close relationships with some of these individuals. Some of them have been key informants, discussing with me the implications of my findings and suggesting new issues I had overlooked. Still other major discoveries were made accidentally as I was hitchhiking or traveling through Canada while on holidays from my work.

Although the direct observation method afforded me a large range of detailed interaction data on American refugees, there were some things it could not answer. It did not allow me to contact a large sample of individuals and one that was as representative as possible. Thus, in order to obtain more systematic information, I supplemented my observation methods with a detailed eight-page questionnaire (see Appendix A). It was organized according to experiences and crucial episodes which had structured the lives of American refugees while they were involved with the draft, the military and Canadian activities. This I gave as an interview schedule to 123 American refugees from the four major Canadian cities in 1970. It consisted of one-half draft resisters and one-half deserters. An attempt was made to include a diverse group, taking into consideration the length of time an individual had been in Canada, regional differences and men who settled in different areas in Canada. These persons were obtained by the "snowballing technique" in which the first few refugees who participated often volunteered their friends and suggested other refugees whose experience was different from their own.

To obtain a somewhat larger sample I also cross-checked some of my information with another questionnaire that was administered by the counselors of the Vancouver Committee to all those men who sought their aid over a two-month period in the summer of 1970.[12] I tallied approximately 425 questionnaires from this source to compare with my own sample.

In addition to the questionnaires, I taped 30 in-depth interviews across Canada with refugees whom I determined to be representative of diverse social types. The interviews probed complex questions on identity and labeling which I was not able to fully explore through field observations or questionnaires. In total, I contacted over 1,200 American refugees across Canada through these three research approaches. The methods of direct observation and the historical approach, when combined with the analysis of questionnaires and in-depth interviews, permitted a systematic study with considerable cross-checking of data and conclusions.

Social Background of American Refugees

Who were the young men that fled to Canada, either to dodge the draft or to desert from The American Armed Forces? To understand them we must look at the individual and social biographies of these young refugees from militarism. The picture we have in our minds based on newspaper and magazine accounts is that most of these young men were radicals of the New Left or hippies who had given up their hope in the American dream. Such a view has not been substantiated. These new immigrants to Canada represented a diverse section of the American youth population as a whole. The first pamphlet of the Canadian aid groups entitled "Escape from Freedom" summed up this diverstiy of American draft dodgers and commented upon their distinctly American origins:

> For one thing, this is the first group of immigrants from the States who can't be stamped with a specific political, social or religious stripe. They are as diverse as Americans themselves; a composite portrait simply cannot be drawn. But certain outlines do emerge. They are the best educated group of immigrants Canada has ever had. ... But the most striking thing is how "American" draft resisters are in most respects. Perhaps what some would call their weakness is that they believe in all the things America is supposed to stand for. Among them are those who would have been America's original thinkers and pioneer spirits.[13]

Let us now look at the background characteristics of the refugees revealed by my questionnaire and interview data obtained during the peak of emigration by draft-age American males to Canada. In my questionnaire sample, one-third of these men had grown up in the western part of the United States. This bias toward westerners was due in part to my sampling technique, as the bulk of the interviews were held in British Columbia. Almost another third of these men had home towns in the northwestern part of the United States. The South and the Midwest were each represented in about 20 percent of the cases. Almost two-thirds of these men came from urban areas. Their average age was 22, with the deserters being a few years younger than the draft dodgers. Most of the men were single. Of the third who were married, most were dodgers. Most of the refugees had American citizenship but there were some Canadian refugees returning home to Canada who had been living in the United States. These Canadians were called by the Selective Service System; they failed to report and were classified as fugitives.[14] There were also seven young men who were aliens living in America and who also had been drafted. An additional seven men were former American citizens who had renounced their citizenship and were also classified as aliens by the Selective Service System.[15]

Almost all of the refugees were white Americans, black Americans accounting for only 3 percent of my sample. From participant observation and my interviews with counselors and other refugees, it is clear that this number of black refugees was representative of the low percentage of blacks who had sought emigration as a solution to their draft or military problems. Those blacks who did come to Canada were from middle-class backgrounds and almost all of them had one to two years of college. Fifty percent of my sample were of Anglo-Saxon descent and fifteen percent were of Eastern

European descent. The remaining refugees had German, Italian, Scandinavian, Indian, Irish and Latin backgrounds.

About two-thirds of the refugees claimed to have no formal religious affiliation. Of those who did, the descending order of preference was Protestant, Catholic and Jewish in the ratio of 4:2:1. Other religions represented included Buddhist, Quaker and Unitarian. Significantly, however, almost half of the refugees felt that religion was important to them, even though only one-third professed formal religious ties as we have noted. The great majority of the parents of the refugees professed some form of formal religious affiliation in the same ratio as their sons, with only 15 percent claiming to have no religious affiliation. This suggested that the religious young men had not departed from the religions of their parents, though there seemed to be an increasing profession of nonattachment to formal religions with succeeding generations. Those men who grew up in religious homes assumed their religious nonconformism as a reflection of their own thinking and development.

Thus it would seem that the refugees' value orientations and beliefs were more crucial than such personal and social characteristics as his geographical location, ethnicity and class in distinguishing him from his parent's generation and his American peers.

Both draft dodgers and deserters had certain common experiences and values that distinguished them from their parents and their peers. They rebelled against their upbringing for the most part and adopted different values and life-styles from their parents. Let us examine the manner in which these men articulated their value distinctions from their parents.

I asked the men to indicate their life-style in a few words and to indicate the life-style of their parents. The responses to these questions indicated strong contrasting value systems. Some of the most vivid responses were found in the following list of expressions, the first one referring to the refugee's life-style and the second referring to that of his parents:

drifter/stable middle class
moving to farm/moved from farm to city
casual/uptight
moving/stagnant
transient/settled

These terms all related to a type of motion or movement. The active, unbound, exploratory movements of the refugee contrasted sharply with the restrained, "stagnant" life-style that described his parents. The second list of expressions related to the differences in values between the refugee and his

parents:
    freethinking/conformist
    freaky/straight
    free/comfortably limited
    radical/moderate
    nonconformist/traditionalist
    communal/capitalistic

The "inner-directed," free-thinking man, personifying the refugee, contrasted with the man who derived his values from the consumer-oriented marketplace, one whom David Reisman referred to as "other-directed."[16]

Many of these Americans dissented in their opinions from those of their peers within their communities. These young refugees indicated in their personal histories and decisions that they should be characterized as nonconformists within their peer group. In relation to their colleagues in the universities or in the military, they were either singled out or felt themselves to behave and think differently from those persons around them. Often, their opinions against the war in Vietnam served to articulate distinctive values, especially in those areas of the South and Midwest where there was relatively little dissent against the war in the early years. Some of them were cut off from their families and hometowns because of their nonconformist ideas and behavior. Others were subjected to strong pressures from their friends when these friends learned of their decision to come to Canada. For example, a black draft dodger reported that his friends accused him of coming to Canada because he was trying to become like "Whitey."

Statistical data supported the theory that these refugees were independent nonconformists (see Table 1, Appendix B).[17] The majority of Americans stated that they were little influenced by what others thought of their decision to leave the country. This demonstrated that their decisions to a large extent reflected their own thought and determination of action. Comparing dodgers to deserters reflected that a higher percentage of the deserters, 39 percent compared with 24 percent of the dodgers, were influenced in their decision to leave the country. This was indicative of the greater degree of pressure on men in the military to conform. In contrast, dodgers were usually students and conformity was not the valued norm for them, at least in philosophical terms.

In addition to having a common background of nonconformist views and actions both the draft dodger and deserter in Canada shared another important characteristic in common, namely, that their flight to Canada was in most cases the first political act of significance in their lives. These men could not be branded as political activists for the most part. Although almost all of them were opposed to the Vietnam War, most of them were not leaders in the resistance movement or antiwar activities either on or off the campus. Most of them participated in one or two large peace demonstrations but for the most of them, this was the first time they had to make a major decision of a political nature. The chief exceptions to this generalization were those draft dodgers who came to Canada in the early period of 1965—67, as well as those derserters who came to Canada during 1968—70. Their actions will be discussed in chapter 2.

One-half of the refugees defined themselves as "radical," including a few as socialists, anarchists and communists. Another quarter described themselves as "apolitical." These latter individuals favored a radical life-style but claimed that they were "beyond politics" or explained that everything in their lives was political. The remaining quarter was predominantly "liberal" with only a few persons describing themselves as "conservative." This political grouping was the opposite of the parents' political orientation, as seen through the eyes of their sons. One-half of the parents were characterized as political conservatives, among them John Birchers, Reagan and Wallace supporters. One-quarter of these men described their parents as liberal and the remaining quarter divided between "apolitical" and "no reply" with only 4 percent of the parents referred to as "political radicals."

Another major area in which dodgers and deserters were similar was that they had neither a criminal background nor an extensive record of previous convictions. The Vancouver Committee sample, together with my sample, indicated that out of a total of 400 refugees who were asked if they had ever been convicted, only 44 men or 5 percent indicated convictions other than parking tickets. The largest majority of these convictions were for petty theft or misdemeanor charges. Approximately 20 were arrested for drug-related charges, mainly the possession of marijuana. Two deserters had been convicted for grand larceny; however, in some states possession of marijuana was considered a felony. The number of convictions among these men did not appear to be overly high for their age range, considering that most of the laws they had violated discriminated against youth as a group.

American refugees, therefore, were similar in most ways to their youthful counterparts in the United States with the exception that they were for the most part nonconformists with strong views against the war. More importantly, however, there were striking differences between the draft dodgers and the deserters in terms of their social background and their career routes to Canada.

The major difference between the dodgers and deserters who came to Canada lies in the circumstances under which they were channeled into the Selective Service System and into the military. The deserters were more recent arrivals in Canada. Although the draft dodgers had sought refuge in Canada since 1965, deserters only began coming to Canada in larger numbers since 1968. Fifty-nine percent of the draft dodgers in my sample had been in Canada from one to three years, whereas only 21 percent of the deserters had been in Canada that long (see Table 2, Appendix B).[18]

A number of factors explain why deserters came to Canada later than the draft dodgers. In the United States, newspapers daily carried stories about war atrocities until the public began to see through the maze of propaganda and generally became more favorable toward the antiwar position. The year 1968 saw the development of resistance groups against the draft and, concurrently, the beginnings of a GI movement against the war. Resistance In the Army (RITA) began an underground press whose primary circulation was directed to GI's. RITA made its presence felt on all major military bases in the form of informal coffeehouses. In Canada, more information about emigration as an alternative to the draft was making its way into resistance circles in the United States from those first resisters who had organized refugee aid organizations. The media carried stories on these men and their organizations, letting other men know there was a way out.

Generally, the deserters who came to Canada during 1966—70 were younger than those draft dodgers who emigrated during this period[19] (see Table 3, Appendix B). When I compared my sample taken in the winter of 1969 with the Vancouver Committee sample taken in the Summer of 1970 a striking difference could be seen in the younger age group of men 17 to 20 years. In my sample only 17 percent of the total number of dodgers and deserters fell within this age group, whereas in the Vancouver Committee sample almost half (43 percent) of the men were between the ages of 17 and 20. In their sample were 127 draft dodgers; none were in this age group in my sample. Here was a strong indicaton of the effect of the new draft lottery system, initiated in January 1970, in which the burden of the draft was designed to weigh most heavily on the younger men. It was also noteworthy that 10 percent of individuals over 26 used the Vancouver Committee to aid them in immigrating to Canada.[20]   Among this group were families with young sons, veterans, a number of whom had already served in Vietnam, all receiving honorable discharges. Fifty-three women, almost all of whom were single, also filled out questionnaires at the Vancouver Committee during these months.[21] All of these diverse groups together represented the broadening of the spectrum of political refugees seeking aid from the Canadian groups in Canada in the early 1970s.

The most important difference between the dodgers and the deserters was in the social class of these men. Since education has traditionally been an important index of relative class position in our society, the educational background of their parents reveals this difference (Table 4, Appendix B). The data of Table 4 indicate that the parents of dodgers had considerably more college education than the parents of deserters. Two-thirds of the parents had some college experience or had obtained their college degrees, the latter group accounting for about half the total sample. By way of contrast, deserters' families having college experience or college degrees made up only about one-third of the total sample. The bulk of such families, about two-thirds, had only some high-school experience or a high-school diploma.

A comparison of the occupational levels of parents of American refugees yielded similar findings (see Table 5, Appendix B). The bulk of the dodger families, about two-thirds, were skilled tradesmen, professionals or managers, whereas these categories encompassed only half of the deserters' families. The other half of the latter group were in the unskilled or semiskilled category, as compared with only about one-third of the dodgers' parents.

Thus we can conclude generally that on the basis of their socioeconomic level of education and occupation, dodgers' parents tended to be middle and upper class, and deserters' families tended to come from the working class. This conclusion agreed with the findings of Kenneth Emerick who surveyed 33 exiles in 1970, as well as many other journalistic observations of these men.[22]

What these latter observers had not sufficiently characterized, however, and what showed up clearly in my data, was the size of the minority in the sample. I noted that about one-third of the deserters' families had some college experience and were in the skilled or professional category. The class distinction between the dodgers and the deserters became more apparent when we considered the educational and occupational levels of the dodgers and deserters themselves. As we might expect, these tended to correlate fairly closely with those of their parents.

The results of my questionnaire regarding the educational and occupational status of the refugees (see Tables 6 and 7, Appendix B) substantiated the claim made by the refugee aid groups that these men were quite educated. My data also verified that there was a strong class distinction between the dodgers and the deserters. While 90 percent of the dodgers had some college experience, 64 percent having acquired bachelor's of arts or professional degrees, only one-half of the deserters had college experience, with most of them only having one or two years in a junior or technical college. As one's educational level closely correlated with one's occupational level in an urban technological society, the occupational data closely paralleled the educational portraits of these men. My data showed that whereas only 5 percent of the dodgers had full-time unskilled or semiskilled work, almost half of the deserters had such unskilled or semiskilled work. Almost all of the dodgers were full-time students or engaged as skilled tradesmen or professional workers.

The Vancouver Committee data on both the educational and occupational levels of these men substantiated the overall conclusions of my data. Since it was approximately three times the size of my sample and represented more of a random sample of refugees collected over a two-month period, it was probably more representative of the larger community of American refugees in Canada (see Tables 6 and 7, Appendix B).[2 3]

Another major difference between the draft dodger and the deserter stemmed from his relation to American law and his experience with jail. A total of 30 men out of my sample of 123 indicated that they had spent time either in jail or in a military stockade, or had received an indictment for their arrest by the FBI for desertion or dodging the draft. Of these men, 20, or two-thirds of them, were deserters. The actual proportion of deserters was probably even higher; many of them indicated that they did not know if they had been indicted, since they had been "on the lam" in the United States and had been living "underground." The use of underground contacts in coming to Canada was also more frequent among deserters than among dodgers. Table 8 (Appendix B) shows that almost three times the number of deserters than dodgers made use of underground contacts in coming to Canada. Two major factors seemed to be involved here. Because a higher number of deserters had been indicted and were being sought by the FBI, they were forced to take more precautions and to be more secretive in their relations and not to rely upon their known friends and acquaintances. Also, there seemed to be a more concerted effort in the various movement and GI counseling groups to direct GI's to Canada and supply them with a list of underground stops and contacts. Resisters or dodgers, especially those who had not already resisted or refused induction, were discouraged from coming to Canada by these movement groups.

It is clear that the deserters were relative newcomers to Canada, coming in larger numbers only since 1968. They tended to rely, more than the dodgers, upon underground contacts in making their way to Canada. They were generally a couple of years younger than the dodgers, though this began to alter as younger men were drafted by the lottery system in 1970. The middle-class background of the dodger and the working-class background of the deserter was the most crucial factor, however, for the individual's relationship to the Selective Service System. In the next chapter we will examine that relationship and explain the crucial episodes that channeled both of these refugee groups to Canada.

NOTES

1. A step-by-step recounting of the series of events that led to the deportation based on the testimonies presented at the federal judicial inquiry is presented in chapter 8.
2. *Vancouver Sun*, October 1, 1973.
3. *Hearings* before the Subcommittee on Courts, Civil Liberties and the Administration of Justice of the Committee on the Judiciary. House of Representatives, 93rd Congress (Washington, D.C.: U.S. Government Printing Office, 1974), p. 794.
4. "Vietnam War Draft Evaders and Deserters: An Official Count," *Congressional Digest* (October 1974), p. 230.
5. Administrative Office of the United States Courts, Washington, D.C.
6. *Congressional Digest*, p. 230.
7. Korean AWOL rates (absentees per thousand men) compared to Vietnam AWOL rates:

1952 — — — — 22.0	1968 — — — — 29.1
1953 — — — — 22.3	1969 — — — — 42.4
1954 — — — — 15.7	1970 — — — — 52.3
	1971 — — — — 73.5

Jack Calhoun, "AWOLs: What They're Like," *AMEX 3* (January—February 1973): 48.
8. *Hearings* before the Subcommittee on Courts, Civil Liberties, and the Administration of Justice, testimony of Walter H. Morse, General Counsel, U.S. Selective Service System.
9. Paul Lauter and Florence Howe, *The Conspiracy of the Young* (New York: World Publishing Co., 1970), p. 193.
10. Roger N. Williams, *The New Exiles* (New York: Liveright, 1971), p. 401.
11. Irving Louis Horowitz, "Capitalism, Communism and Multinational-

ism," *Society* (Jan./Feb. 1974): p. 32—43. In this article, Horowitz sum-
marizes the characteristics of multinational corporations. He feels that the
"emergence of the multinational corporation is the paramount economic
fact of the present epoch. . .What we have now is economics as a managed,
manipulated form of political exploitation and domination" (pp. 32, 33).

12.   The Vancouver Committee questionnaire can be found in Appendix B.

13.   "Escape from Freedom" or "I Didn't Raise My Boy to be a Canadian,"
published by SUPA, Toronto, 1967.

14.   Not all the Canadians who found themselves in the clutches of Uncle
Sam's army decided to leave the country. At least eight of them took up
American citizenship after having fought in Vietnam. *Vancouver Sun,*
December 1970. A number of them died on the battlegrounds in Viet-
nam.

15.   According to the U.S. Nationality Act, expatriation was a right. If your
renunciation was accepted (and Congress had the right to decline to permit
renunciation "in times of stress"), the individual was given the classification IV-C and was subject to the laws of the U.S. as an alien. American
citizens were not encouraged by the Canadian aid groups to renounce
their citizenship until they obtained Canadian citizenship.

16.   David Reisman, *The Lonely Crowd* (New Haven, Conn.: Yale University Press, 1950).

17.   All of the tables can be found in Appendix B.

18.   Table 2, Appendix B. We can see this time differential in Table 2, obtained from data in 1969.

19.   The data of Table 3, Appendix B, indicated that if we compared the
draft dodgers with the deserters in my sample we found that whereas 29
percent of the deserters were in the 17—20 age bracket, only 2 percent of
the dodgers were represented in the same age group. These statistics are
also a measure of how long these men had been in Canada, as the draft
dodgers were resident in Canada longer than the deserters.

20.   J. McRee Elrod, an older war objector, wrote an interesting piece,
"The Over-Draft Age War Objector in Canada," found in Kenneth P. Em-
erick, *War Resisters Canada* (Knox, Pennsylvania: Free Press, 1972),
Appendix E, pp. 314—17.

21.   During the Vietnam War era, American women of ages 15 to 29 who
received landed immigrant status in Canada exceeded that of draft-age
American men. See Canadian Immigration Statistics, 1960—1975 (Ottawa:
Queen's Printer, 1975).

22.   Kenneth Fred Emerick, *War Resisters Canada* (Knox, Pennsylvania:
Free Press, 1972), pp. 17—21, 23—28. See Table F, Parental Education,
Occupation and Current Income, p. 18. See also: Roger N. Williams, *The*

New Exile; Jim Christy, *The New Refugees* (Peter Martin Associates, 1972): Frank H. Epp, ed., *I Would Like to Dodge the Draft Dodgers But* (Conrad Press, 1970); Richard L. Killmer, Robert S. Lecky and Debrah S. Wiley, *They Can't Go Home Again* (Pilgrim Press, 1971); James Reston, Jr., *The Amnesty of John David Herndon* (New York: McGraw-Hill, 1973): Murray Polner, *When Can I Come Home?* (New York: Doubleday-Anchor, 1972); Arlie Schardt, William Rusher and Mark O. Hatfield, *Amnesty? The Unsettled Question of Vietnam* (Croton-on-Hudson, N.Y.: Sun River Press, 1973); documents found in *Amnesty Hearings*, Subcommittee on Courts, Civil Liberties, and the Administration of Justice, 93rd Congress (Washington, D.C.: U.S. Government Printing Office, 1974).

23.   The class distinctions between the dodgers and deserters appear in an even sharper manner in the Vancouver Committee's data than in my own sample. In comparison with their data, my sample tends to be skewed in the direction of the more educated dodgers and deserters. For example, my data indicated that approximately half of the deserters had some college education, two-thirds of them being high-school graduates only or dropouts. My data indicated that half of the deserters had unskilled jobs whereas the Vancouver Committee's data showed that two-thirds of the deserters held unskilled jobs.

2

Career Routes of American Refugees

The Selective Service System and Youth Channeling

The effect of the Selective Service System was to channel the manpower aspirations of millions of American youth. The basic assumptions and goals underlying its policies were bluntly stated in a most revealing document entitled "Channeling" issued in July 1965 by General Hershey, head of the system from 1935–71.[1] This document revealed that in addition to delivering men into the Armed Forces, the Selective Service System served also to control the lives and life choices of millions of young Americans by the manipulative use of the draft and its deferral and exemption system.

The meaning of the word "service" with its former restricted application to the Armed Forces, is certain to become widened much more in the future. This brings with it the ever-increasing problem of how to control effectively the service of the individuals who are not in the Armed Forces. It is in dealing with these other millions of registrants that the system is heavily occupied, developing more effective human beings in the national interest.[2]

Thus, much of the energies of the Selective Service went toward directing the lives of civilian men in order to promote the country's "health, safety and interest."

The "deferment carrot" under the threat of induction was utilized to direct young men into certain occupations and activities in the "national interest," as defined by the Selective Service. "Service" was synonymous with those professions such as engineering, the sciences and teaching, considered "the ultimate in their expression of patriotism" because they were the new fields involved in the manipulation and social control of the population to serve the ends of the American government. According to "Channeling," many young men would not have pursued a higher education if there had not been a program of student deferment. Many young scientists, engineers and other men would not have remained in the defense effort were it not for a program of occupational deferment. Others would not have joined VISTA or the Peace Corps, which were also defined as critical occupations in the national interest. These men entered these activities in order to remove themselves from the "warm room" leading to induction into the Armed Forces.

If a man decided that he would take control over his own life disregarding this "pressurized guidance" system, he was denied a deferment. The "Channeling" document explicitly warned that "the loss of deferred status was the consequence for the individual who has acquired the skill and either does not use it or uses it in a nonessential activity."[3] Thus the draft served to facilitate control over the careers of all young men by explicitly tracking youth into occupations believed to be in the interest of the state in return for deferments. In this manner, the Selective Service System was used by the American government to exert social control over the entire male youth population.

Let us now examine how the Selective Service System exerted its control differentially upon the middle-class student and the working-class man to create separate classes of draft dodgers and deserters. I will discuss each career separately, as the crucial episodes that describe the experiences of those who remained civilians were quite different from those who became soldiers.

Career of the Draft Dodger

For the draft resisters, the initial precipitating event on the road to emigration was usually dropping out of school. This brought about the loss of their student deferment with reclassification to 1-A status. Reasons given for leaving school included the following: lack of interest in their classes, involvement in more interesting political activity, involvement in the youth and drug subculture which widened their perceptions of nonacademic interests, a reaction against channeling into occupations their parents and society approved but in which they were basically uninvolved. Upon receiving their 1-A reclassification they were forced into a consideration of the alternatives open to them. Some sought solutions within the established structure of the Selective Service System by applying for conscientious objector's status or for medical and physical exemptions. Other individuals, whose objection was to the system at large and not just to their classification in itself, sought solutions outside of and in direct opposition to the Selective Service, such as refusing induction, burning their draft cards or appealing to the courts through legal actions against their draft boards.

In addition to these incidents, many persons cited other political events related to the war and the repressive atmosphere in the United States which alienated them further from their country. These included the 1968 Democratic National Convention in Chicago where the brutal beating of the protesters by the Chicago police occurred, the People's Park struggle in Berkeley with the killing of an innocent bystander, as well as rumors of concentration camp preparations for protesters and racial strife in the cities. These advanced their increasing awareness of the deterioration of the democratic process in the United States. All of these events, in conjunction with their own precarious situation with Selective Service, caused them to turn their sights northward.

The majority of those draft resisters who sought refuge in Canada were in the danger zone. Of those men I interviewed, one-third of the total number of 62 men had already been ordered for induction, and half had indicated that they expected to be inducted soon. The other 20 percent had deferrals and were not in immediate danger of being drafted, yet neither were they exempt. Most of them had difficulties with their draft board in order to maintain their deferrals before they finally decided it was necessary to leave their country.

A little more than half of the men in my sample who had not yet been inducted had corresponded with the draft boards while they were in Canada. Some of them were appealing their cases and hoped to be reclassified as conscientious objectors. Others just wrote to inform their local board of their new address and that they would not be returning; then their cases could be closed. A few sent vindictive letters condemning their boards for participation in the Vietnam War.

Two-thirds of these men stated that they had been active in the antiwar or civil-rights movement activities in recent years. However, contrary to popular

belief they were not leaders or campus activists. Most of them had participated in one or two peace marches against the war, while only a quarter of
them indicated that they had been active organizers in Students for a Democratic Society (SDS) and the resistance movement. Five of them had spent
some time in VISTA or the Peace Corps in order to obtain a deferral while
doing work they would enjoy; nine men indicated that they had been involved in some aspect of the civil-rights movement.

Robert Fulford, a leading Canadian journalist, suggested in an article in
Saturday Night, a liberal Canadian magazine, that the first wave of draft
dodgers between 1966 and 1967 consisted of articulate radicals who had
moved to Canada out of the university ferment and protests of the antiwar
movement. But he stated that by 1968 a draft dodger could be almost anybody — an ambitious sportscaster, a printing salesman, or an ex-*Playboy*
editorial assistant. One man he spoke with was "a believer in capitalism, armies and the draft" and another was "a follower of Ayn Rand."[4] A more
systematic study was done by Robert Akakia, a draft dodger and philosophy
student who gave a questionnaire to 100 dodgers aided by the Toronto Anti-
Draft Program in 1967. He concluded that over half of them were "radical
activist types."[5] The political distinction between the earlier and later draft
dodgers was validated by my own interviews with these men. My questionnaire indicated that over two-thirds of the early draft dodgers who came to
Canada between 1966 and 1967 were actively involved in movement activities
in the States (see Table 9, Appendix B). When asked if they had been classified as "delinquent" by their local draft board as a result of their antiwar
activities, 16 men indicated that they had. Of those men who were delinquent, 11 of them were from the early years and only five of them were newcomers. The use of the draft to punish political activists opposed to the draft
and the war was the only case in which the draft rules functioned in a deliberately negative way against the white middle-class student.[6] An example from
my interviews demonstrates the kinds of actions that were subject to punishment by the Selective Service System before the 1970 Supreme Court ruling
made this punishment illegal: Michael joined the Peace Corps in the summer
of 1966 to avoid the draft, was given a II-A occupational deferral and sent to
India. "After two months in India, they kicked me out of the Peace Corps.
They didn't like me because I was too politically involved and wouldn't play
their game," he explained. When he returned, he didn't tell his draft board of
this change. However, someone informed on him, he lost his deferral and was
reclassified 1-A. After 1970, Michael could no longer be legally classified 1-A

for his action since the Supreme Court ruled it was illegal to use the draft to punish political resisters.[7]

The rate of draft violation indictments in the United States in 1970 was about six times higher than during World War II or the Korean War. Between 1965 and 1970, the annual number of criminal indictments increased ten times for Selective Service violations. By no means, however, were all the men investigated eventually tried, convicted or jailed. In a study of Selective Service prosecutions in the northern district of California it was found that for the years 1967 and 1968 there were 98 defendants indicted. Of these 30 percent pleaded guilty, 39 percent were found guilty and 31 percent had the indictment dismissed or were acquitted, yielding a conviction rate of 69 percent. The rest of the country showed a conviction rate of 66 percent during this period.[8] As a general rule, the defendants who made the most numerous and detailed claims for deferments, particularly conscientious objector exemptions, had the best chance of getting acquitted. Also a number of Selective Service decisions by the courts since 1968 tended to decrease the conviction rate.[9]

Only one-third of the individuals in my sample indicated that they had been indicted on draft violation charges. This finding was substantiated by another independent study of draft dodgers in Toronto. The author stated that by 1967 the Justice Department had signed warrants for the arrest of only 75 of the some 10,000 draft exiles estimated to be in Canada at that time.[10] A greater proportion of the draft dodgers who received indictments were from the early period of 1965–67. The larger numbers of individuals refusing induction, or not even appearing for their induction and fleeing to Canada, accounted for the backlog of cases and the lengthy time before an indictment was issued. Many of these cases were lost somewhere along the way. For example, by the summer of 1970, well over 4,000 men along with several women accused of destruction of draft records had been convicted of Selective Service violations. Four thousand indictments were still awaiting trial at that time.[11]

Of the total of 61 draft dodgers whom I interviewed, eight had renounced their American citizenship after they came to Canada (see Table 10, Appendix B). All of the dodgers who renounced citizenship emigrated before 1969 and had more than one year's residence in Canada at the time of the interview. The possibility of renouncing one's citizenship was explained in the early organizational literature sent out by the Canadian aid groups. A leaflet from the Vancouver Committee in 1967 advised that "in order for renunciation to have the effect of removing the threat of arrest while on United States soil, one must renounce before he has committed any offense against the Selective Service law." The first printing of the *Manual for Draft-Age Immigrants to Canada*[12] recommended that draft dodgers not renounce their citizenship because "you renounce the benefits as well as the obligations of American citizenship" and it can be "very awkward for you as a stateless person." The subsequent editions of the *Manual* eliminated reference to renunciation. This explains why so few renounced, since it was not necessary to do so in order to become a landed immigrant. It was significant, however, that 25 draft dodgers I interviewed said that they had considered renouncing their citizenship. This was almost half of the entire sample of draft dodgers. It appeared to be one indicator, along with the others mentioned, of deep cultural alienation from the United States. This was expressed in the reasons given for considering renunciation of citizenship. Many of the refugees saw renunciation as "disaffiliation from a criminal government." These same individuals suggested that alienation from the American culture in terms of its "technocracy, up-tight atmosphere, violence and suffocation of creative solutions to problems" was their major reason for coming to Canada, in addition to their draft status. In a position paper "Americans in Canada," printed in an exile publication, several draft dodgers explained their feelings: "Most of us came here because we refused to be part of an organization that is systematically committing genocide on the Vietnamese people. Our decision to come up here was for many of us, an expression of our desire to disassociate ourselves from a violent society."[13]

The broader career patterns of the draft dodger were responses to the pressure of channeling. However, in order to capture the dynamic interaction of the individual confronting the Selective Service System, I present here some case studies to portray more specifically the manner in which the individual coped with the system. How the functionaries or rule-makers and enforcers labeled the individual had important consequences for the way he viewed himself and ultimately how he determined what his relationship would be to the system.

Interviews best present the complex interactions of these men, as well as their rationale for their own actions and reactions. The labeling process was best disclosed by this method. In fact, it was possible to view the various changes of self-image an individual had undergone in reference to changes in his self-typing or labeling. To aid the reader in obtaining an overall glimpse of the major changes in each man's self-image, I have attempted to diagram the institutional sequence of steps the individual took in relation to the Selective Service System. The crucial events and turning points in each individual's Selective Service career are indicated. I have selected the more "typical" or normative case first, and then, the case representing the minority of dodgers.

Case # 1 Draft Dodger

Year	Age	Selective Service System Events		Crucial Events and Turning Points in Labeling Process
1962	18	Registration		
1966	22	II-S Deferment		Undergraduate (B.A., Anthropology)
		II-A Deferment	working within system →	VISTA volunteer (Confrontation with black regarding draft-exempt status. Left VISTA after 1 year with guilt feelings)
1967	23	1-A Reclassification		Social Welfare Worker (Case worker with NYC Welfare Dept. with middle-class image)
			turning against system →	Radical Activist (Worked with young militants to control community)
1968	24	Induction Notice		Turned against middle-class social work system, quit social work job
June 1968		Induction Day	leaving system →	Draft Dodger and Fugitive (Split to Canada with wife on induction day in yellow Ford truck)
				Landed Immigrant (Became immigrant at border point)

Jimmy and His Yellow Ford Truck

Background

I come from a military background. My father's a Marine. All my family are military officers. He's basically a Roman Catholic, Midwestern Republican. It's an easy background to react against because they give you certain contradictions, even though they're reactionary, you know. And these contradictions will affect the way your life is. I mean, they give you certain liberal concepts, and then they give you the reality of the system. If they're not willing to fight it, then fuck it. Like my mother wrote me this unbelievable letter. I couldn't believe it. My father's getting shoveled off to some nonexistent camp in Georgia somewhere because his son split. And like my mother turns around and says, "You know, basically the Marine Corps is being really decent about the whole thing; they're giving us two more years." And that just seemed like sleep-talk to me. And if people think that way, then I can't help it. Half of slavery is voluntary anyway. But maybe it's impossible for them to change. As far as I'm concerned, if they're not willing to change, they're going to reap the harvest.

Avoiding the Draft as a VISTA Worker

I got a B.A. in Anthropology. When I was in college I was active in SDS. I was even chairman for awhile. But I never got anything organized.

I thought I'd like to get into community organizing. The summer I graduated I became a community organizer in VISTA in New York City.

But then I finally came to a realization; I think Stokeley Carmichael really influenced me in this direction; that we had this kind of middle-class social worker's mystique. That was that we were supposed to go out and help people. And this black guy came up to me and he said, "How long are you going to stay out of the draft?" And I said, "Maybe a year, maybe two." And he replied, "What the fuck are you doing in our neighborhood, you know, you can't even solve your own problems. You got to come down here and tell us, who live here, how to solve our problems." So he was right. I thought, O.K. that's groovy. The only thing I can get out of this is to maybe stay out of the draft for a year and maybe we can do a couple of good things with the government's money and the government's car.

Thwarted and Disillusioned Again

But you couldn't do anything in the end. The government was so arbitrary that they could just cut out anything you did. They could take the car away, which they did when they knew I started working on this bail bond project. I was getting guys out of jail. And we were ready to take over the community action board with this election and a bunch of young militants from 16 to 19 years. But as soon as we planned to do that they changed the voting age to 21, so these guys couldn't vote. So we thought, well, fuck, we'll just use the government car and take people to work if they want to work. If I can help get people out of jail, I'll do it.

A Turning Point: "I Had To Organize My Own People"

After my year in VISTA was up, I stayed in New York and became a welfare case worker for the New York City Welfare Department. And it really became absurd. Like I was supposed to be helping these Cuban refugees. And I was saying to these people ...; well I was in fact adapting these people to a system that I couldn't buy. So what I finally thought was, you have to organize your *own* people. My own people aren't the working people. My own people are the people who said, "Fuck off... the factory's as much slavery as the university is." I got active in the Yippies and the Mother-Fuckers on the lower East Side. But not too heavy. Most of the time I was just part of the masses.

Heading North on Induction Day

Then I got my induction notice to report. I knew I wasn't going to stick around. I was pretty paranoid. The week before we planned to split, my brother and I camped out in a motel way out on Long Island. We were really paranoid. I expected the FBI to be at my door as I split. When we got up here we realized that the FBI is just as red tape bound as any other bureaucracy. They take two or three months to get around to running you down.

I think the groovy reaction was on the part of my mother and father-in-law. They're from North Carolina; they're farmers, and they're real bigots and racists. If they didn't consider themselves to be "civilized," then they'd probably be members of the Klan. But the Klan's just too "white trash" for them. But they're just as racist. So's my old man, for that matter. But their reaction was "great ... get out of this country. ... it's out to destroy us. ..." The FBI shows up there and they say, "Get off our land." They don't want to have anything to do with the government. For the same reasons that they would react against federal civil rights legislation, they would also react against the draft. It's not their thing. They don't know what good it's doing, so they don't want to invest their kids in it. And they were even thinking of splitting and coming to Canada. too, except that they've got a bit of a stake in that they own land down there... about 25 acres. My father-in-law is about 55 and he's reached the point where tobacco farming is supporting him.

Anyway, my wife and I came up to Toronto in our yellow Ford truck. We split on my induction day.

Getting Landed

We got landed as we came across the border. It was pretty easy. We had money when we came up. I looked pretty straight. I had cut my hair for them. But it was really weird. I'm sure he knew I was a draft dodger. [Jimmy showed me a picture of himself at that time.] This was last year when I got landed, June 1968. I had very short hair. [Jimmy now had shoulder-length hair held together by a leather band.]

Case # 2 Political Activist

Year	Age	Selective Service System Events	Crucial Events and Turning Points in the Labeling Process
1958	18	Registration	
1962	22	II-S Deferment	Undergraduate (B.A., Mechanical Engineering)
			Graduate Engineer (1st year)
			Radical Activist (Involvement in peace demonstrations against Vietnam War; arrested twice in 1965)
1963	23	I-A Reclassification	Published bitter letter against war in *New York Times*
		Induction Notice	Legal appeals
		Induction Day	Did not report for induction. Draft Delinquent (more appeals). Appeals to local board rejected. Appeals to higher authorities
Summer 1966		Delinquent Status	FBI-Suspect (visit # 1 from FBI, visit # 2 FBI threats)
		turning → point	Draft Resister (Interview with NY State director of Selective Service. Decision to leave country)
September 9, 1966			Draft Dodger (Preparation to leave for Canada)
		Grand Jury Indictment	Fugitive from Justice (Indictment mailed to McGill University. Framed indictment as badge of heroism)
			Political Criminal

Steve, A Political Draft Resister

Background

I'm from Brooklyn, New York. My father died a couple of years before the business with the draft began. My little sister, who was 11 years old at the time, lived with my mother at home. My family had a Jewish background, but we were not traditionally religious. In my life I have kept the socially relevant parts of Judaism. For example, I wrote a radical Jewish script for a Seder here. My mother's very apolitical, although basically liberally inclined.

Political Activist

I've always been active in the political sense in my college years. I was extremely active as an undergraduate at New York University up at University Heights in the Bronx. I was chairman of the Student's Policy Board there at the time, and a columnist and contributing editor of the Heights *Daily News*. I was responsible for bringing all kinds of radical speakers to the campus. In fact, I'm kind of proud of having driven Norman Thomas up to the campus, from his residence. One summer I spent some time in civil rights work in Mississippi and Alabama. I received quite a beating in a little town called Pasagoola, Mississippi, which is a whole adventure in itself. I was involved in all kinds of teach-ins against the war, which was a big deal back then (1965—66). Not everyone then was automatically against the war. You know, everyone wants peace today (1969). Richard Nixon wants peace. *Time* magazine wants peace — which is bullshit of course, but at least peace has become like Motherhood. There was a time not terribly long ago when everybody was going all the way with LBJ, you know. Even the mention of peace was sort of subversive. I was involved in talking up the war as much as possible. In fact I'd been arrested a couple of times in demonstrations and things. I also tend to be a rather prolific writer of letters to editors, which evidently didn't sit too well either with someone in my local draft board or higher up. ...

Ordered Inducted: Punitive Action Taken Against My Antiwar Stance

I vehemently object to this war. It's a barbarous war. In fact, if there is such a thing as aggression, if there is such a thing as right and wrong, this is as black and white as anything could possibly be. I see the German movement all over Europe as being no more hideous than the American decimation of the Vietnamese people. The things I was writing back in 1963 and 1964 even as an innocent freshman, even before Kennedy's assassination, reflect my views. I've been considerably worked up over this for a long time. I should say too that I'm quite convinced that the *coup de grace* as far as my draft board was concerned was a particular letter that the *New York Times* published from me back in May of 1966. It was a rather long and bitter kind of diatribe against Lyndon Johnson. I'm reasonably certain that someone at my draft board saw this letter, because it was not long after that I received the order to report.

I had already graduated from college in mechanical engineering, and was continuing graduate work in Boston, Massachusetts, and still had my II-S deferment. Then they decided they wanted me in June 1966. I didn't report.

I Appealed at Every Level through to the President, To No Avail

Instead I wrote all kinds of letters of appeal to my own local draft board, which, of course, they refused. Then I went higher up, wrote other letters to New York City headquarters, then the New York State Headquarters, and then through to the president. I was refused at every level. They declared me delinquent. This was through the summer of 1966.

On two separate occasions that summer, the FBI investigated me. They came to the Mechanical Engineering Department, found out where I was living, and came over to me. The first time they just inquired as to whether I knew that I was supposed to report. I told them that I did know, but that I was in the process of filing these appeals. It was obvious anyway, that I knew because I had communicated by writing to my draft board. The second time they just sort of wanted to impress upon me that they weren't fooling around, you know, and that in fact the next time they might not leave me alone! They were slowly working up. ...

Anyway, it was back in New York in the early part of September, between the summer thing I was doing there and the start of the fall term, when I arranged for an interview with the head of New York State's Selective Service. At the time Colonel Axelrod had his office there in Manhattan on Third Avenue and Forty-second Street. It was a Wednesday, September 7. I spoke to him from about 10 o'clock to 11 o'clock. Anyway, it was almost an hour, and he was very sympathetic. He said, "Yeah, sure, graduate students aren't normally drafted, this is true, but after all it's only your local draft board that's going to decide these things. They know they have a certain quota to fill... . If it's not you, it's going to be somebody else. Besides everybody's got to serve. The draft board's only following orders. ..." Actually, the final thing he said to me as I was leaving his office was, "Well, are you going to go down and report?"

That was the only thing he wanted to know. I of course didn't give him any commitment. Anyway, leaving his office, well, I decided right then that I had to leave.

Exploring Alternatives

Anyway, down from his office, I then just had to kind of face the music. I looked at the alternatives open to me. There was just going back to school, making believe that nothing was happening. But that would have been burying the head in the sand. It wouldn't have been more than a few weeks or a month that they [the FBI] would have come back and dragged me away. It might have been a glorious type of thing to be dragged away in the middle of a rally or something, but nevertheless it would have been the *can*.

Then so far as the legal channels, at least according to the information I had available to me at the time, that is, battling this through the courts, would have been more or less fruitless. A cousin of mine is a lawyer, and I know the Selective Service Act. It says specifically and explicitly that the courts may not review or pass judgment on the criteria by which a draft board decides it's taking someone. Only a very small number of people are getting Constitutional deferments. All kinds of other people, ordinary students, or people working in defense industries, do not have statutory deferments. But these are guidelines only that the Selective Service System itself sets up.

One kid was clearly drafted for political reasons by his draft board. The Court ruled nine to nothing (even Supreme Court Justice William Douglas ruled against him, and if that happens there's no hope) that the guy did not have a right to ask the federal courts to review his draft board's decision to draft him. The courts stated that he had no right to go to the federal court because the Selective Service Act states that the decisions rendered by the draft boards cannot be appealed to the federal courts. The Constitution states that the Congress shall define the realm of jurisdiction. Congress is acting perfectly within its rights in stating that the case just mentioned could not be appealed.

I didn't really consider jail as an alternative. I feel it's very important to do something effective, and I don't see myself, or anyone else for that matter, as being horribly effective behind bars. I might see all kinds of visions of glory and messianic beauty, and what have you, in inflicting pain upon myself in that way, in lying there and vegetating for two years. But in fact, so far as what I'm actually doing by sitting there ... I'm doing nothing to the system; there's plenty of places in the jails. So I had the choice of going back to school and waiting to be dragged away, battling the thing in the courts, which seemed quite closed, or opting out. Actually I've not at all opted out as far as my political activity is concerned. In fact, what I've been engaged in here in Canada is probably very little different than what I would have been engaged in had I remained in the States.

Two Days Preparation for Canada

I decided that very morning, right there on the corner, downstairs from Axelrod's office, that I had to cut out. And two days later I was out. In fact, heading back to Massachusetts I simply got hold of my mother's car and a cousin of mine and my little sister. I was driving them up to school. ... Supposedly I was going to come back with the other kids and my mother lent me the car for this. However, before we left, I rented a U-Haul in New York and took that up to campus and packed all my stuff from up there. I spoke to the chairman of the department and told him it was necessary for me to leave and just why. I wasn't happy about it. I was due to start teaching again on Monday; classes were due to begin. That was on Friday morning that I spoke with him, and on Friday we took the long trip up, driving directly from there.

The reason I found myself in Montreal was simply that Montreal was the big city in Canada closest to Massachusetts and we just headed straight north, right up to the border. I really had a great deal of stuff with me, you know. I had books and most of the stuff you see here in my apartment: bicycle, my golf clubs, everything, the whole bit. And there was some question as to what was going to happen at the border. I was really apprehensive about that. There were no groups at the time to inform me of the procedure as there are now. It was already three months since I was called for induction. For all I knew warrants were already out, or at least notice may have been given. Who knows if we were being followed, or what have you, although we tried to be careful of that. And I had no idea what exactly was involved in crossing the border. ... I had never done this before. There was some question as to whether it would be wise to cross at a busy point, a well-traveled one, or one of the lonelier kind of spots, and what time of day. We wound up going through at a place just south and east, a pretty desolate kind of place at 11:30 at night. Actually, before we even knew it, we were in Canada. I didn't realize that you don't have to pass through the American checkpoint coming up here. And the next thing I knew there was a sign saying "You Are Now In Canada."

I would have passed right through the Immigration Station there. It was like a little gas station on the side. I had to wake the guy up! He came out, and I expected all kinds of questions. Instead he just sort of peeked in, asked nothing at all, didn't even ask where we were going, or the registration of the car, nothing. We simply said we were visitors to Canada. "All right," he said, "Go on through."

I think we slept in the car that night. Then they drove me to Montreal the next morning, and sort of wandered around the streets looking for a place to deposit me: A little sign somewhere, you know, "Room for Rent —12 dollars a week." I unloaded the stuff and my cousin and my little sister left.

I didn't see any purpose in telling my mother about coming here beforehand . . . it would only cause her all kinds of worries. As soon as I got here, of course, I called back and told her just what was what. Of course, they were unhappy. Of the alternatives of going into the Army and leaving the country, she would have preferred, I suppose, my going into the Army. Because at the time [1966] there were only about four or five hundred thousand, or not even that many. The build-up really started in 1965. But now that I made the decision she supports me. She's been up here a couple of times to visit me, and my sister comes up and stays a couple of weeks.

An Indictment for My Arrest

An indictment was sent to me in Canada. Probably I'm one of the first hundred or so draft dodgers to be indicted. [Showed me copy of actual indictment that was hanging on his wall, framed.] Notice I have a criminal number. And they're telling me here to report for trial, at a certain time and place in Brooklyn. The United States Attorney versus me. Notice it also says that if I fail to report, a warrant will be issued for my arrest. It is out for me right now. And here's the actual indictment.

That is all the draft board had to establish, and it seems like a clear-cut case on their part, is that I was properly registered, that they properly notified me to report for induction, that I knew that I was supposed to report for induction and that I failed to report. That's it! Nothing about whether or not I'm a graduate student, whether I'm teaching, whether I'm an engineer; irrelevant, completely irrelevant.

Career of the Deserter

"But you can't just turn your back on all your responsibilities and run away from the Army," Major Danby insisted. "It's such a negative move.

It's escapist."

Yossarian laughed with buoyant scorn and shook his head. "I'm not running to them. There's nothing negative about running away to save my life. You know who the escapists are, don't you, Danby? Not me and Orr."

Joseph Heller — *Catch 22*

Unlike the draft dodgers, the men who entered the military either as enlisted men or draftees were usually not aware of their alternatives to the military. They felt they had no choice. They were completely ignorant about the nature of the Vietnam War and became aware of it only through their direct encounter with the military.

Almost three-quarters of the deserters I interviewed, 44 men (72 percent), enlisted in the Armed Forces at a young age. Although the term "enlist" sounds like they volunteered, there were in fact many other factors that came into play, all of which fell into the Selective Service's general philosophy of granting "choice under pressure" as an indirect way of channeling these youths into the Armed Forces. Seventeen men (28 percent) were drafted into the Army.

Almost half of all men reaching age 26 in the United States served in the military. Those who "volunteered" did so to avoid the draft under the pressure of an induction notice. Eli Ginsberg cites a Department of Defense study that gave draft avoidance as the reason for the enlistment of 38 percent of the regular soldiers, 41 percent of the officers and 71 percent of the reserve and National Guard enlistees.[14]

Voluntary enlistment at the officer level, usually after college graduation, corresponded with the Reserve Officer Training Corps (ROTC) programs offered on 350 university campuses. Only 5 percent of my sample consisted of commissioned officers. A larger percentage stated that they had taken ROTC to secure a good position in the military. Being in ROTC assured the student of his II-S status until he finished his education, while he trained for the privilege of officer status as a second lieutenant.

Among the group of younger men between the ages of 17 and 18, many of them viewed enlistment in the service as a means of upward mobility from their poor backgrounds. Among this group of lower-income youth, voluntary enlistment must be considered within the context of the high unemployment rates in America. Many young men in the cities could not find work. Their enlistment resulted directly from the closing of almost all other doors in the opportunity structure to these groups. The recruitment efforts of the services were aimed directly at these men. Incentives were offered in the form of "free" technical and vocational training, guaranteed only to enlistees, as opposed to inductees. Approximately one-third of those men in my sample were involved in trades programs in the military. Charles Moskos, in his book *The American Enlisted Man,* suggested that although black Americans had a greater likelihood than whites of being drafted and of being assigned to dangerous combat duty, they were more favorably disposed toward military life because their chances of advancing themselves in small ways were better than in civilian life.[15] Thus, in addition to the chance to acquire skills, the enlistee gained a degree of security and pay higher than that found in the ghetto, Appalachia and other slum areas.

The very high rate of enlistments into the reserve program and the National Guard also reflected the incentive of the lower death rates. Because these services had very high physical and mental standards they were more open to the middle class than to the poor and there was much competition and long waiting lists to serve. Death chances in these services were generally recognized to be low, although during the last few years of American military participation in Vietnam, some of these reserve units were sent to serve there. Two of the 62 men in my sample sought refuge in Canada as deserters for this reason. Three men enlisted in the Air Force for motives similar to those who enlisted in the reserves.

These cases were yet additional examples of the Selective Service's "indirect guidance," by which certain doors were open to military careers with lower death chances. This allowed the system to recruit the type of manpower it required. Enlistment opportunities tended to leave mostly individuals with working-class backgrounds in the draft pool. They usually wound up in the Army Infantry and many were sent to the front lines. There was a high percentage of blacks who enlisted in a volunteer army predominantly staffed with white officers. The black reenlistment rate in 1975 was 52 percent, compared with only 35 percent for whites.[16] "Voluntary enlistment" presented a very clear example of how dangerous survival in American society was for the poor. Table 11 (Appendix C) describes the different services represented in both my sample and that of the Vancouver Committee.

Three-quarters of the men in my sample served in the Army. This corresponded approximately with the sample of the Vancouver Committee. There was also a very high percentage of men deserting from the Marines, taking into consideration that they were all enlistees, men who were usually quite patriotic.   The Navy was third ranking in desertion rates, according to both samples. It was also significant to note the growing number of men from the Air Force, Reserves and National Guard in Canada, since these were considered to be the most desirable services. What ranks did these men occupy? Most of the men who deserted from the service were privates, as could be expected, since they were the lowest ranking and were treated the worst. However, there was also a significant minority (15 percent) of noncommissioned and commissioned officers who had sought refuge in Canada (see Table 12, Appendix B). According to Moskos, sharp status distinctions in types of work and privileges remained between the officer and enlisted man despite the change in the grade structure since World War II. This created a growing disparity between these two groups. [17]

Most of the men, especially the enlistees, found military training to be very different from their initial expectations. When asked about this, all but a few mentioned that they were treated more like machines than like human beings and found it "intolerable" and "inhumane." Many of them alluded to the vast "brainwashing" process that they found repulsive to their human dignity. All in all, they felt they were unfairly treated even when they attempted to cooperate.

Contrary to the myth that the deserters left the military primarily because they could not pass basic training, only 20 percent of the men left during the basic training period (see Table 13, Appendix B). Twice as many left after 4 to 11 months and another 40 percent left the military after one to three years. Nine percent of them were Vietnam veterans. This meant that the largest number of deserters left the military with advanced trades and military skills. Most of them cited both the Vietnam War and their military treatment among the major reasons for their desertion.

There were some important differences between the enlisted man and the draftee. We have already noted their different motivations for enlisting in the service. The duration of stay in the military before deserting also reflected the class and motivational differences between the enlisted man and the draftee (see Table 14, Appendix B). Among the enlisted men, over half of them remained in the military from one to three years, whereas among the drafted men, all but one of them left the service after one to 11 months. The enlisted men seemed to be willing to withstand much more maltreatment and dehumanization in the military in order to learn a trade. In addition, most of them had patriotic ideals when they enlisted and it took longer for them to become disillusioned. Most of the draftees, in contrast, did not enter for patriotic reasons. In spite of the fact that most of these men were very dissatisfied with their overall situation in the military they were too intimidated by military punishment to express their discontent in a political manner. Two-thirds of these men were not involved in any antiwar or protest activities while they were in the military. However, a significant and vocal minority of 38 percent stated that they were active in the American Servicemen's Union, which functioned on many bases. This was a GI union that actively supported resistance against the war as well as initiating the struggle for GI rights in opposition to "the brass."[18] Many of these activists spent time in a military stockade or the brig, charged with "subversive acts against military life," which could be anything an officer deemed subversive from refusal of work duties to discussing the Vietnam War to writing for an underground press. The majority of men expressed their protests in a more individual manner by going AWOL (see Table 15, Appendix B). Almost half (43 percent) of the men indicated that they had spent time in a military stockade for the alleged reason of being AWOL. Both the Pentagon and the Armed Forces have consistently insisted that the great majority of Vietnam-era deserters were misfits who had long records of such activity.[19] My data, shown in Table 15, demonstrates the erroneousness of these statements. Approximately half of the men who deserted to Canada never went AWOL before. The remaining portion had only gone AWOL once or twice in an attempt to obtain a discharge. Less than 5 percent could be considered to be suffering from personal problems.

After they went AWOL their final time, two-thirds of the men in my sample spent only a few days to a few weeks in the United States getting themselves organized, seeing friends and getting information about Canada before they headed north. Twelve percent of them had been gone from the military as long as one to two years before they immigrated. Most attempted to live "underground" during this time, and almost all had warrants issued for their arrest. In the next section I will explore how these men lived underground and how they made their way to Canada via the "Underground Railroad."

It is significant that almost all of the deserters stated that their views toward the military had undergone radical changes since they had first entered the service. Three-quarters of them attributed this change to their personal experiences in the military. The remaining one-fourth said they were mainly influenced by friends and the media, including the underground presses they had seen in the military. In light of these facts, the military's charge that antiwar propaganda was the major reason for international desertions was highly exaggerated. The first-hand experience of these Americans within the military in the large majority of cases was enough to convince them that military life was in violation of their human rights as well as the rights of theVietnamese. These Vietnam vets did not need any propaganda to tell them the war was wrong. Their personal confrontation with the reality of the war and the service's complete disregard of human dignity and rights were enough to convince them to disassociate themselves from America's ugly war.

The following two case studies of an Air Force deserter who sought sanctuary in Honolulu and and Army Vietnam vet illustrate in a personal way the dilemmas inherent in the career routes of the deserter.

Case # 3 Enlistee in Navy

Year	Age	Selective Service System and Military Events	Crucial Events and Turning Points in Labeling Process
1968	18	Registration	
		I-A Classification	
		Enlisted Navy	
		Basic Training	
		Radar Operator	
Jan. 1969		Okinawa-Vietnam mission	Ordered to Vietnam for 20 days. No time to protest order
Aug. 1969		AWOL # 1	AWOL GI War Protester (Sought sanctuary in Honolulu on Hiroshima Day)
Nov. 1969		Arrested — Pearl Harbor Navy Brig for 3 mos.	
			Considered applying for CO status while in brig
		Orders for Vietnam	
		AWOL # 2	Intentions to desert
Dec. 1969			Deserter (Decision to go to Canada)

Eric, A Navy Enlistee

Background

I come from a family of five. My hometown is in Riverside, California. My father's a salesman for Ludens, Inc. They sell candies and coughdrops and such things. My mother used to be employed by the Naval Weapons Training Center at Norco. She worked in the airlines, at the travel desk, arranging for scientists doing research. She now works part-time in a travel place. I have a WASP background — White Anglo-Saxon Protestant. My parents are Lutherans but they don't attend church usually. I consider myself to be a free-lance Christian. I think the original message in Christianity has been distorted. And for that reason I reject the traditional Christian church. I believe in personal divinity literally in that it makes up the whole of this concept that the Christians call "God." And I believe in the sanctity of life. I consider myself religious, but not in the formal sense of the word. As far as politics go, my family is split. My father would be on the conservative side: he's a Republican. My mother is an old-line liberal. I consider myself a social anarchist. I'm somewhat brought down by super militant radicals. Although I'm sympathetic with their cause, I don't agree with their militancy.

I graduated from high school. But I was never too interested in school. So I decided to work on my own for awile. I bummed around and spent a half-year living in the Haight-Ashbury in San Francisco, worked at unskilled jobs when I needed bread. I was a waiter, bus boy and a gas station attendant for awhile. I also worked in a nursery. I didn't really feel I was getting anywhere. I had just turned 18. So I thought I'd enlist in the Navy and pick up some skills.

An Airman

So I went down to the Navy recruiting center and enlisted. For little under a year I flew in an aircraft as a radar operator. It was an antisubmarine patrol-type aircraft. And then when I quit flying, I worked on the ground crew, you know, towing airplanes and bringing them in and that shit. The basic job wasn't difficult for me. It wasn't difficult to cope with, and it wasn't difficult to do. I objected to the petty bullshit mostly.

I came to the decision in August of 1969 that I was bullshitting myself in trying to rationalize the fact that I wasn't really involved in the Vietnam war, which I was opposed to. And I came to the realization that my mere presence as an active member of the Armed Forces was involvement enough. It meant one more person was in Vietnam because I was there. A number of things led me to this decision.

Right from the beginning of the time I was in the service, I was reading a lot of the underground press. I thought most of the media was bullshitting people anyway. And it was just a self-realization type thing. I stood back and looked at what I was doing, and realized that I was bullshitting myself by saying that I wasn't involved.

Short Side Trip to Vietnam: A Mind-Jarring Strain

I guess the biggest thing for me was when in January of 1969 we deployed from Hawaii to Okinawa. And I saw a lot of the things that were coming down in Okinawa that I didn't dig. The Okinawans have really been hacked off about the occupation forces there. It's still a military governorship. Okinawa has been asking to be let back to the Japanese rule since Japan was made sort of independent and it's been refused.

Also, while I was there I was told at one point I was going to Vietnam for 20 days. I didn't have time to lodge any sort of protest, and had I been able to, I wouldn't have had to go, because I had a brother who was in the combat zone at the time. Legally, I wasn't bound to go. It's just that the military has ways of putting people off, you know, and I wasn't given any choice. I was almost physically put on the plane. And I found myself in Vietnam for 20 days. I think that was probably the most mind-jarring thing that I'd ever been through. Naturally, it was an incredible strain, because there was absolutely no way that I could rationalize. This was the place that I'd been opposed to for so long, and now I'm here. So I think that really, really got me to thinking. I knew where I stood with the military, and where I was. That was in January, and from that point, I made a number of decisions about myself that eventually led to me splitting to Canada.

Seeking Sanctuary with 37 GI's in Honolulu

When we returned from Okinawa to Honolulu I went AWOL. I read in the local papers that a GI sought sanctuary in the Church of the Crossroads in Honolulu on August 6th, Hiroshima Day. There was to be a march the 11th. It came up at an opportune time and I decided that it was the only way for myself to do it. So that's what I did. I went to the march. At the rally held at the end of the march, I declared sanctuary with five other GI's. It was symbolic sanctuary. Eventually our number grew to 37 and we had to branch out to other local churches. It was one of the largest sanctuaries. I was there for 20 days. On the twentieth day, myself and four other people were to go to San Francisco and spread the word about a peace march led to the gates of the Oakland Embarcation Center. It didn't happen, however, because I was arrested at the Honolulu Airport. I was put in the Pearl Harbor brig for three months.

Considering a CO in the Brig

I had been mulling over filing for a CO for a number of months. When I finally decided that that was what I was going to do in the brig, I was told that I wasn't able to file there, that they weren't my command, and that I would have to go to my next duty station. Now an application for a CO can take a number of months. By that time I would have been launching and recovering planes. And I couldn't have faced that. It was a big mental struggle for me to finally decide to come to the realization that I wanted to file for CO. Because I couldn't in any way find how I could put what I believe down on paper for somebody else's scrutiny, to judge whether it's valid or not. I realized that it was fruitless, and that there would be no CO granted. I'm not sure, but I've been told that there's been less than 50 CO discharges granted since World War II.

But the day I was released from the brig they put me on a plane to San Francisco with orders to be on the attack aircraft carrier #34. And it would have been in Vietnam by the time I'd been able to file for CO. It was really fruitless. That's why I split. The plane just went, and I was gone. Because I wasn't going to wait around to try to file for a CO.

Splitting to Canada with Fellow GI

It was an awfully hard decision to make and I didn't have much time to make it. While I was in the sanctuary, I had thought about splitting to Canada and decided I didn't really want to do that. But when I got in the brig, and I realized exactly what they were going to do with me, I decided that if I got really bad orders, like I did, it would be the only choice left. Had I been given relatively good orders, then I think I could have achieved more in the States, and still made it through. That doesn't mean, however, I wouldn't have stirred up any shit.

I had a military intelligence cat — what a paradox — he wanted to know whether I was going to embarrass the Navy any more. He said he was worried about classified documents and things like that. And I said, well that's cool. I don't feel like going over to the Russians and handing them the plans to some electronics equipment. I had a secret clearance. I said, if you mean am I going to make any more noises about the war, or am I going to just sort of clam up after I've done this, I said, that's absurd to think about. It's like someone losing their virginity. After the first time you might as well go the whole route. So I said, don't expect me to just sort of be a good little boy any more. But then in the brig I decided there was nothing I could do but go to Canada.

I went home for a couple of weeks and saw my people. I didn't ask anyone for their advice. They didn't offer. The relationship with my parents is that everyone in the family has their own personal autonomy and no one violates that. But in my larger family, my grandfather's kind of a reactionary cat. If he saw Christ on his front lawn, he'd beat him with a shovel because he had long hair and a beard. ... So I would have had Thanksgiving dinner with my family, but it wouldn't have been a good scene. Because I wasn't certain that my grandfather wouldn't have called them up and said, "Here he is!"

I called a guy I was pretty tight with in Hawaii. He had been in my squadron. He was released from the Navy while I was in the brig. And I knew he and his wife were eventually going to Vancouver. I told him to get in touch with me when he got ready to go to Canada so we could go together.

Meanwhile I went to the Unitarian Church at Riverside and talked to them there. And they gave me addresses of people to contact depending on where I went. I had the number of the Vancouver Committee. We met in San Francisco and traveled to Seattle by bus. We were separated from each other in Seattle. There I made inquiries about traveling over the border on the bus. They advised me against it. So I was told about an underground group in Bellingham that aids people like me. ... They arranged to have me come across the border in a private auto. They also gave me an address of a friend of theirs who's doing his doctorate at Simon Fraser University in Burnaby, B.C.

Coming across the border I had an intense feeling of freedom. You know, finally, God, after almost three years. Finally I'm free. I can do what I want. I don't shave if I don't want to, and I don't have to cut my hair. ...

Case # 4 Vietnam Veteran

Year	Age	Selective Service System and Military Events	Crucial Events and Turning Points in Labeling Process
1968	18	Registration	High School Graduation (anti-Communist)
		Enlisted Army	GI
		Tank Crewman (Germany)	Nazi (In Germany, applied to Nazi party)
		Court-Martial	Involvement in political activities
		AWOL # 1	AWOL GI (Publicized trial in Frankfort. Labeled by Army as Nazi and treated poorly)
			Hippie-Antiwar (Court-martial and pretrial confinement made him undergo a conversion)
		Transferred to Fort Meade	
			Medic (Switched work duties to medic)
1969		Orders to Vietnam	
			Expressed antiwar sentiments. Given choice of "Nam" or treason charges
		Vietnam Duty	Vietnam Vet (Decorated after one year tour of duty and returned home. Expressed sympathy for NLF in *Time* magazine)
			Saboteur, Socialist (Joined Socialist Alliance. Worked on underground paper)
1969		AWOL	Deserter (5 mos. before discharge went AWOL with intentions to desert)
			Fugitive — Route to Canada
			Mexican—Cuban Embassy
			Underground (US—Canada)

Bill, A Vietnam Veteran

Background

I grew up in Redondo Beach, a small town in southern California. My father is in charge of a small business there. My mom is a housewife. They are both members of the local Episcopal Church. They like to think they are upper-status people. They are conservative-Republican-type people like the rest of their friends. Probably by now they are Fascists. My parents are very anti-Communist and I was very anti-Communist, too. That's just the kind of school I was in. And I had a bitter hatred of them without really understanding anything about Communists. I had never looked to the Left for any answers. I could only find any kind of social answers in the right, in the National Socialists and the Nazi-type philosophies. It seems like the only kind of social problems we are interested in. Like peace ... I actually thought at the time that being anti-Communist was the only way there was going to be racial peace and peace in the world.

Enlisted as Tank Crewman

I enlisted in the U.S. Army when I had just got out of high school. I had had some jobs and didn't want to go to college right away and I didn't really want to get drafted. So I figured I could get a college education in the Army, which later proved to be impossible. I enlisted as a tank crewman, and I was very right-wing Fascist. I really tried hard and wanted to make rank. I finished tank school when I was in Germany, which was really nice for me.

Labeled a Nazi

While I was in Germany I met some people and applied to join the American Nazi party. This is when my trouble began. I had a black C.O. [Commanding Officer] and he found out about it and I got court-martialed for recruiting. They didn't want any soldier involved in political activities. They thought I was up to something. I had gone to Switzerland and ended up AWOL and that's what made them think I was up to something. I spent some time in the stockade in Frankfort on pretrial confinement. I had a very publicized trial, a lot of stuff in the papers. The headlines read things like, "Heil Hitler" and "G.I. Nazi Is Exposed." It kind of marked me as a racist, which I really wasn't. Maybe I was but I didn't want to be. They blew it up into something really sensational.

"I Felt Like a White Nigger" – Conversion Began in the Stockade

Maybe it was a good thing that I was caught. It started me thinking.

The time I spent in the stockade I really got to understand what fascism was all about. The stockade was the old perfect textbook example; like it was right in the old gestapo jail in Frankfort. I finally got a suspended sentence. They couldn't keep me there in Germany. I guess the Germans didn't like it either. The Army transferred me to Fort Meade in Maryland, and I spent some time training there. I quit the Nazi party. ... Actually I never was really in it but I dropped my application. I had some arguments with some Nazis and I turned out very anti-Nazi, very anti-Fascist. The actual court-martial was really responsible for my changes.

In the court-martial I had no rights. That's when I began to realize that's just what fascism, nazism is. I felt like a Jew or a black would feel. Almost overnight I felt a lot of sympathy for blacks. I just felt like a white nigger and that's what I was treated like.

Antiwar Hippie and Medic Ordered to Vietnam as Punishment

I still didn't lean to the Left at all because I didn't trust the Left. I thought it would lead me to the same place that the Right did. So I became a hippie-type and I became antiwar. Whereas before I used to support the war and the bombing of Hanoi, suddenly at Fort Meade I thought all war was bad. I tried to get out of tanks and I had long conversations with the chaplains. Finally they made me a medic. Well, I had a problem with my mouth, and ended up getting into trouble there, too, because I expressed myself against the war. I found myself coincidentally on a levy for Vietnam. It was their way of disciplining me. My C.O. gave me a choice of treason charges or Vietnam. I thought about deserting then. And I finally took Vietnam even though I knew he couldn't make treason stick for this particular offense. It was ridiculous; but it was a change of duty and I wanted to see what it was like. I couldn't really argue Vietnam without going, so I was put on a tank and I went to Vietnam.

A Convert to Socialism in Vietnam; Viet Cong Admirer

It didn't take very long for me to start thinking again about social questions. I was out in the field. We went out on missions and made some sweeps. I started building some really good relationships with some Vietnamese that started me thinking. Anyway, the more I inspected it, the more admiration I felt for the Viet Cong. I expressed that feeling to *Time* magazine. Unfortunately, they printed it and I got into some more trouble. But I got through my year all right. I was decorated and I was sent home. The Army was proud. And my parents were proud. But I was very confused. I didn't like fighting against people that I felt some kind of solidarity with. So when I got to my base in Kentucky, I joined the Young Socialist Alliance.

Working Underground in the Coffeehouse Movement

The Army made me a clerk in Kentucky because I couldn't get a security clearance to get on these new tanks that they had. This was because of my experience in Germany. To the Army I was still a Nazi troublemaker. They never suspected I was a leftist, I don't think. One colonel thought I was a Communist from the day I got in the Army. He thought I played the part of being a Nazi just to make the Army look Nazi. At any rate, I was a clerk. I also began working underground in the newspaper and the copy house. There was a lot of talk in our radical group at Fort Knox of really becoming very activist on a scale that hasn't even been seen yet. It would include sabotage and things like that. We were probably the only armed resistance group in the whole damn state. We were on the posts at night and we did have arms. We organized at the coffeehouse. At that time we were probably the only such group in the States, armed. Not now, though.

Desertion, the Only Honorable Way Out; Like Ché

After awhile though, I couldn't work there. I couldn't stand the conflict of working outside the Army against it, and then coming back and having to salute officers and wearing an Army uniform. Also I was still troubled about Vietnam. So then I thought ... why an honorable discharge? I figured the easiest thing for me to do was to stay in the Army and get a discharge because I only had five months left. And the hardest thing for me to do would be to quit. So I quit. I thought this would be the only really honorable way out. Secondly, I quit because I had this feeling inside that I knew I was going to end up in jail sooner or later. I was just coming to it like a volcano and I didn't want to be around a jail again. So I decided, if I am going to make a commitment, then I may as well make it now.

I think my decision to desert had a lot to do with Ché. I admire him a lot. My friend and I were driving along one day and we saw a picture of Ché Guevara. And it started a discussion about commitments... because Ché believed in something. And even though he had it made in life if he wanted to. He had had it made in Argentina with a good family and a good education. He had it made in Cuba and could have stayed in Cuba. But he didn't think as much about convenience as he did conviction. To me, going into Bolivia was the supreme act of idealism. They teach their children in Cuba to be like Ché. And I in my own way wanted to be like him, and all I could think about doing was leaving. So when one of the lieutenants said to me, "If you hate the Army as much as you make out, you wouldn't be in it," I took his word and left.

My friend, who was also active in the underground, a clerk, deserted with me. This was in August 1969. We went to California together. He subsequently turned himself in and ended back in Fort Knox.

I was trying to figure out the best thing to do. When I had first thought of deserting because I went to Vietnam, I had gone to the Russian Embassy in Washington and talked with them. This was about the time that those four sailors had gone to Sweden. I was thinking I could go to Sweden via Russia. This Russian suggested to me that if I really got into trouble, I could go to Mexico and then go to the Cuban Embassy there. I didn't even know there was a Cuban Embassy in Mexico. This gave me the idea to go to Cuba via Mexico. So I made my way to Mexico City.

Seeking Political Asylum in Cuba

I went to the Cuban Embassy in Mexico. They told me they just weren't interested. A Cuban told me, "You'll get a visa just like everyone else gets a visa, there's nothing special about you." It would take me five weeks. I didn't have enough money to stay in Mexico five weeks. I didn't have any contacts, and I couldn't speak Spanish. So I was just at a loss. I felt let down.

I guess I expected some kind of guys with beards to welcome me with open arms and take me into the back room and out where they would have a helicopter waiting to take me to Cuba. Instead, I got a guy with a suit, a bureaucrat who didn't care who I was. He was only thinking about Cuba and Cubans.

It was explained to me later that Cuba is very touchy with its Embassy in Mexico because it's really its last finger into Latin America. And if it causes trouble or any kind of waves at all, and if it ever became known that American deserters were being channeled through the Cuban Embassy ... well it isn't a very diplomatic thing to do. So that's probably why they weren't very excited about encouraging me. They looked awfully suspicious of me, too.

Safe in Canada At Last

I went back to the States. I knew the FBI would be looking for me by this time because they had a personal sort of grudge against me. So I just didn't want to hang around, because it didn't take them long to start looking for me. So I didn't contact any of the addresses there I had with me. In my little address book I kept every kind of political underground address I could, just as a general reference. I had some addresses of groups in Canada. but I wasn't sure if Canada offered sanctuary to deserters. I had addresses in Toronto, Vancouver and Montreal. But the American De- serters' Committee in Montreal sounded best to me, so I just went to Montreal. Eventually I made contact with the ADC there and found out I was safe at last.

There are all kinds of people like me who don't know about Canada. I had had a lot of discussions with different people and was told that draft dodgers could stay in Canada, deserters no. I didn't know deserters could remain in Canada legally until I went to Montreal. And I was in the Move- ment. So you can imagine all the others who don't know about it. Those who know it sometimes think Canada will be too much of a change ... that there's nothing up here but little villages and snow and ice. They don't know enough about Canada. Like even my mother thought that I was ruining my life by coming up here. They don't realize that you can do the same things here that you can do down in the States.

My mom wasn't too happy about the fact that I deserted. She thought it was kind of a cop-out. She figured that I was so close to getting a dis- charge that I should have stayed. There's a lot of GI's now who have families and they think going AWOL or desertion means ducking in alleys the rest of your life. If they only knew they could just come to Canada and lead the same kind of life and get jobs and go to school, there would be twice as many desertions.

The protests of these refugees and their radical change of consciousness which eventually led them to Canada cannot be explained simply by the two prevalent theories held by many social scientists: the "red-diaper baby" and the "radical-rebel" hypotheses. According to the former hypothesis, radicals came from left-wing families where they had been exposed to radical ideas from early childhood through adolescence. In contrast, the radical-rebel hypothesis posits that these individuals were rebelling against all male parental and societal authority. Kenneth Keniston found that both of these theories failed to account for the complex behavior of the individuals he interviewed as part of the Vietnam summer project in 1967. For similar reasons, I have also discounted these theories in accounting for the politicization process that most of these American refugees have undergone. As Keniston points out, "Both of these hypotheses overlook the actual complexity of radicals' de- velopment and both posit either a total break with the past or total acceptance of it, which rarely occurs in human life."[20] The radicalization process of these young refugees coincided with their struggle against the draft or military and their subsequent decision to leave the United States. As we have seen, it involved a complex process of interaction with these institutions and relationships with significant others.

We have seen how the middle-class student with the good educational background was deferred from the Armed Forces while in college or a critical occupation. When he completed school or dropped out or did not select a critical occupation, he lost his deferral and thus opted to dodge the draft and go to Canada rather than enter the military or jail. Yet the deserter who came to Canada was the working-class student channeled into the military directly from high school. He realized how undesirable the military and war were from his first-hand experiences before he decided to leave his country. Thus it becomes apparent that the channeling of the Selective Service System had a class basis.

As we will see in chapters 3 and 4, the channeling system set up by the American draft meshed with the channeling of the Canadian Immigration Act to continue favoring draft dodgers rather than deserters. This class distinction led to a differential response by Canadian officials to the immigration of large numbers of American deserters to Canada in the late 1960s and early 1970s.

NOTES

1.   Selective Service System, "Memorandum on Channeling," July 1, 1965 (Washington, D.C.: Government Printing Office), pp. 899—1125. This document accidentally fell into the hands of the resistance organizers and was reprinted. As a result of this unscheduled distribution, it was officially withdrawn and reprinted in a less candid form.
2.   "Channeling" document of the Selective Service System, July 1, 1965, GPO, pp. 899—1125.
3.   Ibid.
4.   Robert Fulford, *Saturday Night*, November 1968.
5.   Robert Akakia (pseud.), unpublished manuscript of a draft dodger, "Qualities and Features of American Exiles in Canada."
6.   There is a discussion of the Selective Service's "Persecution of Dissenters" in Jean Carper, *Bitter Greetings* (New York, 1967).
7.   "Prosecutions for Selective Service Offenses: A Field Study." *Stanford Law Review* 356 (197). Some of these court decisions include: U.S. v. Gutknecht (1970) invalidating the delinquency regulations; U.S. v. Haugh-

ton requiring draft boards to state the reason for denying a conscientious objector claim (1969); U.S. v. Atherton (1969) requiring local boards to apply the Seeger test (1965) correctly to conscientious objector claims; and U.S. v. Beltran (1969) requiring draft board members to live within the jurisdictional boundaries of the local board.

8.   Ibid.
9.   Ibid.
10. Robert Akakia, "Qualities and Features."
11. Administrative Office of the United States Courts, Washington, D.C.
12. *Manual for Draft-Age Immigrants to Canada,* chapter 18, "Renouncing Citizenship," pp. 36—58. The subsequent second and third and fourth editions have omitted this section, but the revised summer 1970 edition put it back in.
13. *American Exiles in Canada,* "Americans in Canada" (Vancouver 1968).
14. Eli Ginsberg, *Manpower Agenda for America* (1968).
15. Charles C. Moskos, Jr., *The American Enlisted Man* (New York: Basic Books, 1970).
16. See *New York Times,* February 5, 1975; and Morris Janowitz and Charles C. Moskos, Jr., "The Military Establishment: Racial Composition of the Volunteer Armed Forces"; M. Binkin and J. Johnston, "All-Volunteer Armed Forces: Progress, Problems and Prospects: For Committee on Armed Forces" (Washington: U.S. Government Printing Office, 1973).
17. Moskos, *The American Enlisted Man.*
18. Andy Stapp, *Up Against the Brass* (New York: Simon and Schuster, 1970). The American Serviceman's Union (ASU) was founded by Andy Stapp in December 1967. Only two years later it claimed 4,500 card-carrying GI's and was receiving so many requests for help from AWOL or court-martialed GI's that it was open six days a week from morning until late at night. In his book, Andy Stapp documents the history and growth of this resistance movement within the military in a personal, moving account.
19. Pentagon survey reported in the *Vancouver Sun,* January 2, 1970. Social scientists' research on the behavior of prolonged AWOL have also emphasized their maladaptive characteristics; see Timothy F. Hartnagel, "Absent Without Leave: A Study of the Military Offender," *Journal of Political and Military Sociology* 2 (Fall 1974): 205—20.
20. Kenneth Keniston, *Young Radicals* (New York: Harcourt, Brace and World, 1968), p. 48. Authors like L. Feuer subscribe to the radical-rebel thesis. They argue that the radical is "displacing the psychic conflict," essentially labeling the radical as "sick" in Freudian terminology as a facade for avoiding the real issues involved.

3

Send Me Your Skilled and Educated Men Yearning to Breathe Free

Postwar Canada has been dominated as a resource and industrial base by foreign nations, particularly the United States. It has generally been held that many Canadian industries are branch plant operations of their multinational parents that usually have their headquarters in the United States. In his book *The Vertical Mosaic* John Porter of the University of Toronto found that the elites of both Canada and the United States were closely linked by an extensive network of shared economic interest.[1]

Canadians are well aware of the dependent nature of their economy. This was accepted as a necessary situation in the period preceding the Vietnam War in order to attain a higher standard of living in a country with a small population base of some 20 million in the second largest country in the world.   With the coming of the war and racial tensions in America, Canadians became less enamored of the American way of life and began to question their own desire to emulate the United States. According to a recent United Nations paper on social trends in North America, the growth of Canadian nationalism that emerged in the middle and late 1960s was a reaction in part to the growing domination of the Canadian economy by foreign-owned and controlled businesses, largely American.[2]

This rise of Canadian nationalism in turn resulted in political ambivalence toward the United States. On the one hand, many Canadians favored close economic and political ties to what still was the dominant force in international affairs: the United States and its multinational corporations. On the other hand, many Canadians sought ways of asserting Canadian autonomy on particular economic issues, such as securing energy in Canada for Canadian use exclusive of American needs and on particular political issues, such as permitting American draft dodgers and deserters to seek refuge in Canada.

The resultant economic and political tensions relating to the question of what to do or not to do about the wave of draft-age emigrants from the United States to Canada during the Vietnam War period was resolved by the application of government policy under the Canadian Immigration Act. This act was designed to facilitate the flow of skilled young immigrants to Canada in order to maintain the resource and industrial base vital to Canadian life as well as to the operations of the multinational corporations. It was also used to prevent undesirable political opponents from entering the country. Its policies were not especially designed with regard to American war refugees, but it proved to be the main battleground on which was fought the struggle to secure equal treatment for deserters fleeing the American war machine.

The political debate raised in Parliament over the question of entry of American draft evaders under the Immigration Act more closely reveals Canadian ambivalence toward the United States on this issue. The Canadian Immigration Act effected immigration to Canada in general and the fate of American draft dodgers and deserters because it was a channeling document very similar in its effect to the American Selective Services Act. It served to maintain a continental system of youth channeling that permitted the displacement of rejects from the heartland of America to the peripheries of American-dominated Canada. By this emigration, Canada acted as a safety valve to prevent discontent from surfacing within the American economic system. Even General Hershey, the prime architect and chief administrator of channeling in the Selective Service System, condoned Canada's role as a safety valve for containing the dissidents of the American empire. In a speech in Vancouver in the fall of 1970, addressing a convention of the Army, Navy and Air Force Veterans of Canada, he spoke of the American refugees in Canada as follows:

So I feel sorry for them and I feel sorry for Canada because she got 'em. But I'll tell you, son, I wouldn't want to see it any other way. You'd have a hell of a lot of trouble keeping a few thousand out and letting a few million in, and damn it, who wants a police state? Best to let it lay.

I wouldn't want to see it loused up, this border between the two countries. It's the most wonderful geographic situation in the world — this 3,000 miles of undefended frontier.[3]

Canada and the Vietnam War

Because public opinion in Canada, as in most areas of the world, opposed American intervention in Vietnam, the posture taken by the Canadian government during the Vietnam War years was one of noninvolvement in the fighting but continuation of arms shipments to the United States under a defense-sharing agreement. Although Canada did not have a draft during 1965–75, the Canadian public was well aware that America would have appreciated the presence of volunteer Canadian troops along with the Australians and New Zealanders in Vietnam. While Canada was a NATO member she sent no troops and Prime Minister Trudeau indicated his opposition to some of the particular military methods used there. Yet Canada's refusal to comply with the wishes of its ally did not also hold for the economic and defense sectors of Canadian-American relations.

Military and defense relations between the United States and Canada during the war years reflected the close coordination between the economy of the two countries and the important role defense spending held in each. Under the Defense Production Sharing Agreement, Canada sold the United States more than $500 million dollars worth of ammunition and military supplies for use in Vietnam. These sales constituted an important component of the Canadian economy.[4] This was true, despite the fact that Canada was not permitted to sell arms for use in "international" trouble spots. The policy had been one of "see no evil, hear no evil, but make a buck." Furthermore, while Canada was an ostensibly neutral member of the International Control Commission whose task was to implement the Geneva Agreements of 1954 in Vietnam, she used her International Control Commission offices in North Vietnam to make reports to Washington on "the political and military climate in Vietnam."[5]

The sentiments of probably most Canadians against involvement in the Vietnam War were echoed in George Grant's description of the war as the most recent manifestation of Western imperialism. He saw the relationship of the Vietnam War to Canadian sovereignty as follows:

A central aspect of the fate of being a Canadian is that our very existence has at all times been bound up with the interplay of various world empires.

In that sense our very lives are inevitably bound up in the meeting of that empire with the rest of the world, and the movements of war which draw the limits of that meeting. The depth of that common destiny with the Americans is shown in the fact that many Canadians who are forced to admit the sheer evil of what is being done in Vietnam say at the same time that we have no choice but to stand with Americans as the pillar of Western civilization. Beyond this kind of talk is of course the fact that this society is above all a machine for greed, and our branch-plant industry is making a packet out of the demolition of Vietnam. ...[6]

Yet, while the Vietnam War was one that was singularly unpopular with the Canadian public at large, the Liberal party's policy had been to provide moral and material support to the American war effort there. In 1967, in a public reply to an appeal by 400 University of Toronto professors for disassociation from the war, Prime Minister Trudeau reviewed the benefits that Canadians gained from the integration of defense production and concluded: "For a broad range of reasons it is clear that the imposition of an embargo on the export of military equipment to the U.S. and concommitant termination of the Defense Production Sharing Agreements would have far-reaching consequences that no Canadian government would contemplate with equanimity."[7] Such a statement revealed that the relative political independence of Canada from the United States on the Vietnam War issue was only slight and strongly tempered by its economic dependency on the United States. This had been a constant feature of Canadian-American relations since World War II. It reflected the basic economic penetration of Canada by American-based multinational corporations that had made the industrial sector of Canada into a branch-plant economy. This fact, combined with the tight interlocking military and defense relationships, meant that satisfaction of Canadian public opinion for a total noninvolvement in the Vietnam War could not be a political reality for any government. Recognizing these limitations of Canadian sovereignty in the Vietnam War period led many younger Canadians to react against American domination of Canadian life through support of an increasingly strident Canadian nationalism. The successes and failures on the political front for Canadian proponents interested in granting asylum in Canada for American exiles must be viewed within the context of this growing nationalism and Canadian attempts to attain political autonomy, at least in part, from the United States' dominant economic position in Canada.

Canadian Policy Toward American Refugees: The Political Background

Some of the American exiles in Canada were labeled and tried by the United States government as criminals and found to be in violation of the Selective Service Act. The majority of them fled the country but were not indicted or found guilty of a crime by the courts. They have been viewed by the government as "fugitives from justice" and are subject to penal sanctions for their actions should they return to American soil.

Yet America has tacitly recognized Canada's "right" to grant asylum to military deserters as political refugees even though these men were officially regarded as fugitives. This was indicated by the testimony of Mr. Smith, a deputy administrator in the State Department, before hearings of the Senate Committee on Armed Services in 1968.

> Senator McIntyre: Mr. Smith, can you explain to me why it is that in these Status of Forces agreements or treaties that countries will respect the fact that a man might be fleeing from justice, having committed a crime, but what is the rationale behind the exception being made of the military deserter? This man is guilty of a military crime. There must be some very obvious reason why sanctuary is granted to a military deserter, where it would not be granted to, say, a murderer.
>
> Mr. Smith: The exception from extradition for military crimes is one of long standing and great tradition. I think probably the principal reason is that it is in a great sense considered to be *similar to a political offense.* And some of the same reasons for excluding so-called political offenses from extradition apply in the case of military offenses.[8]

From the Canadian point of view, American refugees were recognized officially as emigrants who could apply for Canadian immigrant status, as any other emigrants. They were not treated officially as political refugees and were not accepted for permanent residence as landed immigrants on that basis. According to Canadian immigration officials, American draft dodgers and deserters "could not be exposed to political persecution" since the concepts of political refuge and asylum had no application to "citizens of friendly countries, particularly those having democratic forms of government ..."[9]

What enabled Americans, who were regarded by the American government as felons, to be considered officially by Canada as emigrants who could apply for Canadian landed immigrant status? How did a felon become a respectable immigrant merely by crossing the border? Canada's tradition of encouraging immigration, her lack of a conscription policy and her extradition treaties with the United States were major historical and political considerations in her acceptance of American draft and military refugees.

Since World War II Canada has had no military draft. The French-Canadians have always had an aversion to conscription. They never enjoyed the prospect of fighting Britain's imperial wars. During World War I and World War II, tens of thousands of French-Canadians refused to register for the draft and rioted in the streets of Quebec. Mayor Camillieh Houde of Montreal was jailed from 1940 to 1944 for openly encouraging resistance to conscription and was reelected from jail. Jean Drapeau, the present mayor of Montreal, was a leader of the anticonscription movement in 1942 and declared at that time, "Why should we fight to support the British Empire?" Thus the French-Canadian resistance movements, with the support of labor and farm groups, eventually led to the end of conscription after World War II.[10]

The admission of immigrants who had refused to perform military service in their country of origin has been one of Canada's oldest traditions. It was also an old tradition of the United States to accept European draft dodgers and deserters. However, for America's own dodgers and deserters this tradition did not apply; they had to seek refuge elsewhere. They remained out of the jurisdiction of American law while in Canada and could not be extradited back to the United States.

Extradition from Canada to the United States could only take place when an individual had been either accused or convicted of a crime committed in the United States, and when that crime was among the 22 extraditable offenses listed in the extradition treaties agreed upon by the two countries. Offenses connected with the Selective Service laws were not among those. This was due to the fact that an offense could only be listed if it was a crime under the laws of both countries. Canada did not have a compulsory Selective Service Act; hence dodging conscription could not be a crime in Canada. Neither was desertion considered an extraditable crime. It was specified in the treaties that "no person surrendered by or to either of the high contracting parties should be triable or be tried for any crime or offense committed prior to his extradition, other than the offense for which he was surrendered ..." It was further specified that: "a fugitive criminal shall not be surrendered if the offense in respect to which his surrender is deemed to be one of a political character."[11]

Canada has willingly accepted fugitives and refugees fleeing from what they regarded as political oppression. For example, the Canadian government took unprecedented steps to facilitate the resettling of approximately 36,000 Hungarians fleeing the 1956 uprisings by removing almost all the usual immigration restrictions. In World Refugee Year, 1960, Canada made special efforts to enable immigrants who would not have normally qualified to enter Canada as part of the humanitarian movement of refugees from Europe.[12] In 1968, after the Russian invasion of Czechoslovakia, thousands of Czechs seeking political refuge were admitted to Canada. More recently, Canada accepted immigrants from Chile as well as 3,000 South Vietnamese immigrants after Saigon's capture by the Provisional Revolutionary Government in 1975.

Although Canada did not have any formal statute providing for political asylum in its Immigration Act or elsewhere, the refugees of Hungary and Czechoslovakia, for example, were handled by the Canadian government as political fugitives.[13] They were granted landed immigrant status whether or not they were qualified officially according to the Immigration Act. All other formalities for them were made easy. In addition, other special measures were taken on their behalf, including increased staffing of refugee centers, the relaxation of some immigration procedures and loans covering transportation and resettlement costs. Financial assistance was provided for students who wished to continue post-secondary education and others were provided with language and occupational courses. According to the report of the Department of Manpower and Immigration referring to the special Czechoslovakian Refugee Movement, "Many Canadian universities and provincial and municipal agencies assisted in the settlement of the refugees. Without this surge of public and private cooperation, the task would have been immeasurably more difficult."[14]

Were American refugees in Canada regarded as political fugitives in the same manner as the Hungarians or Czechs and treated accordingly? The answer has been an unambiguous "No!" According to Tom Kent, former deputy minister of citizenship and immigration, the official explanation of the difference between American dodgers and deserters and Hungarians and Czechs was presented as follows:

> Common usage of the term [political asylum] suggests that it really has no application to citizens of friendly countries, particularly those having democratic forms of government similar in principle to our own. The connotation surely is that someone seeking asylum aims to escape from political persecution by a regime having vastly different standards from ours. A deserter from the American Forces is liable to penalties, as of course

a Canadian deserter would be in this country, but he could not be said to be exposed to political persecution.[15]

Professor Robin Mathews of Carleton University in Ottawa has suggested his own unofficial explanation to account for the different treatment American refugees have received by the Canadian government. He wrote in *AMEX* magazine:

At the present time, as we all know, Canada is not threatened massively (or even slightly) by the imperialism of Hungary or Czechoslovakia. And so the claim that our obligation to United States citizens is "the same" as it was to Hungarians and Czechoslovakians is simplistic, sentimental nonsense. For the United States exile in Canada is different politically, socially, culturally and individually from any other exile we could conceivably harbour, because of the immense effect of U.S. imperialism in Canada, because of his own conditioning before he comes here, and because of the attitude of resident U.S. citizens in Canada.[16]

Both explanations take into account the unique relationship Canada has had with the American government.

Reactions of Canadian Officials

Following America's escalation of the Vietnam War in 1964 and 1965, the draft calls increased. The first individuals who refused to be drafted or jailed fled across the border in late 1965 and the beginning of 1966. By late 1966, these Vietnam War objectors began coming to Canada in greater numbers. This necessitated the setting up of the first Canadian aid organizations in the major metropolitan centers. At this time, Canadian government officials began enunciating their policy with regard to these Americans.

In a letter to *Ramparts* magazine, September 1966, Deputy Minister Kent wrote, "There is not any prohibition in the Immigration Act or Regulations against the admission of persons who may be seeking to avoid induction into the Armed Services and, therefore, provided they meet immigration requirements we have no bases in law for barring their entry."[17]

External Affairs Minister Paul Martin told a press conference in September of the same year, "We don't feel under any obligation to enforce the laws in that regard of any country," when asked about draft dodging.[18]

Between 1966 and 1968, most of the American war objectors coming to Canada to evade the draft were referred to as draft dodgers by the Canadian officials and the public. Most of the Canadian government statements regarding American draft dodgers referred to the fact that the policy toward them was "neutral" and that their draft status was not taken into account in the assessment for the granting of landed immigrant status. However, if we examine the *Hansard*, Parliament's daily record, during this period, as well as various Canadian newspapers and articles on this subject, the ambiguity of Canadian policy with regard to draft dodgers is revealed.

Toward the end of 1966 there was considerable discussion among Canadian members of Parliament and government officials on the topic of draft dodgers. The leader of the Opposition, former Conservative Prime Minister Diefenbaker, brought this question to the attention of the House of Commons repeatedly and received the comments of Liberal Prime Minister Lester Pearson.

> Right Honourable Diefenbaker: Mr. Speaker, in the absence of the Minister of Manpower and Immigration, possibly the Prime Minister will either answer the question or take it as notice. ... According to the estimates of the committee on the subject of draft dodgers from the United States there are some 1,500 to 3,000 draft dodgers who have come to Canada and are now living here, with the expectation that in years ahead they will take out citizenship. What is the attitude of the government with regard to giving consideration to their obtaining citizenship in view of their refusal to accept the responsibilities of United States citizenship which was theirs?

> Right Honourable Pearson: Mr. Speaker, I will be glad to discuss the matter with the Minister, but it would be difficult to give a general answer to a question of this kind in respect of individuals who might be applying in the future for citizenship. I am sure at that time each individual application has to be considered on its merits, and all the factors, including the kind of thing mentioned by my right honorable friend, will have to be taken into consideration. I will discuss this with the Minister.[19]

Diefenbaker's comments were typical of those members of Parliament and government officials who were antagonistic toward American draft dodgers. They would have liked the Canadian government to take a position barring them from Canada. Prime Minister Pearson attempted to appear neutral in his response. He used the argument of judging each dodger on his individual merits, though he did include the man's draft status as one of the factors to be taken into consideration.

Two months later, the conservative MP from Ontario, Michael Starr, also directed a question to Prime Minister Pearson on government policy in regard to draft dodgers. This time Pearson denied the fact that the individual's draft status required any special consideration.

Right Honourable Pearson: Mr. Speaker, the rules regarding the admission to Canada of U.S. citizens would apply in the normal way to men in this category. The fact that these people were draft dodgers would probably be unknown to the immigration officers in any case, and I am sure my honourable friend would not wish to do anything which would interfere with the maximum freedom of movement across the border.

It is difficult to take action in individual cases, but we would certainly not do anything to encourage admission to Canada of this category of United States citizens.[20]

In the face of a negatively intentioned comment by MP Michael Starr, Prime Minister Pearson attempted to take a middle-of-the-road position, assuring him that the Canadian government did not encourage the admission of draft dodgers.

Two years later in 1969, Prime Minister Pierre Trudeau continued to echo Canada's ambivalent attitude in regard to American resisters entering Canada. This equivocation can be glimpsed from the following excerpts from the *Hansard:*

Donald MacInnis (Cape Breton-East Richmond): [He attempts to correct the record of his previous remarks on American deserters.] In reference to deserters from the United States I asked the Minister of Manpower and Immigration whether he was aware of the fact that deserters from the United States Army are more or less criminals. Mr. Speaker, the words "more or less" do not belong there. I referred to the fact that deserters were criminals. I now direct my question to the Prime Minister. Inasmuch as a criminal record bars entry into Canada, how can the entry of deserters be justified?

Right Honorable P.E. Trudeau: I think the honourable member had better put the "more or less" back in there — perhaps more of the "less" than of the "more."[21]

This statement speaks for itself. It sums up the wishy-washy official Canadian attitude toward American war objectors reflected in policy statements.

On the basis of the data from the *Hansard,* one could not conclude whether Canadian ambiguity toward American resisters was intentional or merely fortuitous. No matter which was the actual case, the ambiguous position clearly worked to the advantage of Canada. She obtained additional immigrants who, because of her immigration policy, were highly skilled and educated. All were young and definitely an attractive source of manpower. Ambiguity enabled Canada to pacify those government officials and citizens who were against admitting American war objectors by saying that no special consideration was given to them. At the same time, Canada was able to hold Washington at bay by not accepting these new immigrants as "political fugitives" but admitting them under the normal procedures of the Canadian Immigration Act. The United States accepted this with tolerance; Canada was acting as a safety valve in removing young dissidents from its midst and incorporating them into the Canadian labor force. They would be important in extracting the raw materials and manufacturing the military hardware that America needed to maintain its war in Indochina.

Canadian Immigration Act

The postwar period in Canadian immigration was characterized by increasing governmental control and regulation specifically related to manpower policy. Professor Freda Hawkins provided us with a comprehensive discussion of Canada's postwar immigration policy and program for the period 1945–70. She described the time 1963–71 as "a period of rapid change, the beginning of a great economic expansion, and the emergence, brought about by a combination of factors, of an overall manpower strategy for Canada which has embraced immigration."[22]

Anthony Richmond in his study on *Post War Immigrants in Canada* pointed out that "unlike some previous waves of migration for North America they [postwar immigrants] were not concentrated in the lowest levels of the social structure."[23] Educational preference during this period replaced racial discrimination as the major criterion in the selection and control of immigration in Canada. A recent annual report of the Department of Manpower and Immigration has declared that "the prime objective of immigration policies and programs is to encourage and facilitate the movement to Canada of those who have skills and talents in strong, general or specific demand in this country."[24]

Canada's expanding industrial economy in the postwar era called for a skilled labor force. The need for skilled tradesmen was expanding while the need for unskilled workers was declining. Canada made a major revision in her immigration policy in 1967 to reflect the needs of this growing industrialization that was taking place as part of the gradual but continuous integration of the Canadian economy into that of the American metropolis. The 1966 "White Paper on Immigration" provided the arguments upon which the new immigration policy was based.

Some people conclude that we should open our doors wide to a very large flow of immigrants. ... The fact however is that economic conditions

have changed. We do not have a frontier open to new agricultural settlement. Our people are moving off the land, not on to it. We are not a country of virgin lands and forests waiting to be settled by anyone with a
strong back and a venturesome spirit. Despite its low population density,
Canada has become a highly complex industrialized and urbanized society.
... If those entering the work force, whether native-born or immigrants do
not have the ability and training to do the kinds of jobs available, they will
be burdens rather than assets. Today (and in the forseeable future) Canada's expanding industrial economy offers most of its employment opportunities to those with education, training, skill...[25]

The publicized reason for the new immigration policy was to make it
more egalitarian and to eliminate any racial, religious or national bias in
the selection of applicants. Immigration Minister Jean Marchand stated,
"The main objectives of the new regulations are to achieve universality and
objectivity in the selection processes." The white paper declared that there
should be no discrimination "by reason of race, colour or religion."[26]

Thus, under the new law, each applicant's potential value to Canadian
society was to be assessed as objectively as possible, without regard to race
or national origin. Those granted landed immigrant status were permitted to
work and live in Canada and to become citizens after five years of residence.

However, while this new law gave rise to a "point system" that disregarded
race and national origin, it effectively discriminated in favor of those individuals who had completed their education or who possessed "high-demand"
occupational skills. It specifically excluded unskilled, uneducated persons. An
applicant for landed immigrant status under the point system was rated on
"units of assessment" and given a certain number of points based on his
education, occupational skills and demand, employment opportunities and
personal qualities. The applicant had to compile at least 50 out of 100
assessment points in order to obtain landed immigrant status.[27] Five of
the nine assessment categories concerned skills and occupation. For education and training, an individual could earn up to a maximum of 20 points.
Up to 15 points were given for "occupational demand," i.e., how badly an
applicant's skills were needed in Canada. The occupations in high demand
were determined by the Immigration Department and were subject to constant fluctuations, varying from province to province.

A maximum of five points was given to an applicant for employment
opportunities in the area of destination where there was a very strong general demand for labor. If there was an oversupply of labor in the area, he

received no points. These destination units were subject to change. However, the major industrial cities of southern Ontario and the mining centers in the north ranked consistently high. The point system also allowed for skills independent of current demand, in recognition of the continuing value of the investment of time and money used to acquire such a skill. "Occupational skill" was assessed according to the highest skill possessed by the applicant, ranging from 10 units for the professional to one unit for the unskilled laborer. Ten extra points were given for having employment arranged prior to entry into Canada, but these 10 points applied only if the application was made at the border. (This was altered in 1972.) Thus, 60 possible points out of 100 depended upon the occupation and education of the applicant.

The four remaining assessment categories of age, bilingualism, relatives residing in Canada and the ambiguous "personality assessment" did not affect the application of a professional since he usually did not need these points to pass. However, they were important to the semiskilled or unskilled worker. The age assessment gave an automatic ten points to those between 18 and 35 years old, deducting one point for each year thereafter. Thus youth who could serve a long productive life were favored over more elderly immigrants. Bilingualism was awarded with a maximum of 10 units. If the applicant had a relative in Canada willing to sponsor or nominate him in order to assist him in becoming established he was granted a maximum of five units. Finally, the "personality assessment" category most open to interpretation by individual immigration officers could net an individual a maximum of 15 units. How this assessment applied specifically to American exiles will be discussed in detail in chapters 4 and 5.

The 1967 immigration regulations also reconstituted the Immigration Appeal Board. Once the board could make recommendations to the minister on an appeal against an order of deportation, but these were in no way binding. Thus it had no truly independent status. The new Appeal Board had authority to deal "conclusively in all respects with an appeal against any Order of Deportation, with the exception of security cases." The minister no longer could use his discretionary authority to reverse the board's decisions as had occurred earlier.[28]

The procedure for accepting applicants for landed immigrant status was also altered by the 1967 regulations. Before 1966, immigration applications from visitors already in Canada were not accepted. This meant that almost all immigrants had to apply either by mail or through an American consulate subject to lengthy procedures. In 1966, the Immigration Department began

to accept applications from inside Canada but they were subject to a deferment of one year before an individual received his landed status. In 1967,
the one year deferment was reduced to a few months' time.

Restrictive Immigration Regulations

In November 3, 1972, new immigration regulations imposed restrictions
that were tantamount to the closing of Canada as a haven for most military
war resisters and deserters.[29] Persons who wanted immigrant status could
neither apply at the border nor from inside Canada. All applications were
either through a Canadian consulate in one's home country or by mail directly to Ottawa. As this procedure required a minimum of six months,
immigrating became untenable for fugitives from the military. This regulation was instituted by the outgoing Minister of Manpower and Immigration,
Bryce Mackasey, just before he was replaced in the Canadian cabinet after the
October federal elections. His successor, Robert Andreas, continued restrictive immigration policies.

Andreas's first major act was to monitor and control further additions to
the overburdened population of underground visitors. He imposed six-month
jail sentences and $1,000 fines, as well as the threat of deportation, for
visitors who intended to stay more than three months but failed to register
such intentions with the Immigration Department. Before the new ruling,
the border officials did not mention a three-month limit or record the entry. Under the new regulation immigration officials would register persons
planning to stay beyond three months.[30] Most importantly, the Immigration
Department in 1973 changed its procedure with regard to appeals against deportation. It declared a special adjustment of status program for visitors and
illegal immigrants who were registered between August 15 and October 15
and landed them under relaxed criteria.[31] Many American deserters became
landed under this scheme. Its important consequences for deserters in Canada
will be discussed fully in chapter 8. In November 1974, Andreas took steps to
slow down the number of sponsored immigrants coming to Canada. A deduc-
tion of ten points would occur unless an independent and a sponsored applicant could produce evidence that employment had been previously arranged
or that he would be entering a designated occupation. Andreas stated that
"it was essential at a time of uncertain employment opportunity that the
flow of immigration be closely related to the demands of the labor market."[32] High unemployment in Canada justified these restrictive immigration
measures for Canadian politicians of all parties. The era of liberal immigration
policy in Canada appeared to be at an end.

The full extent of the restrictive immigration policy and its rationale was found in a green paper that was tabled in Parliament early in 1975. It contained a major reevaluation of Canada's immigration policy and was the basis for public discussion upon which the government would bring down legislation to change the 1952 Immigration Act. The "wisdom of the 'expansionist' immigration philosophy that traditionally influenced Canada's outlook" was questioned, especially in light of a rapidly growing labor force in a difficult economic marketplace. The "most effective linkage between manpower and immigration policies" was seen to be the key factor of a newly structured immigration policy.[33]

Since the initiation of the white paper policy in October 1967 explicitly removing racial barriers, there was a "pronounced change in major source countries," with Third World countries providing a considerable portion of all immigrants. In 1966, before the present point system was introduced, 76 percent of immigrants came from Europe and only 6 percent from Asia. This trend dramatically reversed in 1973, with European countries representing only 39 percent and Asia's share growing to 23 percent. India and the Caribbean countries replaced countries such as Germany and France as major sources of immigrants.[34] This immigration trend generated concern as to the absorptive capacity of Canadian society in relation to the immediate market demand for skilled and unskilled labor.

A major problem was generated in 1966 with the creation of a new category of "nominated immigrants" who gained entrance to Canada based upon familial considerations (i.e., they had relatives in Canada) although they were not economically dependent upon them as were "sponsored immigrants." The green paper strongly implied that such "nominated immigrants" were responsible for the "downward trend in the overall skill level" of present-day immigrants to Canada. It was suggested that a continuation of the class of "nominated immigration" could not be reconciled with the "full realization of the economic and manpower objectives which the new immigration structure was designed to support."[35] As one might expect, the major ethnic groups in Canada from Third World countries viewed the green paper as a racist document directed toward restricting immigration from their native countries and making it more difficult for members of their family to come to Canada.[36] Although the green paper of 1975 was tabled after the flow of American refugees to Canada had already occurred, preliminary preparation for its emergence did indirectly affect the nonlanded American refugees, especially in 1973 when Parliament proclaimed the Adjustment of Status Act in order to clear the decks for a new immigration policy.[37]

The Channeling of American Youth during the Vietnam War Era

Most American war objectors during the Vietnam War period emigrated to Canada under provisions of the 1952 Canadian Immigration Act and sought to obtain landed immigrant status under the revised regulations of 1967 and the point system. Certainly the most important feature of these provisions affecting the entry of these exiles was its continuation of the class-based, manpower channeling system that operated in the United States during most of the Vietnam War years through the Selective Service System. As we have seen, under the terms of the Canadian Immigration Act the preferred immigrants were those with education, youth and skill. Necessarily, this would favor the middle-class draft dodger over his working-class deserter compatriot. Working-class youths were not able to meet the educational and occupational requirements sufficiently to raise their scores above the 50 points necessary to gain entrance to Canada as landed immigrants. Since the bulk of the deserter population fell into this category, most of these exiles had great difficulty in moving from underground to landed status in Canada. Thus, the same youths of working-class origins who were channeled into the United States Army in the first place found that the same negative selection operated against them in their efforts to start life anew in Canada after desertion from the Army. (See the graph and table following.)

Among the supporters of American exiles in Canada, Melody Killian and Rick Ayers saw this not as a fortuitous circumstance but rather as part of a continental system of youth channeling that served to integrate the manpower flow in both the American heartland and the branch economy of Canada. In their article in *Our Generation* entitled "The Exploitation of Youth" they pointed out the pervasive influence of the American marketplace on youth throughout North America. "Although these young men have kept themselves out of the military and Vietnam by removing themselves from the Selective Service System, they have not escaped the continental system of youth channeling. Because of Canada's satellite economic status, it is by definition an integral part of the imperial system which exploits youth manpower in the United States and elsewhere."[38]

Having left the United States in order to opt out of the channeling of the draft and the military, the American refugee found himself once again being channeled into the service of the American empire, this time on the economic front instead of the military one. Because of Canada's participation in the Vietnam War as a resource base for the United States, a supplier of manufactured war items and a supplier of information by virtue of its position on the International Control Commission for Vietnam, many American youth recognized that their attempts to integrate into the Canadian economy would necessarily lend indirect support to the American war effort. Only those individuals who dropped into a communal life-style claimed to have opted out of the continental wide channeling system operating in the United States and Canada. The careers of these individuals will be discussed in detail in chapters 6 and 7.

Perhaps the most striking feature of the youth flow from America to Canada was the fact that many of the rejects from America became the preferred immigrants of Canada. This anomaly becomes less perplexing when we realize that most of these young men have emerged with jobs in a Canadian economy dominated by American branch plants. Hence, the outflow of young Americans from the United States favored both America and Canada. Canada gained skilled and educated manpower. America lost dissident youth that it could not control within its boundaries.

Every industrialized state needs a large number of technical and skilled personnel to run its industrial plants and economy. In the United States this large number of skilled workers was supplied through the channeling both of the Selective Service System into the "essential" professions and the educational system. Canada, having no Selective Service system, had to rely solely on channeling within its education system to obtain its own skilled manpower. The post-World War II education system was adapted to the needs of a branch plant economy that constituted part of the American military-industrial complex rather than to those of an independent Canadian economy. The educational system was not able to produce the full range of highly qualified manpower necessary to maintain the Canadian economy and to develop and provide for its economic growth. Thus Canada had to rely upon skilled technicians from the United States and other countries. The consequences of the Canadian channeling of manpower, both for its own youth as well as the surplus youth of the United States, ultimately has been to grease the wheels of the American military machine. As Killian and Ayers have concluded, "Imperialism is indeed a total system, and immigration from one part of the empire to another cannot release one from its grip."[39]

The Canadian vehicle for channeling the flow of manpower coming up from below the border was the Canadian Immigration Act and its point system. An assessment of a representative draft dodger and deserter's relative points would look something like the following:

THE CHANNELING OF AMERICAN YOUTH
DURING THE VIETNAM WAR ERA

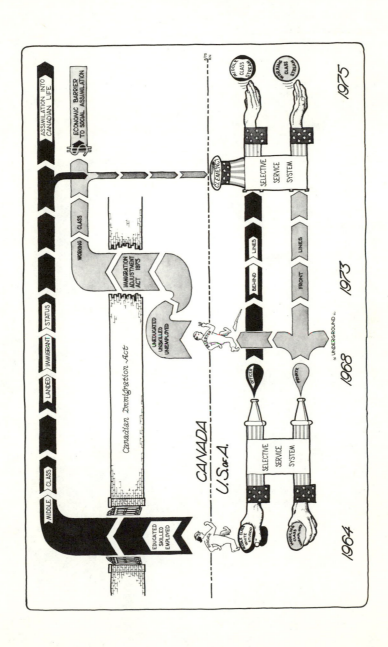

		Draft Dodger	Deserter
Age		10	10
Education		16 (B.A.)	12 (H.S.)
Occupational demand		15	1
Occupational skill		10	1
Area with manpower shortage		0	5
Bilingualism		10	5
Relative in Canada		0	0
Personal assessment		10	10
	Total	71	44

A young, college-educated draft dodger who sought landed immigrant status would automatically accumulate enough points, whereas a high-school educated deserter would not be able to obtain the minimum number, 50, even allowing for a high number of personal assessment points (which was based completely upon the personal discretion of the immigration officer) and manpower shortage points.[40]

Thus the system channeled out the working-class deserter even if he obtained a favorable personal assessment by the examining immigration official. Since many of the deserters would score even lower on the educational assessment than indicated in the table, this picture was certainly not an optimistic one. The American draft dodger was allowed to enter Canadian society to begin the acculturation process, whereas the typical deserter could not even legally enter as an immigrant and had to remain underground. Getting landed meant getting a job either before or after further education. Despite the hazards of seasonal unemployment, the higher unemployment rate in Canada than the United States and competition with Canadian workers, most of the landed dodgers managed to obtain jobs. Thus many eventually found themselves contributing directly or indirectly to the Canadian branch plants of the very same American corporate structures that they had opposed in their fight against the Vietnam War in the United States. The successful intermeshing of the channeling of the Selective Service System and the Canadian Immigration Act had brought these dissidents back "home" again, although they were now residents in a foreign land. By reintegrating these youth into the branch plant economy north of the 49th parallel, they were once more pressed into the service of North American capitalism. Dissent in the United States was thereby maneuvered into a net gain for the multinational corporations, albeit within the confines of the branch plant economy of Canada.

In the following chapters we will look at the career routes of American dodgers and deserters in Canada, the pattern of the support groups assisting them in Canada and the success of their integration into Canadian life. We will also see how the unexpected immigration readjustment amendment to the Appeal Board Act aimed at illegal residents, allowed many deserters to obtain landed status under relaxed immigration criteria. In each of these processes there existed a dynamic tension, political and social, between the institutions in both Canada and the United States which served to sustain American corporate hegemony in North America and the aspirations of the individual war resisters. As we shall see, in leaving the United States in an effort to escape from perceived injustice, the exile usually went through a radicalization in his point of view regarding the basis for that injustice. The migration of tens of thousands of young Americans during the Vietnam War period was not just an effort to escape a particular war but was, in most instances, an effort to shape individual lives around sets of ideals that would no longer incorporate the economic framework that supported such wars. It was the recognition of this dynamic tension by individual exiles and their collective aid groups that explained their hopes for the future and their positions on such important questions as amnesty. Thus these American victims of the Vietnam War were forced to understand American imperialism as it affected the conditions of their lives even after their flight to Canada.

Paradoxically, some of the channeling to which these individuals were subjected upon entering Canada was not only that of the Canadian government's immigration policies, but also that of the Canadian aid groups themselves in their efforts to assimilate these American refugees.

NOTES

1.   John Porter, *The Vertical Mosaic* (Toronto: University of Toronto Press, 1965).
2.   George Kitchen, "Growth of Nationalism in Canada," *Vancouver Sun*, Dec. 18, 1974, quoting from Economic and Social Council, United Nations, December 1974. The following extensively documents the dependency of Canada's economy on foreign ownership: Watkins, et al., "The Watkins Report: Foreign Ownership and the Structure of Canadian Industry," December 1967. The background of this report has been written up in a book entitled, *Gordon to Watkins to You*, ed. D. Godfrey and M. Watkins (Toronto: New Press, 1970).
3.   *Vancouver Province*, September 4, 1970.

4.   *Vancouver Sun,* January 28, 1975. Professor James Eayrs of the University of Toronto in his weekly column disclosed that leaked U.S. Defense Department documents "show that Canadian governments have consistently turned a blind eye to the destination of our exports of arms and military equipment. Ostensibly bound for the U.S., these supplies wound up in Indochina. Ottawa knew it all along, but denied that it was happening."

5   Claire Culhane, *Why Is Canada in Vietnam?* (Toronto: New Canada Publications, 1972).

6.   George Grant, *Technology and Empire: Perspective on North America* (Toronto: House of Anansi, 1969), pp. 63—64.

7.   Booklet entitled, "Ottawa's Complicity in Vietnam" (Student Association to End the War in Vietnam, Toronto, 1967.)

8.   Report by the Committee on Armed Services, United States Senate, "Treatment of Deserters from Military Service," May 21 and 22, 1968, p. 44.

9.   Quote from Tom Kent, Canadian Minister of Manpower and Immigration, found in a personal letter to MP Herbert Herridge, dated January 31, 1968.

10.   For a background on the conscription issue in Canada see R. MacGregor Dawson, *The Conscription Crisis of 1944* (Toronto: University of Toronto Press, 1961); J.L. Granatstein, *Conscription in the Second World War,* 1939—1945 (Montreal: Editions de Jour, 1962; Edgar MacInnis, *Canada: A Political and Social History* (New York: Holt, Rinehart and Winston, 1963); and A.M. Williams, et al., *Conscription 1917* (Toronto: University of Toronto Press).

11.   G.V. La Forest, *Extradition To and From Canada* (New Orleans: Hauser Press, 1961), Appendix I, p. 131.

12.   A. Richmond, *Post War Immigrants to Canada* (Toronto: University of Toronto Press, 1967), pp. 14, 15.

13.   The International Convention relating to the status of refugees and the 1967 protocol defines a refugee as "any person who, owing to well-founded fear of being persecuted for reasons of race, religion, nationality, membership of a particular social group, or political opinion, is outside of the country of his nationality and is unable or, owing to such fear, is unwilling to avail himself of the protection of that country; or who not having a nationality and being outside the country of his former habitual residence, is unable or, owing to such fear, is unwilling to return to it" (Joseph Sedgwick, Q.C., "Reports On Applicants In Canada," p. 11).

14.   Department of Manpower and Immigration, *Annual Report* (1968—1969) on "The Special Czechoslovakian Refugee Movement."

15. Letter written by Tom Kent, dated January 31, 1968, sent to M.P. Herbert Herridge.

16. *AMEX* 2, no.4: 24—25.

17. *Ramparts*, September 26, 1966, letter by Tom Kent.

18. *Weekend*, November 26, 1966.

19. *Hansard*, December 12, 1966, First Session, 27 Parliament, vol. X, p.10982—3.

20. *Hansard*, February 1, 1967, First Session, 27 Parliament, vol. VII, p. 12523.

21. *Hansard*, May 23, 1969, First Session, 28 Parliament, vol. VIII, p. 8994.

22. Freda Hawkins, *Canada and Immigration: Public Policy and Public Concern* (Montreal: McGill-Queen's University Press: 1972).

23. Anthony Richmond, *Post War Immigrants in Canada*, p. 100.

24. Fred A. Hawkins, *Canada and Immigration*, p. 71.

25. *Canadian Immigration Policy* (Ottawa: Queen's Printer, 1966).

26. Ibid.

27. Immigration Regulations of the Department of Manpower and Immigration, Schedule A, October 1, 1967.

28. Ibid, p. 35. The Immigration Appeal Board was a statutory court. The original board consisted of nine members, including a chairman and two vice-chairmen, who had to be lawyers. The board was independent of any government department or agency in the exercise of its judicial functions. An appeal was a full public hearing as in any court and involved presentation by each party of evidence, written and oral, together with legal argument. Refer to Freda Hawkins, *Canada and Immigration*, those pages on the Immigration Appeal Board.

29. Immigration Regulations, November 3, 1972.

30. Ibid., announced on December 28, 1972.

31. Annexed regulations to the Immigration Appeal Board Act, PC 1967 (26084) authorizing the Special Adjustment of Status Program, PC 1973 (2313 and 2314).

32. Immigration Regulation, *Vancouver Sun*, November 1974.

33. Canadian Immigration and Population Study, *Manpower and Information Canada* (December 1974), pp. 26, 36.

34. Ibid., vol. 1, p. 32, 22.

35. Ibid., vol. 1, p. 33; vol. 2, p. 90.

36. *Vancouver Sun*, February 3, 1975.

37. Ibid.

38. Melody Killian and Rick Ayers, "The Exploitation of Youth," *Our Generation* 6 (Fall 1969): 114—47.

39. Ibid., p. 136.

40. Ibid., p. 134.

4

Refugee Aid Groups
and Their Allies

The aid groups that emerged in Canadian cities in 1966 to assist young American refugees played a pivotal role in introducing these individuals to Canadian life as well as introducing Canadians to the realities of the American political refugee. These groups attempted to bridge the gap between the emigrant-exile and the emerging new Canadian.

Although only a relatively small number of American refugees became involved with the aid and exile groups in Canada, their overall influence upon immigration policy and Canadian public opinion was much greater than their numbers would indicate. The individuals in these groups were usually those Americans who were previously involved in draft counseling, protest activity in America or resistance in the Armed Forces, together with those men who had been newly politicized in the process of confronting the draft and the military.

The refugee aid groups assisted anyone who came into their offices seeking their help. The staff members considered themselves nonsectarian and in that sense they did not subscribe to any particular political ideology. However, they did see themselves as being part of the loose antiwar movement in North America.

With the arrival of large numbers of deserters to Canada in the early 1970s, the refugee aid groups were forced to examine their underlying assumption that assimilating large numbers of American draft dodgers into Canadian life as quickly as possible was their primary mission. They began to realize that they were merely successful in processing the middle-class dodger, not the working-class deserter under the Canadian Immigration Act. If so, were they merely perpetuating the class bias of the channeling system in the United States? Questions of this sort began to emerge as serious ones.

How did the various aid groups in Canada serve the refugee community? What were the mechanics of the counseling process? Most importantly, how did counseling manage to become integrated into the channeling system of the Canadian Immigration Act? An examination of the functioning and the mechanics of their operations will reveal some interesting answers to these questions.

Aid Groups and Their Interaction with Clients

Data supplied by the Canadian Ministry of Manpower and Immigration indicate that the peak year for draft-age American male immigrants obtaining landed immigrant status in Canada was 1970 (see graph and Summary). According to the reports from the various aid groups throughout Canada, this corresponded to a period where there was a maximum flow of both dodgers and deserters into Canada. As the dodgers were able to obtain landed status and the deserters usually not, the data supplied by the Canadian government and shown on the graph reflect primarily the flow of draft dodgers into Canada. The exception lies in the peak for 1973, in which the adjustment for illegal residents (to be described in greater detail in chapter 8) allowed deserters to obtain landed status.

The peak flow of American draft dodgers to Canada was from 1968 with an upward curve beginning in 1965. After the draft was ended and the United States had formally removed itself from the Vietnam conflict in 1973, the flow naturally tapered off, although it had already been declining since 1970 when the lottery system for the draft was initiated. The flow of deserters to Canada was low before 1969, peaked in the period 1969–72 and also tapered off in the years 1973–75. During the Vietnam War era of 1965–75, data from the graph and in the Summary indicate that an estimated 40,000 draft-age males were landed in Canada. As the Canadian government made a point of not keeping data on numbers of American dodgers and deserters obtaining

AMERICAN IMMIGRATION TO CANADA:
1960–1975

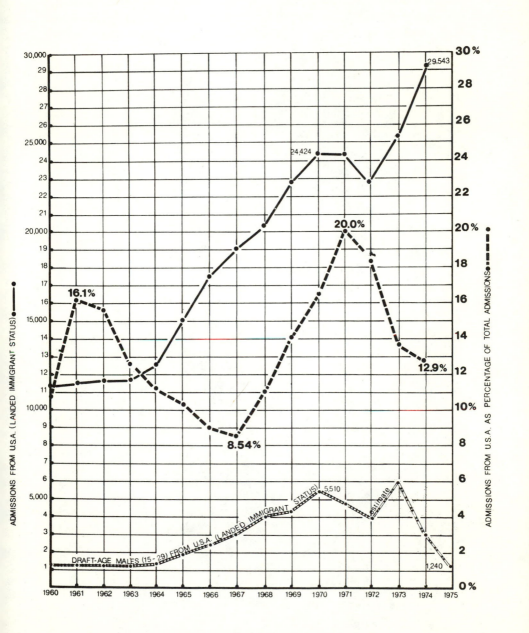

Summary of Immigration of Draft-Age
American Youth to Canada During the Vietnam War Era*

	Draft-Age Males Granted Landed Status	Dodgers and Deserters Granted Landed Status (estimated)*
1965–1972 immigration	30,150	20,230
1973–75 immigration (estimate)	7,200	3,520
1973 Adjustment of Status Program (estimate)	3,000	3,000
Totals:	40,350	26,750

*See Appendix C for complete data and references.

landed status during the Vietnam War period,[1] we can only estimate this population by looking at the American male population aged 15 to 29 for which statistics existed rather than the 18 to 26 population normally inducted into the United States Army. If we assume that the 1,240 draft-age males emigrating to Canada, the yearly average of the pre-Vietnam War years, were immigrants who were not refugees from militarism during the Vietnam War period, then the estimated number of dodgers and deserters landed in Canada by 1973 decreases from 40,000 (high estimate) to about 30,000 (low estimate). This includes the assumptions indicated in Appendix C. Thus we can estimate that by 1975 there were roughly 20–26,000 dodgers and 10–14,000 deserters present in Canada as landed immigrants from the Vietnam War era, making the assumption based on my own estimates and those of various counseling groups that the ratio of dodgers to deserters was 2:1 at that time. This estimate is considerably higher than the 5,000 to 6,000 dodgers and deserters estimated to be in Canada in 1974 by the Pentagon.[2] In addition, while no hard data are available, I estimate that another 10,000 American deserters came up to Canada during the Vietnam War era only to return to the United States after failing to get landed and assimilate there.

This population of landed dodgers and deserters represented about a fifth of the world's total flow of manpower to Canada at the peak years 1970–71, as seen by the peak in the graph. The earlier peak was a result of the decreasing immigration to Canada from the rest of the world while at the same time American immigration remained level in the pre-Vietnam War period.

At the height of the American immigration, there were between 26 and 32 Canadian aid groups functioning to aid American refugees across Canada.[3] They were located in the provinces of British Columbia, Alberta, Saskatchewan, Manitoba, Ontario, Quebec, New Brunswick and Nova Scotia. The largest aid operations were located in the major cities of Montreal, Toronto and Vancouver. Toronto received approximately 70 percent of all Americans seeking aid, with Montreal and Vancouver most of the other 30 percent. It was also estimated that one-fifth of the total number of Americans seeking refuge in Canada never received aid from any of these groups.[4] The following ethnography is an account of the aid groups functioning during the late sixties and early seventies at the height of American influx to Canada.

All the major groups had small store-front offices where most of their work was centralized. Only the small groups carried out their work in one or two homes. The offices had regular hours when they were open to Americans, although it was not unusual to see the office lights burning during weekends and some evenings when there was a mailing or a big fund-raising event being planned. Most of the groups had also changed their addresses a number of times, usually adjacent to or in the vicinity of immigrant areas of town. Most had occasion to be confronted with an eviction notice from an unsympathetic landlord complaining about too many clients and long hair and about peace signs cluttering the walls.

In Vancouver, the underground railroad surfaced in an old warehouse on the fringes of Chinatown. It was in a shabby brick building that was previously a broom factory. This was its third location. Even then the rent was too high and the building was not adequately heated for the winter months. The inside walls were covered with antiwar posters and peace slogans such as We Didn't Go!, and a picture of Uncle Sam with the caption, "Interested in Helping Out? The Committee Needs You." Other pictures related to the Vietnam War: a peace montage pictured one week's dead, a poster of a Vietnamese holding a gun in support of the NLF and a sign, End Canada's Complicity in Vietnam, across two skeletons symbolizing the United States and Canada. In the center of the room was a large bulletin board covered with suggestions for jobs and accommodations as well as personal warnings and notices. On one side was a mailbox system for relaying letters from people in the United States. This was used by many refugees who did not have permanent addresses and wanted a safe place to receive mail from home and the important documents necessary for immigration.

The Vancouver Committee office and atmosphere were typical of all the offices. These aid offices were social places where new arrivals first came to learn about immigration procedures. It was a place to rap and meet new friends who had similar problems. Experiences with other refugees and old-timers were exchanged. For the newcomers, it was the place where you could receive the latest message from home or from your girlfriend off the letter rack. You could casually come off the streets and relax. Nobody would harass you and you could read quietly. Most of the offices subscribed to or received contributions from a number of the local underground presses and magazines, in addition to American and peace publications. Socialist publications, such as the *National Guardian, Socialist Worker,* the English translation of the Cuban *Granma* and the *Vietnam Courier* were available. All day long both newcomers and earlier arrivals to Canada dropped by the office to rap with friends and hear the latest news about draft laws and politics in the States. The original counseling groups such as the Toronto Anti-Draft Program (TADP), the Montreal Council and the Vancouver Committee to Aid American War Objectors (VCAAWO) continued to provide immigration counseling, serving primarily newcomers who wanted to obtain immigrant status. Most of the counseling groups in the later years cooperated closely with the more politically oriented aid groups that continued to provide hostel accommodations to refugees who needed immediate accommodation. They also cooperated closely on fund raising, social events and conferences. The degree of cooperation varied from city to city and at different times of the year. Almost all of these groups were staffed by American refugees of draft age in addition to other sympathetic American expatriates. Over the years, there was a frequent turnover of staff. Since 1969, almost all the offices had both draft dodgers and deserters on the staff, as well as women. A counselor who had been on the staff for over a year was considered a veteran. A full-time counselor working day in and day out usually could not tolerate longer than six to ten months before he became emotionally "burned out" from the extreme demands of the work. After a rest period, a few dedicated souls would come back to continue their work, especially if there was no one immediately available to take over. Usually before a counselor left he would spend a month or two "breaking in" a replacement, working with him until he learned the counseling procedure, office routine and the myriad of details to be handled. Almost all of the offices operated on a shoestring budget dependent on contributions. When funds were plentiful, most counselors received a subsistence salary of $250 per month. After 1970, with outside support from the churches, the salaries increased to $650. These offices usually had one to four counselors in addition to volunteer secretarial help. There was no staff hierarchy or "head counselor"; everyone was considered to be one of the staff. When the media attributed the "head" job to one of the staff interviewed, this was usually ridiculed and cited as an indication that the media "doesn't know where it's at."

By the late period of the Vietnam era (1972–1975), with the winding down of the war and the draft in the United States, and with the subsequent tightening of immigration requirements in Canada, the immigrant aid groups found themselves with few potential counselors. Only the major counseling services were still active by June 1973.[5]

Community Support

The Canadian aid groups relied largely on community support, coming mainly from religious groups, the Canadian student community and leftist political groups, including the Canadian peace movement. Since these aid groups were largely charitable welfare aid organizations, the type of aid and

support they solicited were along these lines. Financial donations were needed to run the offices and pay minimal salaries to those refugees who provided
counseling. Temporary housing and job offers were also provided by these
support groups.

The United Church of Canada, Mennonites, Unitarians and Quaker religious groups were the major supporters of the American refugees from the
outset. These groups provided financial aid, opened their homes to Americans
and from time to time served as political pressure groups in the interests of
these Americans. For example, in Toronto, an Anglican church assigned a
former Canadian army chaplain to counsel American military deserters. The
Unitarians in Vancouver set up Immigration Aid to Refugees of Conscience,
a group that mainly supplied funding to the Vancouver Committee. The
Canadian Mennonites published a book *I Would Like To Dodge the Draft-
Dodgers But* . . . as part of its educational campaign to explain the dilemma
of American refugees to Canadian religious communities and to remind them
of their ethical obligations to this group. The editor, Frank H. Epp, pastor
of the Mennonite Church in Ottawa donated an office to the Ottawa aid
group. In Ontario, the Mennonite farmers went out of their way to hire
American refugees for as long as they wanted, complete with room and
board. They sent delegations and briefs to the federal government petitioning
for political asylum for these men. The Mennonites sent a delegation to meet
with Prime Minister Trudeau as early as the spring of 1970 urging asylum.
Trudeau assured them that Canada would continue to be a "refuge from
militarism."

In Vancouver and Montreal, individuals from the various organizations
formed Canadian assistance groups functioning as sponsors and financial
donors. A young minister of the United Church in Toronto, Eiler Fredericks,
once a German refugee himself, was a long-time sponsor of American refugees
who took many refugees into his own home for varying lengths of time.
According to him, "It takes the kids up to a month just to be able to cope
with the shock of what they have done. And so they tend to be somewhat
disoriented at first and sit around the house for a long time. And then
gradually we begin to encourage them to go out and find a job and do something in the community...."

It is interesting to note that many of the members of these adult assistance
groups were themselves ex-American political refugees. A number of them
were victims of the McCarthy era who lost their jobs because of their alleged
left-wing associations in the past. Many left the United States with their

families during the Vietnam War era as a protest because they felt it was an unhealthy atmosphere for their children and did not want their draft-age boys to be subjected to the unfair decision of war or jail.

Relatively few of those approximately 50,000 draft-age refugees who themselves received aid from the aid groups returned the aid to newcomers via the support organizations. Many of them obtained good jobs, settled into a middle-class life-style and had no further contacts with the aid groups or the Canadian peace movement. The problems that they initially experienced before making the transition to a stable existence were part of their unpleasant past. Aiding newcomers would inevitably bring back memories. Most American exiles did aid the friends they made when they first came to Canada, when they needed financial assistance or were in trouble with the police. The aid groups were partly responsible for the fact that more new Canadians did not in turn aid their fellow refugees. Since they were set up mainly to assist newly arrived immigrants, they did not actively solicit support or maintain any contact with the exiles after they became landed.

In the beginning, most of the aid groups received limited donations from friends in local communities and work was done on a voluntary basis. They were almost always in the red. A major portion of their financial aid in later years came from American organizations.

One of the early Toronto aid groups, The Student Union for Peace Action (SUPA), received a grant of $4,000 through the Canadian Privy Council in 1966 to carry on its activities, writing propaganda and counseling American resisters. However, the original source of SUPA's funds became a major concern of both opposition parties, the Progressive Conservatives (PC) as well as the New Democratic party (NDP). They suspected that Canadian youth organizations like SUPA received funds directly or indirectly from the American Central Intelligence Agency. In the following exchange in Parliament regarding SUPA's source of funds, David Lewis, leader of the NDP queried Prime Minister Lester Pearson, leader of the Liberal party.

> Prime Minister Pearson: The Canadian Union stated in this letter I received that there had been no direct contact between their Union and CIA operatives and when the grants were received from this organization [reference to the Foundation for Youth and Student Affairs] they considered it to be a reputable private organization. They did not know at the time that it had any connection whatsoever with the CIA.
>
> David Lewis (York South): May I ask the Prime Minister whether his reply accepted their suggestion that the Canadian government should

protest this intrusion by U.S. government agencies into Canadian affairs by way of a front organization?

Prime Minister Pearson: Mr. Speaker, the only information on this matter I have received at the present time which would seem to warrant any protest to the U.S. government is in respect to an offer of a small amount of money through a foundation [reference to SUPA's grant], the nature of which I am not entirely clear about, but which appears to be a front organization of the CIA.[6]

It became clear from this discussion that SUPA not only had received Canadian government funds to carry on its central activity of encouraging draft dodgers in Canada, but it was a distinct possibility, acknowledged by the Prime Minister, that Canadian foundations aiding Canadian youth organizations like SUPA were being used and financially supported by the CIA in order to spy on the activities of American draft dodgers in Canada.

The major portion of financial aid to Canadian aid groups came from American religious groups. However, it was not until December 1969 that representatives of both Canadian and American religious organizations met in Windsor, Ontario, to discover how the religious community should respond to the American exiles. They urged the National Council of Churches to become involved in the funding of Canadian aid groups as well as providing other kinds of spiritual support. A direct response was the establishment of the Emergency Ministry Concerning United States Draft-Age Emigrants in Canada in February 1970.[7] They were instrumental in prodding the World Council of Churches in 1971 to sponsor a fund-raising project, raising $210,000 over a three-year period. Of this, $70,000 was to be spent in 1972 for "effective pastoral help for immigrants."[8] The remainder of the funds were used by the Canadian aid groups for expanded counseling and publicity during the sixty-day immigration adjustment program. The Emergency Ministry group, in addition to fund raising, provided spiritual guidance to friends and parents of the American refugees in Canada and maintained a regular communication link through their newsletter, *Contact*. Their leader, Richard Killmer, also reached a larger audience through the publication of his book with other colleagues, *They Can't Go Home Again*,[9] a compassionate account of American refugees. He has continued to be a major spokesman in the National Council for Universal and Unconditional Amnesty (NCUUA) formed in April 1973. NCUUA represents at least 54 national and local groups in the United States, including civil-rights groups, peace and anti-war groups as well as religious groups that have joined together to mobilize the American people to work for a universal and unconditional amnesty for all American war resisters and servicemen.[10]

Counseling Refugees Through the Immigration Process

Most of the committees across Canada had at least one full-time counselor. The major groups in Toronto, Montreal and Vancouver during their peak operation had two or more counselors working full time, depending on the number of immigrants they had to aid. The responsibility inherent in the counseling process was considerable. The counselor had to know the immigration laws inside out and had to keep abreast of changes in its interpretation by immigration officers. Although very few records were kept on each individual, the counselor had to keep many mental notes as to what border points were the best, which immigration officials should be avoided and other kinds of information for obtaining landed status that could make the difference between a person's application being accepted or rejected. Most important, a counselor had to have an understanding of, and empathy with, those he was attempting to aid. Assurance and friendly support were critical ingredients. Perhaps this is why almost all of the counselors were American.[11] As one Toronto counselor put it, "Americans understand what hassles the draft or military puts a man through and can best empathize with him." Counselors relied heavily on the *Manual for Draft-Age Immigrants to Canada,* which was the most complete information on immigration to Canada for American exiles throughout the Vietnam War era. It contained information on the mechanics of becoming a permanent resident of Canada and included Canadian history, culture, politics, standard of living, universities and other pertinent information a draft dodger might want to know. The first edition of the *Manual,* printed in January 1968, sold 5,000 copies. The second printing two months later sold 20,000 and the sales kept doubling. By 1970 the *Manual* was in its fifth edition with the same basic content and minor revisions and had sold a total of 65,000 copies.[12]

Most individuals had only two interviews with the aid group counselor. In the first interview, the counselor explained the procedure for obtaining immigrant status. The second contact was usually from three weeks to two months later, when the individual was getting ready to set up his appointment with immigration officials. He had been preparing all these weeks to do the essential tasks: gathering together all the important documents, lining up a job offer, etc. He had been told both by the counselor and by his compatriots that becoming an immigrant would be the first major event in his efforts to begin making a new life for himself in Canada.

In the early and middle periods of the Vietnam War, until 1972, it was almost invariably recommended by the aid groups that prospective Canadian immigrants enter Canada as visitors and consult with them before applying for landed status. This was relatively easy to do since Americans and Canadians were very open about visitors traveling between the two countries during this period. This procedure was drastically altered in the late period, from 1972 onward, due to stagflationary economic conditions which precipitated a more restrictive immigration regulation.

There were various options one could choose from in order to obtain landed immigrant status during this period. These included making application at the border or applying at an immigration office inside Canada, the process of nomination or sponsorship for those who had relatives in Canada and application by mail or at a Canadian consulate in the United States. The latter two methods were found to be unsatisfactory by the aid groups due to frequent discrimination against draft-age Americans. Only those persons who were highly qualified in education or skill or could not risk applying at the border were usually advised to obtain landed status from within Canada. The majority of draft resisters and deserters were advised to obtain immigrant status by application at the border. This method had many advantages. First, it was the quickest method and the decision was rendered immediately after the personal interview instead of months later. Second, an applicant who was rejected would probably be given an opportunity to withdraw his application so that he could reapply at another border point, a move that was not possible when applying from inside the country. Third, and often most important for those who were not highly qualified under the point system, a job offer counted for an additional ten points at the border but not when applying internally. It was also easier to obtain a job after you had entered Canada as a visitor. Finally, if you applied inside Canada or at the border, you would be dealing with Canadian officers less sympathetic to the official American view of exiles than those at most Canadian consulates located in major American cities.

Over the years the counseling process used by the aid groups directed toward obtaining immigrant status became more or less routine. Each new arrival was given a questionnaire to fill out requiring specific details about his personal background, education and work record, designed to obtain the desired information for obtaining immigrant status. Anticipating that many of the refugees would be in a paranoid state and reluctant to divulge this information, the Vancouver questionnaire promised that replies would be held in confidence. In spite of this, many men omitted their name or hid behind an alias that they had assumed for self-protection. The Committee was also cautious with this information. After the questionnaire was completed and read by the counselor, it was usually filed for a few months until the individual was ready to apply for landed immigrant status. In the Vancouver office, the deserters' questionnaires were either taken home by the counselor or carefully locked up in a file cabinet, whereas the dodgers' questionnaires were often left in an open desk. These were the only records kept on the refugees who were aided by the Vancouver Committee. This lack of paperwork and records on its "clients" was deliberate and designed for security purposes. There was also a basic disdain for paperwork and the kind of red-tape procedures that were used by "establishment" agencies that treated individuals like "objects."

This initial information was used by the counselor to assess the individual's chance of success as an applicant for immigrant status needing 50 points. The immigration point system was explained and the types of experience which gave the applicant additional points were stressed.

A person could be disqualified from obtaining landed status by falling within a "prohibited class" described in the Immigration Act: "The existing prohibited classes of individuals broadly speaking, includes criminal offenders, mentally or physically defective and diseased persons, criminals, members of subversive organizations, spies or sabateurs and a variety of morally or socially undesirable persons, including public charges."[13] More specifically, criminal offenders were "persons who have been convicted of or admit having committed any crime involving moral turpitude," which usually meant any major felonies committed in the United States that were recognized as such by Canadian law. This usually included drug users who were engaged in or suspected of engaging in unlawful activity with narcotics. Morally or socially undesirable persons include prostitutes, homosexuals, chronic alcoholics and persons "who are likely to become public charges." The category of political subversives was defined as people who had been associated with organizations subversive to democratic government or persons "concerning whom there are reasonable grounds for believing they are likely to engage in or advocate subversion." Also prohibited were "persons concerning whom are likely to engage in espionage, sabotage, or any other subversive activity directed against Canada or detrimental to the security of Canada."[14]

In the Vancouver Committee sample a total of 63 persons out of a total of 424 answered that they had a conviction record that might place them in a prohibited class. Of these, 20 men had been convicted of charges relating to marihuana possession, 38 relating to misdemeanor charges involving things like vagrancy, loitering, trespassing, delinquency, joy-riding and alcoholism and four were felonies like grand larceny. One individual was convicted for desertion from the Navy.

If the individual did not fall into a prohibited class the counselor then rated the prospective immigrant as if he were the examining immigration officer. If the person came out low on points, he was given suggestions for picking up a few extra ones. For example, he might be told that if he were to get a good job offer and apply at the border, he would be likely to be successful. Alternately, he might be advised to apply in another province where it was known to be easier to get landed even though he did not qualify in the province of British Columbia. He might be told to develop a skill that would be considered useful in Canada. If the newcomer already had previous correspondence with the aid group or had read the *Manual* he would already be familiar with the above procedures. However, more often than not he had no previous correspondence with any Canadian aid groups. In my sample of 123 persons, only 29 percent indicated that they had previous correspondence with an aid group; 71 percent indicated that this was their first contact.

A copy of the actual immigration application form was given to the individual to fill out in advance and he was advised to bring it to his second interview session with the counselor. His responses were carefully checked over, especially those questions dealing with education and employment. The refugee was advised to obtain as many official documents as possible. This usually included his birth certificate or passport, high-school and college transcripts or other school diplomas, trade certificates, a marriage certificate if applicable, and proof of good character in the form of letters of recommendation. In addition, he would show proof of financial assets and support. These documents were carefully checked by the counselor to make sure they had American addresses, so it would not appear that the individual had actually obtained them in Canada. If he had secured a job offer while in Canada it was also scrutinized.

In personal cases where a refugee was not able to obtain some of his documents because his parents had disowned him, for example, several of the aid groups would supply a high-school diploma or trade certificate. They would also lend some individuals who were borderline cases a Canadian identification. It was to be used only if they were turned down for immigrant status and could not obtain a visitor's pass to reenter Canada. They could then use the Canadian identification to reenter at another border point. This was especially important for the less-qualified deserters who had a warrant out for their arrest.

All applicants were also advised to divulge their ready cash and any proof of savings to the immigration official. Three hundred dollars was recommended as the minimum for a single individual with a good job offer and $500 for a married couple. For those men who were less qualified in other areas, additional money would speak in their favor. In the Vancouver Committee sample many more draft dodgers came up with enough money to meet this criterion than did deserters (see Table 16, Appendix B). Approximately one-half of the draft dodgers had $200 to $500 on them when they first came to Canada. One-quarter of them had over $500 and up to $5,000, whereas 60 percent of the deserters in the Vancouver Committee sample had only $50 or less, almost half of them having no money at all. Most of the deserters did not have enough money on them to qualify as landed immigrants. Those men who had no money of their own would be lent the required amount of money for this occasion by the aid counselor.

The individual was advised to be neat and clean and present himself as a solid middle-class person determined to work hard and be a productive citizen. They advised those who looked "hip" to shave and get their hair cut and appear "straight" for the day since it usually brought about the best results. The Vancouver Committee lent out suits and ties for this occasion. Before going to the immigration office, the counselor helped prepare the exile by giving him a mock interview in anticipation of the real one. The counselor usually stressed that other refugees had some problems with border officials. Thus the individual was prepared for the worst possible situation. Mike, an ex-Navy man, had the following mock interview at the Vancouver Committee to Aid American War Objectors in preparation for his immigration appointment:

> Counselor (taking the role of the border official): Have you ever been down to the Vancouver Committee?
> Mike: What committee? I don't understand what you're talking about. (Mike is playing dumb, as he was advised.)
> Counselor (looking at official papers): I see you don't have a service discharge.
> Mike: No sir, I don't. (Always be honest.)
> Counselor: Why do you want to immigrate to Canada?
> Mike: Canada's a big, beautiful wide-open country with plenty of oppor-

tunity (emphasizing the positive virtues).

Counselor: Have you ever visited Canada before?

Mike: Yes, while I was on leave from the Navy last August. I spent a week as a visitor here and really liked it.

Counselor: Does the fact that you're a deserter influence your decision to immigrate?

Mike: Well, I have many other reasons, but it's a contributing factor.

The above mock interview was compiled from various experiences with individual deserters who had sought the aid of the Vancouver Committee. It specifically inquired about the man's exile status, even though officially this was considered illegal by the Department of Immigration. Unofficially it happened quite frequently. The Committee's interview was designed to help the deserter or draft dodger feel confident even if direct questions about his exile status were asked.

According to the *Manual for Draft-Age Immigrants to Canada*, "personality assessment" was the category most open to interpretation by the individual immigration official. Usually these units were not calculated until last, and an immigration officer could use the personality assessment units to accept or reject a borderline case. For a maximum of 15 points, the officer judged the "adaptability, motivation, initiative, resourcefulness, and other similar qualities" of the applicant.[15] The language of the desired personality characteristics in the immigration proceedings was reminiscent of that used in the "channeling" document of the American Selective Service System. These qualities all involved the individual's ability to conform and to be useful to the economy.

Since there were so many immigrants applying for landed status at Canadian border points, it was usually recommended that an advance appointment be made. This would also avoid unnecessary waits. Car transportation to the border was best since it indicated the person has led a "stable and prosperous life." Most of the aid groups had a committee of "border runners" who drove people to the border for their appointment. In Vancouver there was a group of ministers and law students who regularly accompanied refugees to the border. It served to assure the individual and, most important, it seemed to impress upon the immigration official his responsibility in obeying the rules. In the event of an irregularity of procedure, a witness was always important.

Each border crossing was somewhat different. Many of the larger crossings like Blaine/Douglas in Washington/British Columbia had a "turn-around area," similar to a parking area, where the car could turn around without directly crossing into American territory. This was advantageous for a refugee who was fearful of a warrant out for his arrest. At the smaller borders, like at Sumas in British Columbia, there was no place to turn around. It was usually advisable to cross to the United States at a larger border crossing where each car was less conspicuous and then proceed to the border where the exile's appointment had been made. This gave the appearance that the car was coming directly from the United States.

If the interview went well, the individual was granted "provisional landed status" and permission to work; then his new life as a law-abiding immigrant in Canada was underway.

Early Beginnings of the Refugee Aid Groups

If this account of the counseling process sounds like the workings of a well-oiled bureaucracy, it could not be further from the truth. In reality, the aid groups were centered around the personalities of a few individuals. They were small groups run on the basis of personal contact; face-to-face relationships were considered to be important. The continuity of these groups often depended upon the intimate friendship networks that remained critical to the group's functioning and output of work. This will become apparent as we examine the origins of the aid groups.

In Vancouver in 1966 a small, concerned group of six university faculty members at the University of British Columbia and Simon Fraser University, together with four wives and an attorney, formed the original working group that called itself the Committee to Aid American War Objectors. Its chief spokesman was Benson Brown, a 27-year-old mathematics professor and a native of Montreal who did his graduate studies at the University of California, Berkeley.[1,6]

The group's first task was to study the Canadian Immigration Act as well as the extradition treaties between Canada and the United States and other legal aspects involving the status of fugitive Americans in Canada. These areas had to be thoroughly researched in relation to draft dodgers and deserters since there were no recent precedents involving this type of political refugee.

When the Vancouver Committee felt it had collected enough information to be knowledgeable about the Canadian Immigration Act, it began counseling young draft-age Americans in their homes. By word of mouth, individuals began referring their friends and acquaintances to these homes. In a short time, their phones were ringing day and night and there was an unending stream of individuals passing through these homes. It became a matter of practical necessity to set up a more formal meeting place where this counsel-

ing could go on and where correspondence could be answered more efficient-
ly.

An office was opened in October 1966, bearing the name of the Vancouver Committee to Aid American War Objectors. For the first few months of
operation the Vancouver Committee was busy setting itself up in its small
store-front building. The one front room accommodated visitors and "clients" and occasionally volunteers performing their services. There was a small
back room used for the counselor's office. Two women, Myra Riddell and
Margaret Brown, took on the total burden of the office work. Between
them, they counseled full time and operated a counseling service by mail.
They attempted to integrate the formal legal information they researched
with the practical experiences they gained by talking with these young men
about their individual draft situations. They continued to inform their work
by research and translated their information into basic informational pamphlets.

One of the early pamphlets of this type addressed itself to the problem of
"Immigration to Canada and Its Relation to the Draft." It was written by
Meg and Benson Brown together with the lawyer in their group, Doug Sanders. The pamphlet carefully raised the moral dilemma facing draft-age Americans and cited Canada as one of the viable alternatives available to them. It
stressed the point that an American who evaded or resisted the draft, regardless of his draft status formally, would have no greater difficulty entering and
remaining in Canada than any other American. All the relevant statuses (landed immigrant, student or visitor) that a non-Canadian could hold in Canada
were described. The landed immigrant status was recommended as the best
because it would lead to permanent citizenship. The individual's eligibility for
landed status, his application and how he qualified were spelled out in detail.
All of the information was carefully related to draft-age Americans. Subsequent editions of this pamphlet were printed and its use was continued by the
Vancouver Committee and the Montreal Council.

In the beginning of 1967, this pamphlet was published and mailed to
approximately 200 individuals in the United States who had sent inquiries
to the Vancouver Committee, as well as to a few American antiwar groups.
The 60 Americans who had been counseled by the Vancouver Committee in
its first few months of existence had gotten the word out to their friends in
the United States. Even the *New York Times* wrote a story on its existence,
quoting the spokesman for the group as stating, "A lot of draft resisters have
found it easier to get their landed immigrant status from our advice."[17]

Other important research was also done during this period. The legal consequences of renunciation of American citizenship were carefully researched by Meg Brown and Doug Sanders and a position paper was written. Other practical information sought by draft resisters included a description of colleges and universities in Canada, teaching jobs in British Columbia, advice for young men under 18 years of age who wanted to immigrate, advice on entering Canada as a visitor and on making the decision to come. All of these items and more were worked into leaflets and made available to potential draft dodgers. Many of these were eventually incorporated into the *Manual for Draft-Age Immigrants to Canada* a year later.

As the numbers of draft dodgers increased monthly to four or five new arrivals daily, plus two or so old faces who came in for additional counseling and aid, community support became necessary. Community contacts were sought in order to secure such things as short-term housing, legal aid, medical aid, job and vocational advice for new arrivals. Doug Sanders offered his legal services free of charge to draft dodgers. Funds were solicited from the community in order to run the office and assist those in dire financial straights. Valuable contacts were established with resistance groups in the United States as well as with newly emergent aid groups in other parts of Canada.

Montreal, Quebec

Steve, a draft resister we met earlier in chapter 2, came to Montreal in 1966 before the existence of any aid groups. Although he was quite sophisticated in dealing with his draft board, he had practically no information about Canada before he arrived there. After living and working in Montreal for one year, he found himself in the awkward position of having been arrested in an antiwar demonstration in Montreal and having no formal legal status in Canada. He had never become a landed immigrant. When he came to Canada in 1966 he did not realize that it was necessary. According to Steve, "I was faced with this problem within a week before my court trial of somehow legalizing myself because I'm a nonentity, so far as the Canadian government is concerned. This despite the fact that for better than a year I'd been earning a salary here and paying my income tax, too."

He decided against applying from within Canada, which was possible under the new regulations in force in 1967 since it would have taken months before he received his papers. Instead he worked out the following plans:

I had some friends drive me out to the eastern townships, in some very
    desolate section of the border, got some detailed geographical survey

maps, and we found a little dirt road that went within a mile of the border. I got out with my compass and went sloshing through the woods, until I came to a stream. I followed this until I passed under a road on the other side of the border. Meanwhile the car was going by a normal road back down to a checkpoint and met me on that bridge, picked me up, and then we very cautiously went through a couple of towns. They'd let me off before the town and drive through to see if things were clear and come back and pick me up and go through. It was like I thought I could have been in Nazi-occupied Europe in the Second World War. . . . It was that kind of thing; there were at least five years of my life involved. They drove me to the airport at Burlington, Vermont. I then flew to Dorval Airport, a border point in Montreal, where I applied for landed immigrant status.

Steve, being highly qualified, was landed with no difficulty, but there was much anguish and worry of deportation surrounding his experiences. Had there been an aid group to assist Steve, he might not have found himself in such a predicament.

Three months after Steve became a landed immigrant, on March 16, 1967, the Montreal Council was registered in the Superior Court of the Province of Quebec as an "official business." The Council was introduced to the public with a benefit performance of French-Canadian entertainers at the Café Campus near the University of Montreal. Over 500 persons jammed the café to celebrate this occasion.

Similar to the early Vancouver and Toronto groups, the Montreal Council offered its counseling services to any American refugee who asked for aid, regardless of his political orientation. It considered itself nonpartisan and was primarily a counseling group.

The formal organizational structure consisted of a five-member board of directors which met to make policy and review the work of the Council. The executive secretary, a board member, was the major coordinator of all the Council's activities. He was responsible for all personal correspondence as well as carrying out the counseling service. Since it was formed later, this group benefited from the research done by both the Vancouver and the Toronto groups and utilized their immigration pamphlets. Other board members included a public relations officer, who served as the official spokesman for the Council, a corresponding secretary, who handled communication with other peace and social action groups, a treasurer, who coordinated fund raising and finances, and a chairman, who convened and prepared the agenda for the monthly meetings. In its early stages it was the most structured of all the counseling groups and the only one to be formally registered within the city as a business organization. Like the other groups, legal aid was provided by volunteer lawyers to Americans who had immigration or other legal problems. Additional personal aid was provided by a group of social workers and a psychiatrist. Community support for the Council was provided by sponsors, who were prominent community leaders willing to lend their name to the group, as well as by families in the Montreal area who provided direct assistance to Americans through temporary housing, job opportunities and financial support.

The Montreal group started in much the same manner as the others. It began as a small group of concerned citizens and resisters who began counseling in their homes. There was more demand for their counseling services as more resisters came north. It then expanded and set up an office operation with regular persons in charge of counseling and other duties.

Toronto, Ontario

Since Toronto had the largest number of refugees, it was not surprising that it also had the largest number of aid groups. In Toronto the Student Union for Peace Action (SUPA) was the first Canadian organization to aid American resisters in late 1966. SUPA had been founded in the fall of 1964 and was the chief organization of the Canadian New Left. It consisted of a loosely organized group of students in the Toronto area who were attracted to the American New Left. The specific inspiration for SUPA projects came from the Economic Research Action Projects, which were loosely affiliated with the Students for a Democratic Society (SDS) in the United States. The Newark Community Union Project, which attempted to create "an interracial movement of the poor" in Newark, New Jersey, served as the model for SUPA projects. Personal contacts played a large part in transmitting this kind of activity from Americans to Canadian New Left persons. For example, the personal magnetism and ideas of Tom Hayden, a leader of the Newark project, had a pronounced effect on the attitude of SUPA leaders in Toronto and Montreal.[18]

SUPA, in alliance with SDS in the United States, had organized one of the largest research indexes of Left literature in North America. In early 1967, when Meg Brown's pamphlet "Immigration to Canada and Its Relation to the Draft" was published, it was placed on their literature list. According to Heather Dean, an organizer for SUPA during this time, "We received so many responses for further information and questions unanswered from this pamphlet, we spent much time doing nothing but answering letters about emigration to Canada. Eventually we were forced to hire a draft resister who spent full time answering this correspondence." In this manner SUPA became involved with draft counseling.

The draft resister hired was Richard Paterak. In many respects he was typical of the early resisters. He graduated from Marquette University in Milwaukee in the spring of 1965, was against the Vietnam War and wanted to avoid induction. As he saw it:

I graduated [from the] university and still being a starry eyed liberal do-gooder, I joined VISTA. I must say that the war was the first major crack I saw in the System, but that crack allowed me to see in deeper and see that the war wasn't the problem but a manifestation of it. The problem was the System. As I trained for VISTA I became what I thought was more radical.[19]

Richard and his wife worked for VISTA for a year in Louisville and Chicago doing community organizing in lower-income communities. Referring to his work he commented, "All of a sudden it seemed purposeless. We felt it would be better to fight the war than to fight slums and work and pay our taxes to the government." He came to the conclusion that the only way "I could maintain my integrity and my radical self" was to go to Canada. He felt it did not make sense to "just sit passively and let them draft me . . .so I decided to get on my horse right away."

Paterak had his office in the run-down brick building that was SUPA's headquarters near the University of Toronto. A pink slip posted on the green front door of his office read "Support the South Vietnam National Front For Liberation." He was paid by SUPA an occasional $25 a week to do full-time immigration counseling.

Under Richard Paterak's leadership and with the aid of other draft resisters, SUPA printed a 12-page guide to immigration entitled, "Escape from Freedom, or I Didn't Raise my Boy to be a Canadian." The second part of the title came from a cartoon panel on the cover. It pictured a mother trying to override her son's objections to burning villages and dropping bombs but objecting herself when her son fled to Canada.[20] The pamphlet was similar in content to the Vancouver immigration pamphlet, though it was more flamboyant in the New Left style. The Union sent over 1,000 of these booklets to various antiwar groups and individuals in the States. Although many draft resisters were aided by this kind of immigration literature, only a minority of the resisters, according to Richard, made use of SUPA's counseling service.[21]

In the United States, the Students for a Democratic Society were not happy that SUPA was involved in counseling and creating propaganda designed to encourage more men to come to Canada. The leaders in SDS, like Tom Hayden and Rennie Davis, expressed the fear that their revolutionary forces in America might "split" to Canada instead of working for the "Revolution" at home. They put enormous pressure on SUPA to disassociate itself from the counseling of draft dodgers. Being loyal to SDS, SUPA eventually bowed out of these responsibilities. At the end of 1967, SUPA split into two factions and ceased to be the major Left group leading the movement in Canada.

Around this time, American refugees in Toronto who were involved in immigration counseling founded their own organization, which became known as the Toronto Anti-Draft Programme (TADP). Mark Satin, a draft resister, became the full-time counselor for the first ten months of TADP's existence. Mark grew up in northern Minnesota and then moved to Texas with his family where he spent most of his high-school years. He attended a segregated school and got "beat up" a number of times by the local blacks. After graduation Mark spent the summer working as an activist with the civil-rights movement in Holly Springs, Mississippi. This was his introduction to movement activities. Thus he became sensitized to racial conflict and social action in a very personal way. Mark continued his activism in college, was restless and sought answers to social problems. At Illinois University he wanted to be a city planner so he could be involved in solving urban problems. But according to Mark, "A professor there talked me out of it. He said I would never be able to get around to the real problems but would end up dealing with trivia." He then attended Harpur College in Binghamton, New York. There he was an activist in SDS and in radical campus politics. During this time he became increasingly concerned with the Vietnam War and his own relationship to the draft system. By September 1966, at the end of his second year at college, Mark decided to immigrate to Canada. He applied for landed immigrant status by mail. After much discouragement and six months later, his application was accepted and he came up to Toronto.[22]

Mark worked frenetically, 15 hours a day, running TADP. He felt that, "There was enough information on how to get here. But once a guy arrived, not nearly enough to acquaint him with Canada or help him find a place to live or a job."[23] So Mark set to work to establish contacts in the Toronto religious, business and student communities who would assist draft resisters.

He organized a housing file of over 600 families who opened their homes to American refugees. In addition to local contacts, Mark established links with other cities across Canada and assisted them in setting up their own anti-draft aid groups. The contribution for which Mark Satin was best known, however, was his *Manual for Draft-Age Immigrants to Canada.* This helped thousands of Americans to make their way to Canada, often unaided except for this booklet.

In addition to TADP, there were several other types of aid groups in Toronto to assist American exiles. Each had its own philosophy of counseling; some were more explicitly political than others. In 1968 13 draft resisters, including Mark Satin and Rick Paterak, constituted the Union of New Canadians. This name was carefully selected to make a good image for Canadians and to bring in the largest base of Americans and other possible immigrants. Their major goal was to "work for the neutrality of Canada." They saw themselves as having two functions: to spread propaganda and to attract sympathy from Canadians and Americans. They did this through their pamphlet "Escape from Freedom" and a newsletter *The New Canadian.* For the individual draft resisters, the group served as a fraternal organization to explore their own ambivalences and feelings toward their action and their new country. Americans of all political persuasions were brought together with weekly picnics in High Park sponsored by the Union of New Canadians. Personal contact with other Canadians was their way of letting others know "that we are human beings first and then draft resisters."[24]

Other exile groups followed. Although they adopted more political rhetoric as part of their program, they also served primarily as fraternal meeting places for American refugees. They sought to explore their own identities and become more comfortable in their new surroundings, not too unlike refugee groups representing other nationalities.

The Union of American Exiles (UAE) succeeded the first union. Its name explicitly identified its members as Americans who were still looking southward for their direction. They had not yet made the transition to thinking of themselves as "New Canadians." This group began in April 1968 as an "organization seeking to bring together exiled Americans for the purpose of self-help and social action." Many resisters felt that the immigration counseling of the TADP was not sufficient for a new immigrant to get his bearings in Canada. Thus resisters who formed the Union attempted to supplement the services of the TADP by operating housing and job services from their offices at George Street. The Union office had a staff on duty seven days a week to speak personally with the new arrivals about jobs, housing, Canadian life and social and political issues. Two draft resisters attempted to explain the impetus that spurred them to form the Union.

> It is clear that the need for expanded immigrant aid services alone would never have been enough to generate the movement toward an organization of American exiles. Union members recognize the identity of social and political factors that have shaped and continue to affect their personal lives. For this reason the Union as an organization is a place where talk, information and action can be found that relates one's life in Canada to the broader, repressive aspects of North American society and politics in general.[25]

According to these resisters, with the passage of time, Americans began to recognize the influence of American culture and politics everywhere in Canadian life. "The new immigrant sees that significant numbers of Americans like himself have come and continue to come to Canada and that this group, of which he is a part, expresses the continuing connection between North American political and social crises and his personal life."

At its peak, the Union had a mailing list of about 70 people, with about 20 activists who worked on their newsletter, *The American Exile in Canada (AMEX)*. After about one year, the activists working on *AMEX* separated themselves from union politics and became an independent publication, re-naming itself the *American Expatriate*. Its function will be discussed later in the chapter. Some of the Union's members had been activists in the United States, while many more had never belonged to any resistance or antiwar group and were on the periphery of action. Tom, a resister who became the public relations man of the UAE, said, "I couldn't find any group that suited me in the States. Nothing that was me. But this is something that I see myself in very much, with all the new people coming up here, and the activities of the Union, I just have to be involved with it." It was not uncommon to go down to the UAE's basement headquarters and hear Marxist and Maoist rhetoric being espoused. Many men were just beginning to become more politicized as a result of their experiences and were trying on different political philosophies for size. The majority of individuals who were attracted to the UAE were self-styled anarchists.

Since the majority of individuals disliked structure, they had a loose, decentralized type of organization. Anyone could join and participate in the weekly open meetings of an elected coordinating committee, in addition to special orientation nights for new arrivals and general political discussion.

General membership meetings for everyone were held every other Sunday. They also sponsored a number of teach-ins for resisters as well as for the larger community. Some of the seminar topics for discussion were: the revolution of 1964 confronts the revolution of 1969; should an American draft dodger or deserter actively seek participation in Canada or bide his time until he could return to the United States?; the New Left in Canada. The group only became more formalized with a constitution and program coordinators when its membership was waning and its existence was threatened by factional disputes.[26]

Despite the fact that few exiles actually considered themselves members of the UAE and took an active role in the activities of the group, the organization in its two years of existence helped thousands of refugees find temporary housing and jobs during the first lonely days of their stay in Toronto. The majority of people they helped did not become actively involved in exile politics but were grateful for the aid UAE provided them.

In 1970 new aid groups emerged. The Black Refugee Organization (referred to as BRO, short for "brother") was founded by three black draft resisters in Toronto that spring. E.I., one of the founders from Cleveland, and his friends were aided by the Toronto Anti-Draft Programme when they first came to Canada and felt extremely isolated, especially from the black community in Toronto. TADP did not even mention to them that there was a black community sympathetic to resisters because they did not know about it. They formed BRO to fill this gap for aid to black resisters and deserters. It operated as a fraternal organization to provide immigration information, counseling and housing with black families for newcomers. Additional problems that blacks had in Canada, such as the existence of subtle racism, were discussed. In some ways BRO functioned as a parallel organization to TADP, yet there was cooperation between them. Most counselors referred black refugees to BRO.

Communication Links

Red, White, and Black occupied the same cubby hole as the Union of American Exiles. An off-center black star appeared on the basement wall to symbolize the entrance of this new exile group. Their first statement appeared in February 1970. It explained:

Red, White, and Black is a broad-based organization, nondogmatic, ecumenical, inter-racial, international — created to bridge the gaps — cultural, social, economic, organizational, political — between the expatriate and the exile, the idea and the act, the old involvements with the crises in the U.S. and the new involvements with Canadian life. Red, White, and Black is designed to serve primarily as an information and communications exchange, both inside the "EX" community, and between it and the other people of North America.

To avoid some of the problems that afflicted the UAE, especially in regard to becoming totally American oriented, they began a free school with its main features being a Canadian affairs seminar and classes in conversational French. They still closely followed news from the United States. In fact, their major source of funds for the first few months came from contributions from the United States. They also cosponsored such things as a theatrical production of the Chicago conspiracy trial and a funeral for the Kent State students. Their major role, however, was in internal communications within Toronto, especially dealing with press relations. In addition, it served as a coordinating group between all the Canadian aid groups. Before the summer of 1970, there was almost no regular communication between aid groups in different cities. From the outset there were only three major times when the various aid groups effectively communicated and cooperated together. Initially, during the early formation of the groups, there was sharing of research on immigration information and contributions made to the *Manual to Aid Draft-Age Immigrants to Canada.* In the face of a common crisis, when the borders were closed to all deserters, all groups pooled and contributed information to briefs presented in Ottawa. Finally, all of the groups exchanged information at the first Pan-Canadian Conference in Montreal in the spring of 1970. At this conference, Red, White, and Black announced its new role as coordinating group.

It did this through its weekly *EXNET* bulletin that was usually sent fortnightly to the 31 existing aid groups as well as some antidraft groups in the States. It relayed the contributions of first-hand sources from the various groups regarding their internal functioning and problems. For example, it covered difficulties with the border scene, official changes with regard to landed immigrant status, job possibilities and unemployment. It contained warnings regarding specific Americans who had "ripped off" families and groups who had aided them and placed these individuals on a blacklist so they would not receive further aid. Its newsletter also helped to introduce new immigrants to other cities besides Toronto (which was overburdened with new arrivals) where they could receive proper aid.

AMEX magazine, the organ of American Expatriates in Canada, written by Toronto draft resisters who were once affiliated with the early Toronto

Union of American Exiles, also attempted to coordinate exile news. It has been the only exile publication to survive for more than eight years and the only one to come out regularly every few months through 1976. In 1975 it had a circulation of approximately 4,000 in Canada and the United States.[27] It also reached libraries in both countries since it was available on microfilm. Although *AMEX* attempted to cover comprehensively all issues of interest to the American exile community, it largely reflected the view of the politically oriented refugee.

Although it was a staff collective effort, its editor, Stan Pietlock, was instrumental in shaping its form and content for the first five years. Stan was an early draft resister whose attempt to obtain a conscientious objector status was rejected, and so he came to the "North Country Fair" to begin life anew. Although he had not been an active antiwar movement person in the United States, he became politicized like many other refugees as a result of his exile status. In many ways Stan resembled the typical new convert, the new Canadian. This emphasis was so evident in the pages of *AMEX* that Ron Haggart, a well-known columnist for the *Toronto Telegram*, remarked in a description of *AMEX*, "and just beneath the surface seems to lurk a rather vague disappointment that Canadians are not more chauvinistic about their own country."[28] Roger Williams, a correspondent for *AMEX*, stated, "Although editor Pietlock soon became one of the most 'Canadianized' of all American war resisters, he never forgot he was an American exile as well." He points out, "AMEX adopted a dual character reflecting the reality of the situation, and became the expatriate publication of American exiles."[29]

AMEX, like any other publication by and for the immigrants, was full of information about job opportunities in various parts of Canada and helpful hints about Canadian laws and customs. But a significant part of its content has always been devoted to informing Americans about Canadian institutions with a special emphasis on their relation to the multinational corporations and the threat of American imperialism. This has been the source of some controversy. For example, one draft resister who subscribed to *AMEX* interpreted this political slant to indicate *AMEX*'s priorities to be to "aid the revolution in the United States, ... rather than to fit into Canadian life." He suggested a reverse of priorities. The *Toronto Star* wholeheartedly agreed with this critique.[30] To this criticism the *AMEX* collective retorted:

We don't fit into the [Canadian] mosaic very nicely, I guess. Many European immigrants I've talked to say, "Canada is free, but not as free as the

United States to make money." Well, we've been through all of that and it turned sour. We are a brand new kind of immigrant and Canadians will have to get used to us.[31]

Old Myths and New Realities

The basic assumption made by the aid groups in the early period of immigration (1966–67) was that the more men who opted out of the war and came to Canada, the more the war effort would be hindered in its operations. Mark Satin, an early Toronto resister, said, "I felt that if I could have helped 50,000 individuals come to Canada in protest, the Vietnam War would have to end soon." This optimistic belief was expressed in one of the earlier propaganda sheets written by the staff of the Vancouver Committee to Aid American War Objectors and circulated in the United States. It spoke of several thousand Americans evading the draft and the thousands of others who might follow in their footsteps if they had accurate information about immigration to Canada. It chastized the American antiwar groups for not distributing this information and stated the political reasons why dodging the draft was part of the antiwar effort.

(1) Those who oppose this war should not only be trying to change the policies of the American government but should also do whatever possible to obstruct the prosecution of the war. We hold that large-scale draft evasion is at least a minor obstruction.

(2) While we encourage and expect these young men to refuse military service, we must at the same time assist by providing them with information on all ways of avoiding induction into the Army. *Every* act of noncompliance with the military should be welcomed as an obstruction of the war effort. . . .[32]

After these aid groups had counseled more than 15,000 men who had fled to Canada in 1966 and 1967 and the Vietnam War continued to escalate and demand more recruitments of men, their original assumption that draft evasion impaired the war effort had to be seriously reexamined. Most of these resisters knew that the option of assimiliating and becoming good Canadians was open to them. After these refugees got over the initial shock of discovering that Canadian society often imitates that of America and were forced to lower their expectations, the majority of them decided to "fit into the Canadian system rather than fight it." However, this option was not open to most of the deserters who sought the aid of the refugee groups.[33]

For the first few years the immigrants to Canada from the United States were draft resisters and the aid groups were highly successful in landing these men. However, the lack of success with deserters in 1968 again made them question their original assumptions regarding their immigration counseling.

Some of the more politically oriented exile groups had memberships that consisted of deserters who did not, for the most part, have the option of assimilating. These groups pointed out that the major function of the counseling groups had been in immigration counseling favoring the attainment of landed immigrant status. Thus, whether they realized it or not, they had implicitly supported the class-based channeling process maintained by the Canadian Immigration Act. They concluded that to merely evade the draft by coming to Canada and becoming an immigrant was in itself an insufficient act to combat American militarism. The individual merely wound up contributing to the multinational corporations in Canada. These corporations, based in the United States, were the chief benefactors of the economic boom during the height of the Vietnam War. The American Deserters Committee (ADC) publication, *Yankee Refugee*, in 1967 explored this question in depth:

Refusing to serve in the military is both a valid and necessary step towards halting the war machine. Yet we need to be aware that that is not all there is to it. Every time one of us refuses to be inducted someone else is drafted in our place, very likely a ghetto black, a Mexican-American or a poor white, few of whom, as a rule, can afford a student deferment, legal aid, etc. Obviously this does not mean we should have gone in. But it does mean that since North American society is constructed along class lines, and we are for the most part from middle-class families, it was class privilege that allowed us the opportunities and resources that make dodging the draft and coming to Canada possible.

We must be aware that simply dodging the draft is in and of itself an incomplete act. Avoiding the military is only significant morally and politically when we use our freedom from conscription to struggle to free our brothers and sisters who are brutalized by United States imperialism. . . struggling on the reservations and the cities against American genocidal racism.[34]

In an editorial after the Pan-Canadian Conference in the spring of 1970, *AMEX* noted that whereas in early 1968 resisters could feel justly proud when carrying a placard saying "We Refused to Go" around the streets of Toronto, in 1970 it was not enough to "merely be an expatriate and Canadianize oneself, forgetting about the United States forever." It was the American exile's role to "lead the fight, physically, against the United States from our exile."[35]

This major change in the thinking of *AMEX* and the aid groups was brought about when the aid groups began helping deserters on a large scale. Eventually their presence precipitated a crisis among the aid groups and forced them to reevaluate their aims as well as their nonpolitical stance.

NOTES

1. Immigration officers were not permitted to note a man's military status on his record.
2. *Amnesty Hearings,* subcommittee on Courts, Civil Liberties and the Administration of Justice. Committee on the Judiciary House of Representatives, 93rd Congress, March 8, 11 and 13, 1974 (Washington, D.C.: U.S. Government Printing Office, 1974).
3. *Manual for Draft-Age Immigrants to Canada* (Toronto: House of Anansi, 1970). Mark Satin was the original author. Subsequent editions were revised by others.
4. This figure is merely an educated guess by number of aid counselors in various Canadian cities who were familiar with the American exile scene over the years. A number of these men showed up in the aid offices after being in Canada over a year on their own.
5. *AMEX* 4 (May—June 1973): 30
6. *Hansard,* February 1, p. 12523 and February 2, p. 12569, First Session, 28 Parliament, vol. XII.
7. Richard L. Killmer, R. Lecky, D. Wiley, *They Can't Go Home Again* (Philadelphia: United Church Press, 1971), pp. 35—37.
8. *Vancouver Sun* (UPI), December 8, 1970.
9. Richard L. Killmer, et al., *They Can't Go Home Again.*
10. *NCUUA Amnesty Update* (bimonthly publication of the National Council for Universal and Unconditional Amnesty), April 1974, issue no.I.
11. A smaller aid group for the cities of Kitchener—Waterloo, 70 miles west of Toronto, was the one exception. It had three Canadian counselors, two professors and a graduate student from the University of Waterloo. A description of this group can be found in Richard Killmer, et al., *They Can't Go Home Again,* chapter 3, pp. 40—49.
12. *Manual for Draft-Age Immigrants to Canada* (Toronto: House of Anansi, 1970).
13. Immigration Act R.S. c. 325 s. 1. *Canadian Immigration Policy* (Ottawa: Queen's Printer, 1966), p. 24.
14. Ibid.
15. "Immigration Regulations," Department of Manpower and Immigration, Schedule A, October 1967.

16. "History of the Committee to Aid American War Objectors," mimeo, May 5, 1970. Much of the information in this section is based upon this history as well as on interviews.

17. *New York Times,* January 28, 1968.

18. For a discussion of the SUPA organization and its political orientation see an article by James Laxer, "The Americanization of the Canadian Student Movement," in *Close the 49th Parallel, Etc.,* ed. Ian Lumsden.

19. Alice Lynd, *We Won't Go* (Boston: Beacon Press, 1968), p. 112.

20. This cartoon was originally published in the *Toronto Globe and Mail,* 1966.

21. Lynd, *We Won't Go,* p. 113.

22. Appendix in Brief on "A Note on the Handling of Draft-Age Americans in Their Entry to Canada." See Mark Satin.

23. Anastasia Erland, "Faces of Conscience: Mark Satin, Draft Dodger," *Saturday Night,* September 1956.

24. Notes from the first meeting of the Union of New Canadians.

25. *Manual for Draft-Age Immigrants to Canada* (4th ed., 1970) ch. 31, pp. 77–87.

26. For a history of the Union of American Exiles see *AMEX,* March 30, 1969.

27. Personal communication with the editor of *AMEX,* January 1970.

28. *Toronto Telegram,* Ron Haggart's column.

29. Roger N. Williams, *The New Exiles* (New York: Liveright, 1971), pp. 81, 82.

30. *Toronto Daily Star,* December 17, 1970.

31. *AMEX,* vol. 2, no. 7.

32. "History of the Committee to Aid American War Objectors," mimeo, May 5, 1970.

33. This option only became available to deserters and other "illegal visitors" in Canada in the fall of 1973 with the Immigration Adjustment of Status Act.

34. *Yankee Refugee,* publication of the Vancouver American Deserters' Committee (ADC), 1969.

35. *AMEX* 2 (June 1970).

5

Struggle for Equal Status in the Treatment of Deserters

The deserters presented the aid groups with new problems. Whereas the majority of draft dodgers simply needed information on landed immigrant status and could obtain funds to support themselves until they received it, the majority of deserters were in need of more extensive counseling and financial aid. Most of them left the United States on short notice, coming to Canada with nothing more than the shirts on their backs. A number of them were living a hand-to-mouth existence as fugitives. As a group, they needed constant reassurance that they were safe in Canada and could not be extradited by the American government. Many of them needed immediate medical and psychological care. Most of them needed a long rest and some time to "get themselves together." The deserters, coming in larger numbers, bogged down the counseling groups' flimsy organization and introduced a new dimension to their existing problems. In fact, the initial reaction to the larger numbers of deserters on the part of the Canadian government eventually brought the situation to a major crisis.

Treatment of Deserters by Refugee Aid Groups

Only a trickle of deserters came to Canada seeking refuge in the first few years of the aid groups' existence. In Toronto, SUPA, the first aid group to counsel American refugees, made the assumption that deserters could not legally remain in Canada. Their yellow pamphlet "Escape from Freedom or I Didn't Raise My Boy To Be a Canadian" listed deserters as members of one of the prohibited classes in Canada, together with drug users, certain political offenders and other criminals. Under desertion it stated, "Any American deserter would not be accepted as a landed immigrant." Mark Satin, one of the original counselors of the Toronto Anti-Draft Programme when it was still located at SUPA offices, observed that the first deserters to come to Toronto seeking aid were informed that they would have to return to the United States on the advice of the TADP lawyers.

According to Bill Spira, a naturalized American expatriate and now a retired Canadian businessman who worked with American refugees for many years, the distinction between draft resisters and deserters was first made by the aid groups themselves rather than by the Canadian government, before the groups knew the law regarding deserters. He substantiated the view that initially the aid groups thought that desertion was illegal. It was only after the counselors did their homework on this subject and researched the Canadian Extradition Treaties and the Canadian Immigration Act with regard to prohibited classes that they found desertion to be omitted from these classes.

More deserters began to come to Canada in late 1967 and 1968 according to Nancy Pocock, an active Quaker who supported the TADP from the beginning of its operations. She and her husband were both on the executive board. She described how newsmen were very anxious to get the story about deserters during that time. She relates, "They knew they were coming and they were poking and prying all the time. They haunted the TADP office. So we decided the best thing to do was to handle the deserters separately." Bill Spira explained that some of these early deserters had to be placed underground "and we used all kinds of cloak and dagger methods to keep them away from the public view." He was one of the counselors who worked with deserters who came to Toronto.

I was on the executive board of the TADP at the time. Whenever they would get a deserter they'd send him over to me. When deserters came to the TADP, the standard answer was, "Look, we can't help you here, but here is the name and address of a fellow who will help you." One weekend I found myself with 17 deserters in my basement. I had wall-to-wall people. At that point I realized I just couldn't handle it myself and I inaugurated a sub-program of the TADP which was a group of Canadians that was to specifically counsel and house deserters.

In this manner Bill Spira carried on his subterranean program and counseled over 600 deserters for a year and a half until early 1968. "I'm proud to say that I have played a key role in the fact that we have 5 divisions in Canada instead of in Vietnam." Thus even after the counselors knew that deserters could legally immigrate to Canada, they made the tactical decision to separate the draft resisters from the deserters who sought their aid. Bill Spira commented on the reasoning behind this decision.

> For quite a while we separated the two operations in Toronto because we simply worried about the public image of the Toronto Anti-Draft Programme and of donations, etc. So whenever we were asked, for example, by reporters about deserters the standard answer was, "Oh, there must be some of them up here." We anticipated that the Canadian public opinion toward deserters would be more negative toward them than toward draft resisters.

Upon further questioning of Bill Spira as to the accuracy of their assessment, he responded that their judgment had been incorrect.

> There was just as little reason to separate draft dodgers and deserters under the Immigration Act as there was little reason to think that the Canadian people would react differently towards them. In so many things we were really swayed by the American public opinion and American attitudes and not by Canadian attitudes.

Thus, the Americans running the Anti-Draft Programme were playing a pivotal role in continuing to impose on deserters in Canada negative judgments that they had assumed would prevail in Canada as they did in the United States. It was for this reason that they did not want any publicity on the deserters who were beginning to enter Canada in larger numbers. An additional reason for not making deserters public, according to Spira, was "the fear of American pressure and the fear that the Canadian government in response would close down the border." The Toronto group's counseling advice itself was the deserters' worst enemy during the early years.

In 1968, when the first edition of the *Manual for Draft-Age Immigrants to Canada* was published, it was very cautious in dealing with the deserter question. It deliberately did not come right out and say that deserters were welcome in Canada. Nor did it bluntly say that desertion was not an extraditable offense. It simply reprinted the Extradition Treaty in an appendix, with no additional comments.

According to Mark Satin, this caution was based on a gentlemen's agreement that TADP and the other aid groups had with the Canadian government at that time. The Canadian government would not interfere with the counseling operations of the aid groups as long as they did not publicize that the government "welcomed deserters." This approach was supposed to minimize American pressure on the Canadian government; Canada would then be able to take a "neutralist" attitude toward them. This may explain why the Canadian government did not keep any statistics on the number of draft-age Americans in Canada in any of its official publications. There was some evidence, however, that the government might privately have been keeping track of at least the military deserters. During the May 1969 debates in Parliament, the Honorable Alan MacEachen, the Minister of Manpower and Immigration, commented on the numbers of American deserters who had landed status.

> I might note that in the past 15 months since the new policy was put into effect for military personnel applying from within Canada, some 72 persons identified as United States servicemen have been allowed to stay in Canada, and another 27 are currently being processed; 7 decided to return to the United States before their applications were disposed of, and 19 were turned down because they failed to meet normal immigration criteria. . . .[1]

However, the Canadian government's public stance when American agencies inquired as to how many draft dodgers and deserters were present was that they did not officially record these statistics.

Aid Groups Press for an Open Door Policy

Both the Canadian aid groups and the Canadian government officials were closely informed of each other's activities. The Canadian aid groups serving American refugees continually sought Canadian government attitudes and policy clarifications with regard to the status of American refugees in Canada. In the first few years of their operations, their major efforts in aiding war objectors consisted of lobbying Canadian government officials. They wanted the Canadian government to maintain its attitude of neutrality toward the refugees. The first major confrontation with the Canadian government involved the white paper on the new Canadian immigration policy. A policy document designed for implementation, it spoke of the need to reevaluate those classes of people who should be barred from Canada because they represented a threat to the public health and safety. It stated: "The problem is to describe precisely the categories of persons who represent such a threat and to ensure that the reasons for prohibition remain an accurate reflection of true dangers."[2] It then proposed a new prohibited class of immigrants, "fugitives from justice."

Those individuals involved with the Canadian aid groups saw the creation of this new prohibited class as a potentially dangerous immigration policy that could be construed to view those Americans who did not comply with American draft or military laws as "fugitives from justice." They feared that this new category would provide the legal prerequisites necessary for those officials in both Canada and the United States to bar entry of American war objectors.

The major Canadian aid groups in Montreal, Toronto and Vancouver collaborated in submitting a brief entitled "A Note on the Handling of Draft-Age Americans Who Apply for Entry to Canada" to the Minister of Immigration Jean Marchand and to Prime Minister Pierre Trudeau. Through careful argument they demonstrated that including "fugitives from justice" among the prohibited classes might jeopardize the free entry of Americans who refused to participate in the Vietnam War. Underlying the brief was a feeling of general mistrust and suspicion with which the Canadian aid groups viewed the Canadian government officials.

The brief raised the issue of whether immigration officers were inquiring into the draft status of those Americans who applied for entry into Canada. Its intent was to demonstrate that inquiries by immigration officers into the draft status of Americans was the rule rather than the exception; that some officers judged any male American of draft age chiefly on the basis of his actual or supposed relation to the draft; that these judgments led some officials to obstruct the entry of applicants who, by the department's stated policies, were qualified immigrants; and that the whole matter raised serious questions of responsibility for senior department officers. Statements taken from 36 Americans who had contact with Canadian immigration officers portrayed this.

These statements emphasized examples of mistreatment and overt discrimination against them by immigration officials. For example, Larry, 25 years old with a master's degree in zoology, stated he was given the "runaround" and deliberately misinformed about the correct immigration form to use to apply at the border. He was told he would have to return to the United States to apply for landed status. When I interviewed him two years after he had obtained it, he related the following recent experience with an immigration officer. After doing field work near a small Pacific highway border crossing he went to a nearby pub, where he overheard the following conversation in which a Canadian customs official was discussing his personal feelings about the Vietnam War and American refugees with some friends. According to Larry, "His words were so disturbing to me that minutes after the topic of conversation changed, I left the pub and wrote down, almost verbatim, his statements." These statements are quoted below. They were made along with other disparaging comments about Americans of draft age and nostalgic recollections of World War II.

> The simplest thing to do is to round them [deserters and dodgers] all up and ship them back — let them get what they deserve back there. I never had so much pleasure as when they shipped one deserter back because they knew he had smoked drugs....One son of a bitch actually admitted to me that he was a physical coward when I asked him why he had deserted. Now all of us are afraid of getting cut up, shot or hurt, but to admit it outright aloud. That bastard really got me pissed. You can be sure he never made it. . . .They are nothing but cowards. You give them a chance to defend Canada, if endangered, and they will say "No" here also. Ninety-nine percent are physical cowards. I don't even have to ask, I can see it. They are parasites. I turn them back whenever I can. What the hell's wrong with the United Church giving these bastards ways of avoiding the immigration laws?[3]

Another draft dodger, Stephen Porsche, testified that when he attempted to get instructions on becoming a landed immigrant, he was informed by a Canadian immigration officer in Vancouver that he would need a letter from an American consulate stating he had no obligation to return to the United States before he could receive an application. This, however, was not part of any officially required procedure. He was also asked if he had served in the Armed Services.

> When I answered "No," the officer said that I had missed a very important part of my life. He then asked me what my draft status was and whether I had any objection to serving in the Armed Services. I said I had a student deferment and that I am against the war. He said that he was against war, too, but that the only way to fight evil is with force. He then went on at length, with no encouragement from me, to justify that war can only be stopped with war. He recounted his childhood experiences as a victim of Nazi aggression in Holland. He also told me that as a naturalized Canadian citizen he had served for 10 years in the Canadian Navy, including 6 years in Korea. He had also served in Cyprus and had been in what capacity he

did not say in Vietnam. "And now do you want to tell me about war?" he asked, the implication being that I had no right to hold pacifist views without having been personally involved in three or four wars myself. While he was saying these things I had no idea whether I was going to be landed or not. The official concluded his remarks by saying, "I hate the son-of-a-bitch who refuses to serve his country."

These statements were indicative of the prejudicial attitudes of some of the border officials who had almost total discretion over the 15 points of personal assessment that they could deny to an American refugee in a legitimate manner. Although it was in direct violation of the Department of Immigration's rules at that time to take into account the draft status of a person, there was very little supervision by superiors in Ottawa to enforce this regulation on low-ranking officials in the various provinces. Even within the central Immigration Department in each major city, there seemed to be little supervision.

The brief concluded with recommendations for action by the Immigration Department to enforce their own stated policies and to delete "fugitives from justice" from the list of prohibited classes in the new Immigration Act.[4]

Deputy Minister Tom Kent officially replied to the brief in a letter to the Vancouver Committee to Aid American War Objectors. He found the report "distressing" and stated: "I do not in any way resist the immediate conclusion that some of our officers at least have not been fully following their instructions." He responded to the brief's recommendations by saying:

Our instructions not to inquire into draft status could not be in plainer English (and French), more precise or more explicit than they have been for nearly two years. . . .We have more recently emphasized to our senior field staff that any departures from these instructions must be treated as a serious disciplinary matter. . . . This, as well as the new regulations, may help to account for the improvement you note. I am optimistic that the follow-up of your report is the one remaining thing needed to drive the point home fully and conclusively.[5]

A second letter referring to the brief followed three months later, after immigration had investigated the "border incidents" documented by the brief. Tom Kent was more defensive of his department's interest this time. In clarifying immigration policy, he asserted:

The acceptance of immigrants at the border is not our normal practice. It is a concession extended to United States citizens only when a job has been arranged with a definite starting date and possibly other practical reasons. If we are not taking it [draft status] into account, we cannot make it a reason for granting immigrant status at the border, any more than it is a reason for refusing such status.[6]

Deputy Minister Kent attributed the misunderstandings that occurred in the "border incidents" to the fact that the Immigration Department was in a transitional phase before introduction of the new regulations and also to the bad advice of aid groups to Americans to "go to the border."

In summary, the deputy minister's response to the brief excused his department's mishandling of a few cases of draft dodgers and asserted that he was "unable to determine that in any case the personal views of the officer were allowed to determine a decision contrary to government policy." He shrugged off the whole affair. He also urged the aid groups to provide complete and realistic information about the immigration process.[7] This follow-up report, however, did not conclusively put an end to the "border incidents" between American resisters and Canadian immigration officials. Neither did it lay to rest mutual feelings of mistrust between the two groups. Two years later, in 1969, the same issues exploded into an even larger controversial public arena, focusing on a different group: Americans who had deserted from the Armed Forces.

Correspondence between the Canadian aid groups in Montreal, Toronto and Vancouver give us some insight into how deserters were faring at that time. A letter from the Vancouver Committee to a former Vancouver counselor living in Montreal in February 1969 referred to the "earthquake of rumors and half facts" they had received from the east coast on the status of deserters. They described the situation as "screwy." Along similar lines, the TADP in a letter to the Vancouver Committee referred to the "deserter scene as complicated as hell and changing every day now." They also alluded to the "rumor problem" and for this reason suggested that the contents of their letter should be handled as "classified information." Thus, this letter had "top secret" scrawled on it in the Vancouver Committee office. More specifically, the letter cited that "the border from Sault Sainte Marie east is bad all the way for deserters." The letter continued:

> Not only are they having trouble with Canadian immigration, but it is becoming about impossible for deserters to get out of Canada into the U.S. [see "border runners," p. 93] due to strict checking at customs. Hence we have almost completely stopped sending deserters to the border for the time being.[8]

The letter concluded with detailed instructions on how Vancouver should handle its deserters.

These correspondences from Canadian aid groups indicated that they sensed something was awry with Canadian immigration's treatment of deserters. They anticipated the Canadian government's unannounced shift of policy, making it extremely difficult for deserters to enter Canada legally and to obtain landed immigrant status.

In Ottawa, the possibility of making deserters ineligible to live in Canada was being considered in the Department of Manpower and Immigration along with other amendments to the Immigration Act that possibly would be submitted to Parliament later in 1969. The Immigration Department had already issued a memorandum the previous July to tell its immigration officers at the border points that they could exercise their broad discretion over applications for permanent residence and to take into account active military duty as a possible breach of contract.[9] Thus, although no policy decision had been declared in this controversial issue, the Immigration Department had already made it highly unlikely that most deserters would get landed immigrant status.

In direct response to Ottawa's blatant shift of policy in regard to deserters, the Canadian aid groups prepared for a "head-on fight with immigration" as one TADP counselor put it. They planned to coordinate a two-pronged attack on the new immigration practices, utilizing legal briefs and the mass media. They wished to accomplish the following:

> One, we hope to clean up the border situation as best we can by publicizing the irregularities. Secondly, we hope to exert enough pressure to get Ottawa operating the way it used to. And thirdly, by using good publicity about draft dodgers and deserters in general, we hope to create, if possible, a climate of public feeling which would react against the bill were it ever to get as far as the Liberal caucus or Parliament, which seems doubtful, if the latest information is to be believed. [Reference is made to a possible immigration bill.][10]

After admitting qualified deserters under the point system in 1968 and 1969, the border was closed by the Minister of Immigration to deserters. No one could get through. At that point, according to Bill Spira, "We decided to take the wraps off the deserters."

> The first thing we did was to start a publicity campaign showing deserters to the press; in other words "Meet Your Local Deserter and See That He Doesn't Have Horns." That made big news and the stories the guys had to tell made big news. Everyone knew that there were 200 to 300 deserters

living in Sweden but finally to meet some of their own deserters delighted them. The press gobbled it up. A lot of human interest stories came out. That was really the beginning of our campaign to let the Canadians see and meet deserters in the press, on T.V. and radio shows.

According to Jack Pocock, who was selected by TADP to handle press relations, aid groups contacted a steady stream of newsmen from all over the world: West Germany, Japan, Sweden, Russia, every country in Europe and every state in the United States. A full-scale publicity campaign was launched throughout the major cities in Canada. The first two weeks in February, the Montreal *Star,* the Toronto *Star,* the Toronto *Globe and Mail,* the Ottawa *Citizen* and the Vancouver *Sun* carried articles bringing before the Canadian public all sides of the controversy on the status of American deserters in Canada. Headlines blared: "Ottawa Accused of Prejudice,"[11] "U.S. Army Deserters Find Canada Closed," "Collusion at Border Admitted"[12] and "Draft Dodger Crackdown Denied."[13] The aid groups exposed the discriminatory policies of the Immigration Department and accused it of straying from both the spirit and the letter of its own Immigration Act. The Montreal Council To Aid War Resisters was reported to have said that what galled them most was the fact that the Immigration Department "admits it speaks with a forked tongue." According to the Montreal *Star:*

> They accuse the Immigration Department of acting as the long arm of the U.S. government, either slamming the door in the face of deserters at the border or starving them out once they are inside the country. They matter of factly note that the RCMP act as informants for the FBI, grilling deserters and some draft evaders for the U.S. Federal agency.[14]

Canadian immigration officials were forced to clarify their policies once again. In response to reports that immigration officers, acting on the July 29, 1968 memo, had put into effect tougher admission procedures, the immigration office denied that this was the case. They announced that there had been no change in their policy toward American draft dodgers and deserters. They admitted, however, that though desertion from the United States Armed Forces was not by itself grounds for barring an American from entry to Canada as an immigrant, it was "one of the factors" taken into account in determining his admissibility, according to an immigration spokesman.

During this period the Canadian Institute of Public Opinion presented a cross section of public attitudes and sympathies toward dodgers and deserters. A survey suggested that Canadian opinion was polarized. Fifty-two percent were sympathetic to the Americans, 47 percent unsympathetic and 19 percent gave qualified support. Canadian youth, including high-school and university students, was the largest group supporting American refugees. Persons 40 to 49 years old were less sympathetic and more indifferent to the problems of these Americans. In the group surveyed, a larger percentage of women than men was sympathetic.[15]

Opinions of prominent Canadians were also sought on the question of whether Canada should accept deserters from the United States Armed Forces as immigrants. These were published in the Toronto *Daily Star* in the "Question of the Week" column featuring a Canadian author, a member of Parliament, a government official and religious and student leaders. Each of them answered the question affirmatively, with the exception of Mr. MacEachen, the Minister of Immigration, who qualified his statement much as he had done before. Some of these individuals felt very strongly on the issue. Farley Mowat, a leading Canadian author, stated:

> The very real if unveiled unwillingness of the Canadian government to admit deserters from the U.S. is indefensible on humane, moral or legal grounds. If the victims in question were deserters from the British army, French Foreign Legion, army of the Hungarian People's Republic, or almost any other Armed Force in the world not under the direct American control, they would be evaluated as to their worth as immigrants strictly on the legal criteria our laws have established. The fact that they were deserters would be irrelevant. The truth is that Ottawa has received the word from Washington that deserters from the U.S. Armed Forces are to be denied sanctuary in Canada. The truth is that the Ottawa satraps are doing their best to obey their overlords and are making a mockery of law in order to do so.[16]

This issue did not divide the members of Parliament along the usual liberal, conservative and labor lines. Conservatives as well as labor members were outspoken in their support of American deserters. Gordon Fairweather, a Progressive Conservative MP boasted:

> Canada takes some pride in having a basically humanitarian and liberal attitude towards immigration. . . .Canadian history is a veritable chain of movements to our shores of individuals and groups wanting another chance at life. I cannot imagine an immigration officer questioning any of the 12,000 Czechs who have come to Canada since the Soviet invasion of last August about their military status. Neither was this issue raised at the aftermath of the invasion of Hungary in 1956. Canada is filled with men,

women, or their sons and daughters who came here at great risk, and often as refugees. So it should be with American servicemen, whose protest of the futile and ugly Vietnam war results in their seeking a new country.

One nation's deserter may be another's hero; one nation's humanity must not be turned off to suit another nation's draft law.[17]

In addition to utilizing the normal channels to present their case before the Canadian government and people, some members of the aid groups, together with Toronto students, made a more dramatic presentation of the facts. Five Toronto students from Glendon College each masqueraded as the deserter William John Heintzelman from the United States Air Force and applied separately at five different Ontario border points for landed immigrant status in order to test Canadian immigration policy. They all carried the same appropriate papers and references of the actual American deserter which would qualify them as admissable immigrants, in addition to their own identification and passports. If they were caught in a bad situation, they could unmask and prove they were Canadians doing a journalistic project for the Glendon College newspaper. According to Bob Waller, one of the participants:

The authorities actively turned me away while I was posing as a deserter, as were my four comrades. This is directly contrary to immigration department policy. The Canadian authorities unlawfully gave information to officials of a foreign country referring to definite proof of collusion between the Canadian and U.S. Immigration offices.

This story was widely carried by all the major newspapers. Most of the stories carried put Canadian government practices in this incident in an indefensible position. The Ottawa bureau of the Montreal *Star* accused the Canadian government of sanctioning collusion between Canadian and American border guards in order to apprehend United States Army deserters. Mr. MacEachen was said to have conceded that the discretionary powers enjoyed by officials at the border are wide enough for them to personally bar a deserter from Canada.[18] Mr. MacEachen also said. "Canadian officials have the right to inform their American counterparts that a U.S. citizen has been rejected. The American must then check in at the U.S. border station after he has been turned away at the Canadian side."[19]

Although Mr. MacEachen stated that officials were not allowed to advise Americans of the reason for rejection, one of Mr. MacEachen's aides said later, "Mind you, it's very easy for those guys [the U.S. officials] to put two and two together and figure out that their boy is a deserter."[20] Thus

the reactions of Immigration Department officials were full of contradictions.

This incident reopened the debate in the House of Commons on deserter
policy. Mr. MacEachen asked for a report on the Glendon College student's
incident and concluded: "The officers have behaved properly and in accord-
ance with the regulations. The action they took in advising their U.S. counterparts is one which I understand is routine at the border."[21]

This led some members of Parliament to ask the minister of immigration
whether there was a difference in policy applied to draft dodgers and deserters at the border points and when this distinction became operative. The
question was raised for two weeks without receiving an answer and finally
MP David Lewis, leader of the New Democratic party suggested that the
document containing the guidelines of July 27, 1968 be tabled for the consideration of the members of the House. Mr MacEachen, after much vacilla-
tion, reluctantly agreed but added that "these documents are internal in the
department and are not normally tabled."[22]

It is clear from the July 1968 memo issued by the Department of Manpower and Immigration that the highest-ranking authorities gave the lower-
ranking immigration border officials complete discretion in their personal
assessment of deserters. In fact, the intent of the memo was to promote the
discouragement of American deserters and at the same time shift the ultimate
responsibility for this action onto the individual officials.

The case of the five Glendon College students impersonating the same
deserter showed that the Canadian border officials did cooperate with American border officials when handling American refugees.

At the same time that this House of Commons debate occurred, the
Canadian aid groups persistently applied pressure on Ottawa via the press
and personal delegations visiting with the cabinet ministers. A note from the
Toronto office of the TADP, keeping the Vancouver Committee informed, related that "the battle with immigration is getting rough."[23] Each of these
activities was part of an overall strategy to pressure the Canadian government
to open its border to American deserters. Bill Spira described this strategy:

> The first stage of our campaign was simply to have the public meet their
> local deserter. The second stage was to prove that MacEachen was a liar,
> which we did with the Glendon students impersonating deserters. The
> favorable publicity we got in the press with this case, plus all the other
> things we did, proved that we had an excellent lobby going. The media
> constantly gave us a sympathetic show; all three Toronto papers gave full

editorial support to our opposing MacEachen, and the pressures simply started building up. . . .

During this period, the Vancouver Committee was busy keeping its clients informed of the changing situation for deserters and interpreting its significance for them. It sent out mimeographed sheets to those who requested them, noting that the official policy from Ottawa as of January 1969 was "that deserters will not be landed at the border." The policy change was attributed to American pressure on Ottawa after President Nixon's election in 1968 and was interpreted to mean that deserters were more "vulnerable to the vacillating discretion of an immigration official in terms of the 15 points for personal assessment since they no longer can obtain 10 points for a job offer at the border." A new counseling approach was necessitated by the change and three alternatives were spelled out: qualified deserters could get landed from within Canada, a deserter could initially enter as a visitor and marry a Canadian girl to assure his admittance as a landed immigrant or Canada could be used as a "jumping off point" for going to other countries that accepted deserters as immigrants or political refugees.[24]

The Vancouver Committee also informed the embassies of all the countries considered friendly to American deserters such as Sweden, France, Cuba and Yugoslavia of the recent predicament. These letters stated that "such action is the result of pressure from the United States government which knows that large-scale desertion is threatening its war effort." They also stated their political position:

We feel that desertion is a politically effective act and as such we encourage it. We also feel that aiding desertion is a means of lending more than just tacit support to liberation struggles throughout the world, most especially of the Vietnamese people.[25]

These letters suggested that these particular governments could provide a haven for some of the American deserters.

Commenting on these Vancouver pamphlets and the total situation, the Ottawa aid group had strong opinions. In its estimation, to keep fighting and sending deserters to the border and attempting to land them was very important, even knowing some qualified persons would be rejected. They disagreed with the policy of sending deserters quietly underground to Sweden and other countries. They encouraged the Vancouver Committee as well as the other aid groups to send deserters to Ottawa so they could get sympathetic members of Parliament to accompany them, as this seemed to work better.[26]

All the Canadian aid groups agreed to present a brief documenting discrimination against Americans as part of their public strategy of keeping the pressure on the Canadian government with regard to deserters. The brief addressed itself to the Honorable Alan MacEachen, Minister of Manpower and Immigration. It contended that "the present discrimination against the deserters and the effective enforcement of American law by Canadian officials at the border goes against Canadian law and government policy and harms Canada's reputation abroad."[27] The brief documented the background of the government's policy with regard to American refugees and contrasted this with its present discriminatory practices, referring to the affidavits presented with the brief. It specifically charged that "the department is allowing the prejudice of immigration officers to flout the intent of the Immigration Act and the 1967 regulations." The petitioners did not seek to change the Immigration Act or the regulations, nor did they seek preferential treatment for deserters. They merely urged the minister to "ensure fair treatment without discrimination for young Americans, so they may enter Canada on the same terms as people from any other part of the world."

There were 32 signatures affixed to the brief, those of Andrew Brewin of Canada's NDP, Gordon Fairweather of the Progressive Conservatives, Mark MacGuigan of the Liberal party, Reverend John McRae, an Anglican clergyman from Ottawa and Dr. Pauline Jewett of the Political Science Department at Carleton University in Ottawa and presently the president of Simon Fraser University in British Columbia. It was presented to Mr. MacEachen on March 5, 1969, in his office by a delegation consisting of a cross section of the concerned community. The purpose of this brief, according to Professor Jim Wilcox of the Ottawa aid program, was: "The foundation it laid for the lobbying that was my main task from March 5 until May 22, the day the Minister announced in the Commons the government's decision to accord deserters exactly the same treatment given to all other applicants for immigration. The lobbying process resembled a chain letter: I not only asked for an individual MP's support, but also for the names of other members whose sympathies might be enlisted."[28]

Jim Wilcox attempted to educate the members of Parliament on the chief features of the Selective Service System and American military as well as the Canadian immigration point system. Most of the MPs were not familiar with either in any detail. Jim noted that "many were surprised to learn Canada did not extradite deserters, though an equal number were quite unaware American war resisters had any problems in immigrating."[29] Many of the MPs who represented first and second generation immigrants were most sympathetic since they felt that a policy permitting discriminatory treatment against American deserters in 1969 could be utilized against their constituencies in future years. A major turning point in the lobbying efforts, according to Jim, was his meeting with Marcel Prud'homme, a Montreal Liberal who had several weeks earlier started his own campaign espousing the cause of deserters to his peers. This lobbying effort contacted approximately 130 MPs and held three caucus study meetings with them organized by Prud'homme.[30]

During its lobbying efforts the Ottawa aid group wrote a letter to the Vancouver Committee commenting on the odds for a favorable decision: "Who can say? All our sources in the Government indicate that the vast majority of the Cabinet and Parliament are favorable and that a lot of pressure is being exerted on MacEachen and Trudeau. But ultimately it will be MacEachen and Trudeau who decide and they have the right to make a fairly autonomous decision."[31]

The aid groups together with their Canadian supporters geared up for the final phases of their media campaign. In Toronto, Bill Spira of the TADP pointed out to the press some aspects of Canadian history. For example, he indicated that Canada had proclaimed the Chinese Exclusion Act, which prevented all Chinese persons from immigrating and becoming citizens. The result was that there were tens of thousands of Chinese working and living in Canada, though they were not legally in the country. Spira suggested that "Mr. MacEachen was creating another Chinese situation with the American deserters."

The United Church of Canada also exerted considerable pressure on both MacEachen and Prime Minister Trudeau to expose what they referred to as the "secret guidelines," referring to the memo of July 29, 1968, which would have negated the effectiveness of the immigration regulations concerning American deserters. The Moderator of the United Church sent a telegram to the Minister of Immigration charging the guidelines to be an "immoral and intolerable evasion of public responsibility." MacEachen publicly replied that such statements were "illfounded and erroneous to the point of irresponsibility."[32] This exchange of telegrams was brought to the attention of the House of Commons by MP David Lewis, leader of the NDP. He and other MPs had requested a clear policy statement on immigration procedures again and again. This time MacEachen attempted to explain the Canadian policy:

> We do admit members of the Armed Forces of other countries. If such persons apply in this country and satisfy normal immigration criteria they are admitted regardless of military status. Since January 1968, a number of such persons have been admitted.
>
> With respect to applicants at the border or overseas, the immigration officer is expected to exercise overall discretion in determining admissibility.[33]

After further pressure from the NDP,[34] MacEachen tabled copies of a press release containing quotes from the guidelines. It told border officials that a qualified individual's application could be denied "if in his opinion there are good reasons why these norms [the point system] do not reflect the particular applicant's chances of establishing himself successfully in Canada." It designated three reasons for such rejection: excessive financial debts, marital desertion and military desertion. According to Jim Wilcox, the aid groups were appalled that immigration authorities would equate the voluntary obligations of marriage and indebtedness with the involuntary obligation of military conscription. When the church leaders, members of Parliament and the press learned of these guidelines they were equally appalled.[35]

The climax of the controversy peaked two weeks later with a decision favorable to the deserters. The public campaign organized by the Canadian aid groups across Canada utilizing the news media, briefs, private telegrams and consultations over a four-year period had succeeded in bringing enough organized pressure from a cross section of the Canadian community. According to caucus scuttlebutt, the Cabinet vote on the issue was an even split until MacEachen cast the deciding vote in favor of a more tolerant policy toward deserters. There was so much favorable pressure inside the Liberal caucus that the Cabinet had to settle the controversy or face divisive friction within the party. They chose the former.[36]

On May 22, 1969, MacEachen retracted his secret guidelines and announced a major policy change in his talk before the House of Commons. After reviewing Canada's past immigration policies and practices, he declared: "We have now decided to carry the policy a step further. Membership in the Armed Service of another country, or desertion, if you like, potential or actual, will not be a factor in determining the eligibility of persons applying for landed immigrant status in Canada, whether such persons apply from within Canada at points of entry or at Canadian immigration offices abroad." In response some honorable members commented, "Hear, hear." He affirmed

Canada's autonomous position vis-à-vis the United States in regard to an individual's military status: "Our basic position is that the question of an individual's membership or potential membership in the Armed Forces of his own country is a matter to be settled between the individual and his government and is not a matter in which we should be involved. The result of the decision is ... to bring our policy on military deserters into line with our treatment of draft resisters."[37]

The official rationale for this turnabout in government policy, according to External Affairs Minister Mitchell Sharp, was based upon the legal-historical precedent that from 1939 to 1941, before the American entry into World War II, Canadian deserters were permitted to enter the United States to settle there without fear of reprisals. Sharp, commenting on this point, said: "We found that Americans had accepted deserters from the Canadian Army without question during the period when we were at war and they were not. So we said, well that's fine, the Americans are in a war now and we're not, so we will apply the same policy in Canada that they applied to us."[38]

Political factors explain this policy reversal. In his early years as minister MacEachen had no experience in immigration and relied heavily on the advice of his assistant deputy minister and his senior civil servants, who were both known to be unsympathetic to American deserters. They were, in fact, the persons who wrote and signed the July 1968 guideline memo sent to all Canadian immigration officers. It became clear MacEachen at first did not have a full understanding of the guidelines' political implications. By the end of May 1969 there was so much political pressure about them that the Cabinet had to settle the controversy.

Many Canadians supported this issue "not because they gave a darn about the boys, but they did care about Canadian sovereignty," according to Nancy Pocock of the TADP.

It was a great upsurge of the feeling of Canadian nationalism that had a lot to do with it. Most people felt if we wanted to take a deserter from another country, it was none of the other country's business to tell us whether we could take them or not. It was a feeling that the U.S. was trying to dictate to us in internal matters. They weren't deserters from *our* army and why should *they* tell us who *we* should have and who we shouldn't.

Was it commonly known to Canadians that American pressure at that time was the reason why the Canadian border was tight? Nancy Pocock replied, "Oh yes, everybody in Canada knows that the United States is always putting pressure on us to do what they want to do." Bill Spira also had strong words to say about American pressure on Canada:

> At the height of the campaign against MacEachen, I was interviewed on
> T.V. and the interviewer asked me, "Was there any American pressure?"
> Now everybody knows that there's American pressure but the average
> Canadian citizen really doesn't have any proof, and I have no proof. . . .
> So I simply said, "All I can do is to refer you to what Mr. Sharp answered,
> 'No,' in the House yesterday." The next question was, "Why do you
> think then that the Canadian government is reacting that way?" To that I
> said, "The Canadian government is like a well-trained prostitute that
> spreads her legs even before she is asked." As a result of this remark I re-
> ceived 400 phone calls within the next few hours, all but two supporting
> what I said. So this should give you an idea of what Canadian public
> opinion was like.

Thus, the American refugee question seemed to be a ready-made peg on
which many Canadians could hang their anti-American feelings and assert
their own sovereignty.

The Canadian aid groups and individual refugees in Canada celebrated this
new declaration of policy. "It was the first and only political action that I
was ever engaged in that was successful. After we were successful we said,
by God, what did we do wrong — we've succeeded!", said Bill Spira. The
task at hand for the aid groups then became a campaign to inform the potential refugees and other resisters of the new policy reversal. A new release
from the Montreal bureau of the Liberation News Service serving all the
underground presses in Canada and the United States carried the story
"Canada is Open to Deserters."

> Deserters from the U.S. Armed Forces will be welcome immigrants to
> Canada, according to new regulations announced by Canadian authori-
> ties. . . .
>
> The American Deserters Committee in Montreal hailed the govern-
> ment ruling as a victory, noting that it was the result of considerable pub-
> lic pressure from antiwar groups, the United Church of Canada, the New
> Democratic Party and even the established media.[39]

Thousands of new pamphlets were issued, describing the announcement
and interpreting it into common-sense procedures.[40] Since the open-door
policy on deserters, the numbers of deserters seeking refuge in Canada has
equaled and sometimes surpassed the number of draft dodgers. There was
very little interaction between the aid groups and the Canadian officials
throughout the rest of 1969. Most of the efforts of the aid groups were

directed toward more effectively assisting the larger numbers of deserters entering Canada.

Early Beginnings and Present Operations of American Deserters Committees
Montreal

When deserters came in larger numbers, counseling groups were unsure of how to handle them. Their counseling, once primarily oriented around obtaining landed immigrant status, was inadequate to meet the qualifications. A number of politically active draft resisters involved in counseling and aiding deserters in the Montreal area recognized the necessity for forming a group primarily for handling deserters' problems. Thus in the fall of 1968, the American Deserters' Committee (ADC) was founded. Its name and ideology were modeled on the already functioning American Deserters' Committees both in Paris and in Stockholm.

Jerry Borstein, a former New York sociologist and Congress of Racial Equality organizer and an early draft resister, was one of the founders of the Montreal ADC. He suggested that the emergence of American exile groups like the ADC in 1968 was closely related to the "critical mass" of American refugees beginning to gather in Canada; approximately 7,000 had already crossed the border. The developing resistance movement on the college campuses and the beginnings of the GI resistance movement encouraged political activists like Jerry and his friend Bill Hertzog to support the American movement in Canada. The American refugees who became a part of the ADC recognized that desertion from the United States Armed Forces had to be publicized in order for others to understand its political significance.

The American Deserters' Committee differed at the outset from the other existing aid groups by openly proclaiming itself to be a radical-political aid group. Its first manifesto took a strong position against imperialism and oppression both in the United States and abroad and expressed solidarity with the NLF of Vietnam and other groups that were struggling against oppression:

We deserters and associates view ourselves as an integral part of the world-wide movement for fundamental social change. We express support and solidarity with the NLF of South Vietnam and with the black liberation struggle at home. [We are] forced to view ourselves as victims of the same oppression as the Vietnamese and the American people, not only the minority groups but also the broad masses of American people who are becoming more aware of the need for change.[41]

This manifesto was published in left-wing presses like the *National Guard-*

ian and other underground newspapers in the United States.

The ADC's major ideological and psychological links were with the radical antiwar and antiimperialist movements in America. Jerry Borstein clarified the relationship between those refugees in Canada and the United States movement in the first issue of *The Rebel*, an early publication of the Montreal Americans in Exile that wished to "link exile activity with the movement at home":

> Those who have fled to Canada have left a movement which is growing in strength and in militancy and in the potential ability to bring about revolutionary change in the U.S. . . .That movement is just now waking up, becoming alive and growing. . . .Moreover, the development of an active exile community here with close links to the Movement in the States is crucial to the success of that Movement. . . .[42]

During its first few months of existence, the ADC held that desertion was the only antiimperialist strategy open to GI's. At a conference in February 1969, this original position was altered. Desertion was viewed as a complementary strategy to the primary struggle, which was resistance offered within the military itself. This position was reflected in *The Rebel* when its editorial staff encouraged Americans to "stay and fight" and viewed exile status as a last resort. Two years after the founding of the ADC, this strategy remained unaltered. In fact, the Montreal ADC has been instrumental in persuading other aid groups to adopt this strategy, too. In the first issue of its new publication, *Antithesis*, it was suggested that deserter groups be responsible first to resisters in the army, potential deserters and to the men and women of Indochina. If these responsibilities were not met, desertion became escape.[43]

The members of the American Deserters' Committee viewed themselves as Americans in exile in Canada and frequently compared themselves with other exile groups. Uriah Underwood, a member of the Montreal ADC, compared the ADC and a Greek exile group in a discussion of the political role of deserters and resisters. Both the Greek and American exiles came to Canada because of political conditions and convictions. Both groups were also working in Canada for a revolutionary change in their native lands. However, while the Greeks in Canada raised money for the opposition groups in Greece, the American exiles were dependent on the movement in the United States for financial aid. Another major difference was that for the Greeks there existed a real and imminent possibility of their return after the revolution. For Americans, however, their stay in Canada was likely to be long-term with a revolution far away.[44]

The issue of reconciling an exile state with assimilation into Canadian life had been a continuing debate in almost all the political exile groups, including the ADC. The ADC recognized that it was desirable on a practical basis for a deserter to become a landed immigrant wherever possible so that he could be somewhat secure and less vulnerable to problems with American and Canadian police. Yet it did not view immigration counseling as its major or sole activity as did most groups. The Vancouver ADC recognized that "the Canadian Immigration Act must never be our criterion for whom we help. Every GI must be helped." The Montreal ADC felt that those individuals involved in the counseling group had focused on immigration because they misunderstood the nature of desertion. These men did not understand that desertion was a "total life commitment." An ADC position paper stated that: "To envision aiding a deserter as only immigration and a rough mapping of the direction to integration is to recognize only a portion of the totality of desertion — an essential portion, yes, but in its incompleteness, a destructive one."[45] Although providing immigration counseling, food and shelter and opposing discriminatory practices were concrete and essential, this was hardly sufficient. Aid groups did not hold out promises of getting American deserters and resisters "to freedom" in Canada as encouraged in the *Manual*.

The Montreal ADC had attempted to fill the gaps of the counseling approach of the Montreal Council by providing a more comprehensive program for deserters. It included more kinds of aid for those men who were not yet landed and those who were not likely to become immigrants. Medical aid and guidance were provided as well as an educational program for those who had not yet completed high school. It also took into account other spiritual and educational needs by including organizational projects of community aid to introduce deserters to other groups in the local community. Emphasis was given to self-help programs that taught the deserter about democratic participation in the functions and decisions of the aid organization and a program of political education.[46]

For the first cold Quebec winter of its existence, the Montreal ADC used all its energy to survive and was politically inactive. It rented a small three-room apartment in the French-speaking district on Wolfe Street and used it as a hostel and social center. In the spring, the members became more active and public as they became involved in the campaign to combat discrimination against deserters by the Canadian Immigration Department. The summer of 1969 was a transitional period in which there was an increased flow of deserters northward. At a June meeting of about 30 deserters and their wives and girlfriends, a major policy decision was made to reorganize the ADC and reevaluate its political position. It was decided that the original founders of the group, the draft resisters who had been controlling and running the organization, should step aside and let the deserters take control. In early September a new declaration of purpose was accepted at a general meeting. It stated its opposition to "imperialistic and oppressive policies throughout the world" and specifically condemned United States militarism and economic exploitation of the peoples of Canada and Quebec. Members pledged to work closely with other Deserters' Committees in Canada and Sweden in distributing information to GI's. They would aid the American exile in important matters and participate in the Quebecois and larger Canadian community.[47]

They began acting upon this manifesto the fall and winter of 1970. The Friends of the ADC was set up to provide respectability and financial support for the group. The ADC was a participant in the Vietnam Moratorium activities at McGill University and in Montreal high schools. The general membership came out in unanimous support of the self-determination of the people of Quebec and began to set up a French language course for deserters. Larger headquarters were found and a new hostel was opened that accommodated 25 persons. A big "Christmas Dinner in Peace" was held by the ADC in the University Settlement Community Center for all the deserters it had aided as well as the friends and allies it had made over the past year in the Montreal community. One hundred and fifty American deserters came with wives, girlfriends and other friends bringing the total to 250 persons. Several French Canadians and 7 Vietnamese students belonging to the Vietnamese Patriots joined them for dinner along with Claire Culhane, a Canadian nurse who spent a year in the Canadian hospital in Quang Ngai.[48]

Other activities during the winter and spring of 1970 included making a four-hour videotape on Montreal deserters, putting out a newsletter, issuing press releases and holding discussions with various United States movement groups. The overall counseling program continued with approximately 20 to 30 newly arrived deserters counseled each week. Weekly meetings attracting 35 to 45 persons were held. An ADC delegation marched in Ottawa together with other Canadian groups to protest Canadian complicity in the Vietnam War. They also marched with Canadian students on the American consulate in Montreal to protest the United States invasion into Cambodia and the Kent State murders. On May Day, the ADC marched with the Confederation of National Trade Unions and other groups in a workers' solidarity parade. The rest of May was spent organizing a pan-Canadian conference for all deserters and resisters.[49] This conference created policy changes that have had major consequences for the aid groups.

Other Canadian Cities

The Vancouver American Deserters' Committee sprang up a few months after the ADC in Montreal and was organized by a few draft resisters and deserters. Its political objectives and major activities were similar to the Montreal ADC. The group put its major efforts into political propaganda, such as a GI pamphlet distributed on many American bases and a newsletter called the *Yankee Refugee,* which was mailed to American exiles and sympathizers on the west coast. It usually operated one or two hostels for American exiles.

The Vancouver ADC from its outset attempted to build strong relations with other leftist groups in Vancouver, such as the unemployed, trade unionists, students, natives, women and "street people." It demonstrated against the Vietnam War with these groups under the banner "U.S. Deserters Oppose American Imperialism." It also cosponsored a march against oppression for all minority groups with political grievances. The ADC saw itself primarily as a catalyst for American refugees working with the local Left movement in Vancouver. Often it would meet the crews of American Navy ships berthed at the port of Vancouver and manage to slip a GI desertion pamphlet between the covers of "See Beautiful B.C." tourist brochures, sometimes with positive results!

In 1969, new ADCs sprang up in Toronto, Ottawa and Regina in the prairies. Each was involved in a comprehensive counseling program for deserters and in operating hostels. Each of the ADCs viewed political action and propaganda against American imperialism as an important priority. Unlike the other aid groups, the objective of their counseling was not a smooth adjustment to Canada. Canada was not viewed as a "liberated zone." They saw themselves as rebels exiled in Canada whose major commitment was to stop the Vietnam War by means of international resistance to American imperialism and to struggle against all forms of oppression.

Who were the political allies of the American deserters' groups? Despite the American orientation and focus of the ADCs and other exile groups, they were not recognized by the New Left and other radical peace groups as part of the American peace movement until the amnesty campaign of 1973. Until 1970, they were deliberately shunned and assumed to be "cop-outs" from the movement. There was no direct financial or moral support from these groups until the early 1970s. When the ADCs had attempted to publish news in the GI press and Liberation News Service, they were met with deaf ears. Thus, they were forced to seek allies in the student and religious community in Canada. One interesting ally of the Montreal ADC was a small group of Vietnamese deserters and draft dodgers calling themselves Vietnamese Patriots. Although their personal backgrounds were quite different from those of the American deserters in that they were highly educated and skilled and sought advanced training, they were victims of the war just as the American refugees. In 1970 their association consisted of 60 active members and 150 supporters, all of whom were students or ex-students from South Vietnam. Their major objective, according to one of their leaders, was to "unite with all peace loving Vietnamese in Canada and the U.S., to assist and cooperate with all American and Canadian antiwar movements and other Vietnamese organizations in foreign countries, and to support totally and unconditionally the struggle of the Vietnamese people against foreign invaders and to unite with their native allies leading to independence, neutrality, peace, democracy and prosperity in South Vietnam."[50] In their bimonthly magazine *Tien Phong* there was an exchange of articles written by American deserters who described their experiences in Vietnam. *AMEX* and other exile publications carried articles written by the Vietnamese Patriots.

The Pan-Canadian Conference: From Social Welfare to Resistance

Despite the fact that in 1969 deserters were viewed with equanimity under the law many of them still did not qualify for landed immigrant status under the point system. Many of the aid groups became overburdened with work and experienced more and more frustration because they could do little to aid those deserters in immigration counseling. Thus in the spring of 1970 the Montreal ADC took the initiative in sponsoring a pan-Canadian confrerence of deserters and resisters in a major attempt to bring together all aid groups across Canada, as well as some antiwar groups in the U.S. It was no secret that the Montreal ADC wanted to politicize the other aid groups and move them to a more radical posture in regard to the deserter. For this reason it held a separate caucus of all members of the various ADCs across Canada the evening before the conference.

The Union of American Exiles had attempted to organize a similar conference a year earlier, but due to the victory in the battle with the immigration laws the aid groups did not feel the urgency of the crisis and were disinterested. Also, the union lacked the coordination necessary to organize such a conference. The ADC sent out organizers before the conference to visit all the major Canadian aid groups to stimulate ideas and to promote the idea of a national conference. Preregistration was necessary for security reasons.

All the Canadian aid groups were represented at the conference; American peace groups from Maine, New York and Vermont, SDS, Women's Strike for Peace, GI coffeehouse organizers such as Fred Gardner, the American Friends Service Committee and others attended. The keynote speaker was Tom Hayden of the Chicago conspiracy trial and Carl Ogelsby, New Left activist and past president of SDS. Included were presentations by the Canadian aid groups on coordination, financial and legal problems. Their relationship with American aid groups was discussed and information was exchanged about the political role of American refugees in Canada and their effectiveness in helping to end the Vietnam War. As had been anticipated by the ADC, the most controversial and important discussions dealt with the political role of American refugees.

Many called for a different approach and orientation of the aid groups. Naomi Wall, TADP employment counselor for the past four years, felt that although their program had attempted to remain apolitical, the individual counselors could not. She summed up her personal feelings by stating that the "aid groups are no longer relevant unless they begin playing a political role" Her statement elicited general agreement among the other counselors who came from as far away as Vancouver, Demetrios Roussopoulos, a radical of the Canadian New Left and editor of *Our Generation*, spoke of the "charitable Red Feather" orientation of the aid groups for the past years. "Five years ago it was predicted that deserters and war resisters would flood the ranks of the antiwar movement and this didn't happen," according to Roussopoulos "These men have placed themselves in an untenable limbo." Roussopoulos urged the groups to "transform the antidraft consiousness of Americans into a political and social understanding of anti-U.S. imperialist institutions." He felt that in relation to Quebec, the aid groups, especially those in Montreal, should seek the expulsion of American imperialism and enunciate the self-determination of the Quebec people. His analysis began a discussion as to whether American refugees should engage in exile politics or join a Canadian movement of political groups.

The Montreal ADC, represented by Larry Svirchev, opted for a strong political stand by Americans. Svirchev visualized a new era in which exiles "must become the revolutionaries of Quebec, to work together with other French Canadian revolutionaries." Thus far, however, the ADC and other exile groups had been relating vicariously to the American struggle rather than joining the struggle of the Canadian Left. Most of the conference's invited guests were from the American movement. Both Hayden and Oglesby assumed that the refugees present at the conference were part of the "American Revolution."

Roussopoulos and other Canadians involved in the movement were particularly critical of exile groups relating only to the American movement. He warned against the dangers of Left imperialism and felt Canadian Left groups had to be vigilant against the "uncritical importation of U.S. ideas and tactics." Some of the older American ex-patriates strongly agreed with him. They argued that exile politics focused the refugee's attention on American issues and reinforced his old identifications and guilt feelings, which only prolonged his misunderstandings of Canada. Linking up with the Canadian peace movement and leftist groups was their suggested alternative to exile politics if the individuals wanted to be relevant as new Canadians.

The women of the Montreal ADC sponsored a women's caucus , where there was agreement that women in both Canada and in the United States had been denied meaningful participation in the movement. They stressed the necessity of building a community in Canada where both men and women worked together to fight oppression with new approaches and new life-styles. They too were political refugees; they too had to make the political decision to leave the United States, whether they came with a draft resister or deserter or whether they came alone. Their desire to work equally in these aid groups led to some concrete changes in the groups' structures and goals.

The conference concluded with an address by Tom Hayden, who was the only person, strangely enough, to raise the issue of amnesty. The majority of delegates did not share his concern. A telegram received from the Vietnamese National Liberation Front to the Montreal conference was read. It sent fraternal support of resistance and asked the conference to demand a complete and immediate withdrawal of the American troops in Vietnam. This received unanimous approval.

The proposals that received approval from all the conference delegates concerned financial and coordination procedures as well as new political positions. It was agreed that avoiding the draft and coming to Canada at this time was an act of little political consequence in relation to the American political struggle. Yet desertion was seen to have strong political consequences. Therefore, keeping the border open for deserters had the highest priority. The proposal urged draft resisters who had not yet been inducted into the Armed Forces to:

> either refuse induction and agitate in U.S. schools and industries or to en-
> list with the express purpose of organizing and agitating within the service.
> We realize because of the repressive nature of U.S. society, flight to Cana-
> da must be maintained as an alternative for those involved in active resist-
> ance. This conference therefore calls for increased political involvement
> and resistance and the protection of refugees here in Canada to defeat the
> U.S. system.[51]

This new political position was to be implemented by a preinduction training program for potential refugees who wanted to work politically in the
military. They would first come to Canada to be trained by deserters. More
effectively, political counseling would also encourage draft dodgers to return
to the United States and resist until their only option was jail or exile.

The Montreal conference marked a turning point in the direction of the
refugee aid groups. An editorial in *AMEX* discussing the conference stated
that "regardless of what the masses of regulars decide to do from now on, one
thing for sure, the organizations assisting new American arrivals no longer
look on their function as merely dispensing aid. . . . I think we are going to
witness a new breed of war immigrants."[52]

The ADC has had a political ax to grind since its inception. For example,
it declared its support for the struggle of the Quebec people when it became
increasingly difficult to remain apolitical in the midst of a growing French-
Canadian separatist struggle. This became especially significant during the
Quebec crisis in October 1970 when the Front de Liberation de Quebec
(FLQ) engaged in political kidnappings.

In response to these kidnappings the War Measures Act was declared by
Prime Minister Trudeau. This was the severest measure the Canadian government had invoked since World War II. All civil liberties were suspended for
over six months. The prime minister even had considered total censorship of
the media, though Parliament did not back him on this specific measure.
The media, however, did not need an external authority to censor their content during the crisis; the major newspapers and magazines, with only a few
exceptions were supportive of the government's action and practiced self-
censorship.[53] Public opinion polls showed that even the ordinary Canadian
citizens supported this resort to martial law, believing that law and order
had broken down. For example, the dismissal of teachers in both Ontario
and British Columbia for mere discussion of the FLQ and the War Measures
Act was supported.

The province of Quebec was especially subjected to a military state of repression by the federal government. All members of the Royal Canadian Mounted Police, Quebec police and the armed services were on 24-hour duty. They patrolled all major streets armed with machine guns. Together they made more than 2,000 raids and arrested approximately 500 Canadians on suspicion that they were connected with the FLQ. Those arrested were held incommunicado without counsel. When they were eventually released it became clear to most that these were respectable Montreal citizens, members of citizens' groups and trade-union spokesmen, such as Michel Chartrand. Montreal draft resister Roger Williams reported in the *New Republic*, "Newspapers disappeared from the newstands; distributors had been warned by police not to handle 'revolutionary materials' and one distributor, an American deserter, had all his stock confiscated and was threatened with deportation if he chose to reopen his business." He, like many other American refugees, was very shaken by these suspensions of civil liberties. Comparing this experience with that of his fugitive days Williams wrote:

[I had] lived as a draft-refusing fugitive in the U.S. before coming to Canada and I can honestly say that I was never then as afraid of the authorities as I was in Quebec in October. In the U.S. there would have been bail, court proceedings, appeals and a degree of support from the movement had I been arrested. And one is innocent until proven guilty. . . .Under the provisions of the War Measures Act, the defendant is forced to prove his innocence before the authorities who consider every suspect guilty.[54]

During this period the ADC hostel in Montreal was raided twice by the police and most of the active deserters were forced underground. Their close association with the Vietnamese Patriots Association, 40 of whose members were arrested and subjected to deportation hearings, and their announced support of the French-Canadian separatists, made these Americans prime suspects.

The War Measures Act radicalized the aid groups in other major Canadian cities even though most of the military activity connected with repression of the FLQ occurred in Montreal. In Vancouver, British Columbia, there were also repercussions from the enforcement of the War Measures Act. Mayor Campbell took advantage of it to crack down on what he considered to be undesirable groups and stated in an interview that he favored using the emergency law to "pursue American draft dodgers, drug traffickers and other types of criminals."[55] In part, therefore, the aid groups were also radicalized due to the scapegoating of these exiles by prominent Canadian conservative politicians. Some examples of this type of blame were evident in incidents that took place in Vancouver and Toronto in 1970.

In the spring of 1970, Mayor Dennison of Toronto used a large demonstration against the expansion of the Vietnam War into Cambodia as a pretext for public condemnation of American refugees. Of the 5,000 persons who participated, 91 were arrested for their "violent acts." According to the chief of police, these included the breaking of windows and throwing paint bombs. Although only 15 of these 91 individuals were Americans, most of them were not draft dodgers or deserters. Rather, they included a lawyer and other political refugees. Nevertheless the mayor blamed American exiles for the violence that occurred.[56]

The Toronto aid groups, feeling themselves to be under attack, feared that their public support would suffer as a result of Mayor Dennison's statement. They confronted him at a press conference to deny their involvement in the violence and the demonstration and attempted to explain that American refugees were trying to "Canadianize" themselves rather than "Americanize" Canadians. Mayor Dennison preferred blaming the "outsiders" to coping with the real problems that existed among Canadian youth.

In a similar manner, Vancouver's Mayor Tom Campbell often attacked transient youth and American refugees. In the summer of 1970 he said that if he had his way, he would close the United States' Canadian border to American hippies and draft evaders "and let the United States have back the ones already here." He continued: "It will be a national disgrace if American draft dodgers are housed in Canadian hostels. If they won't fight for their own country, what are they going to do for Canada? If Canada was in trouble, they'd flee to another country."[57] Thus American exiles came to be looked upon by some Canadian officials as part of the larger Canadian "youth problem" and were treated as Canada's newest scapegoat.

In the months after the Montreal conference there was a visible change in the operations of the major aid groups. Most of them began a serious evaluation of their function. They could no longer be based only on a charitable approach because this meant a continuation of the individualism by which a draft evader could only be relocated within the American empire in Canada.

In December 1970 the Montreal ADC announced its dissolution and the formation of a new group, the American Exile Counselling Centre. It provided political rather than humanitarian counseling. The new counseling procedure presented Canada as an economic satellite of the United States. Women were also treated as exiles and encouraged to do political work with the exile group. Men with draft and military problems were aided either to return to the United States legally or to continue their struggle in Canada. The Montreal exiles accepted Tom Hayden's analysis that the major struggle for Americans was in the "motherland" and that Americans in Canada should realize that they were there for political reasons.

The Toronto aid groups also underwent a major transformation. The ADC dissolved and became a new group called the Committee to Aid Refugees from Militarism. It moved into "The Hall," which became a Canadian-American neighborhood center with other political and cultural activities. Its counseling services became more political and its programs were more coordinated.

The Vancouver Committee to Aid American War Objectors had also changed its counseling approach as a direct result of the Montreal conference discussions. It gave counseling and aid mostly to those individuals who had exhausted or were trying to exhaust all possibilities that would allow them to remain in the United States. All others, men who were I-Y, IV-F or overage, were simply being given printed information on Canadian immigration laws. In its mailings, the Vancouver Committee sent out an analysis of why people came to Canada, which included a description of the War Measures Act, the repression in Quebec, the content of Vancouver Mayor Campbell's statements against draft resisters and the British Columbia government's attack on the freedom of speech of teachers since the War Measures Act had been in effect. One of its mailing statements reflected the new policies:

> We feel that Canada should be a last resort, a step to be taken only if all else fails. We do not feel that anyone should go so far as to go to jail, but you should at least try every possible means before leaving for Canada. ...Once here, most immigrants become politically ineffective and often end up working for American branch plants, thus having done nothing except relocate. ...

The aid groups' new political counseling had some impact on the flow of American refugees. According to both the Toronto and Vancouver groups, since the changed counseling tactics, the numbers of refugees had dropped sharply by one-third. The Toronto aid group stated that newcomers dropped from about 25 men a day in early October 1970 to about 8 a day in January 1971. The Vancouver group noted that it was only handling 20 a week instead of its usual 30 in the same time period.[58] Some of the major factors responsible for the decrease were the new counseling advice telling men only to come as a last resort and the proclamation of the War Measures Act. According to the aid counselors, there was widespread concern about this act among potential draft resisters; many letters were received asking about its implications. Also, in 1972 the draft was winding down since the shift to the lottery system in December 1970. In Canada, the tightening of immigration requirements in the same year discouraged American refugees. On top of this was an increasing unemployment rate that especially affected these youths.

During the height of the American refugee influx in 1969 and 1970 there were as many as 26 aid groups operating to service both the social welfare and political needs of these men; by 1972 most of these aid groups had substantially wound down their service. Even some of the larger centers shifted their counseling operations to the homes of a few dedicated individuals who served as main contacts. The Canadian Council of Churches, which had distributed United States funds to the aid groups, tapered off its financial support.[59]

Although they continued counseling, most of the aid groups that were still operating spent most of their time working on political aspects of immigration, such as petitions to the Canadian government for political asylum for nonlanded refugees. They also did educational work around the issue of amnesty which was raised as an issue in the United States as a result of the McGovern campaign for the presidency in 1972. The new aid groups that formed after 1972 were basically political exile groups. The prototype of one such group was the Exiles Association in Vancouver which appeared on the scene in November 1972. Its antiimperialist orientation was similar to that of the original American Deserters' Committee, although its membership included both draft dodgers and deserters. Its main objectives were to provide a "focus for the ongoing antiwar commitment of American resisters in exile"[60] and to organize exiles around the amnesty issue and demand a universal, unconditional amnesty for all war resisters and deserters. However, it did offer some "repatriation counseling" to those exiles who wanted to investigate the possibility of returning to the United States before unconditional amnesty was achieved. It actively boycotted the amnesty offered by President Ford in 1974. Similar groups, such as the Toronto American Exiles' Association and the Montreal American Exiles for Total Amnesty formed in 1974 as a direct response to Ford's earned reentry program to mobilize around a program for a universal, unconditional amnesty.[61]

Exile Groups Encounter Canadian Nationalists

Many sympathetic Canadians did not approve of the politicization of

American refugees organized as exile groups. These Canadians, some ex-refugees, felt that these Americans should become part of the Canadian mosaic and express their political beliefs through Canadian political groups. Eiler Fredericks, a young minister of the United Church in Toronto who had aided more than 15 American refugees in his home, as well as helping some of the exile groups, expressed typical Canadian opinion on this matter. Once a German immigrant who had become a Canadian citizen, he stated:

> I think that anyone who comes to another country has to make a very basic decision about what his attitude to that country is going to be, if he sees himself as a political exile. I think personally, and I suspect that most Canadians, are quite prepared to welcome anyone under the sun, quite literally, if they are prepared to become Canadians. I think that we are highly suspicious of people who call themselves exiles. And I have never been in favour of that group calling themselves "American exiles." [Reference is to the Union of American Exiles.] The thing with some Americans is that they keep to themselves and perpetuate with their organizations the idea that they are going to return to the U.S.

Fredericks compared such an attitude on the part of these Americans with that of the "right-wing Cuban exiles who operated out of Florida, in that they were obsessed with their homeland and couldn't make any contribution to their new country." He welcomed Americans who were actively involved in Canadian political events.

American refugees who always hoped to return permanently to the United States did not adjust to a normal life in Canada. Fredericks commented, "Now those kids who always wanted to return just don't make out in this country in terms of jobs, in terms of anything. There isn't any kind of stability."

Bill Spira of the Toronto Anti-Draft Program, a major organizer and fund raiser, also had strong feelings against Americans organizing as exiles in Canada. Bill was an Austrian who became a naturalized American and then a Canadian citizen. Because he was active in the left-wing Waffle caucus of the New Democratic party at the time, he was particularly sensitive to what he called "Left imperialism":

> Americans are not generally known for their understanding of the national aspirations of other people and even the American radicals that come, especially the American radicals, are very insensitive about it. While many of them bring their bodies here, it takes a good two to three years till their heads catch up with them. For the first two years they're still fight-

ing the battle of the imperialists. If Canadians and those Americans really want a way of ending the imperialist role, they should try for Canadian independence. Because, in effect, we're an American colony and we have to wage an anticolonial struggle in Canada.

Professor Robin Mathews, an outspoken Canadian in favor of Canadian nationism and coediter of the book *Struggle for Canadian Universities,* argued that the United States draft dodger in Canada was part of imperialism in Canada: "Many exiles are blindly ignorant of the Canadian fact. As a result they act in Canada as if they were in the U.S. . . . In recent years U.S. citizens have increasingly taken over posts that should have gone to Canadians. That is where the U.S. draft dodger is today. He is part of U.S. imperialism in Canada."[62]

Dr. Ron Lambert, a sociologist who counseled American exiles in the Kitchener-Waterloo aid group in Ontario, challenged many of Mathews's assumptions. His major argument was that the "exiles do not, in any significant sense, articulate with the power structure of Canada." He challenged Mathews's colonial self-portrait of Canada as imperiled by strangers in her midst that she cannot successfully absorb.[63] Most American refugees were sympathetic to Lambert's position. They took strong exception to Mathews's views and in fact felt that they had personally made a contribution against American imperialism by choosing exile in Canada rather than fighting in Vietnam.

In summary, then, the counseling groups in their first five years of existence basically served the function of social welfare-benevolent organizations as would any other immigrant social groups. They oriented tens of thousands of young Americans toward assimilating into Canadian life and society. However, the 1970 crisis and the struggle to legitimize deserters in Canada made them aware of the political nature of the class-based continental channeling system. The deserters could not quietly integrate themselves into Canadian society. This realization forced the aid groups to review their initial counseling approach. At the first pan-Canadian conference, all the aid groups, following the lead of the Deserters' Committees, rejected their individualist approach to counseling whereby the war objector would merely be relocated within the American empire in Canada. With this new political consciousness, the aid groups in 1970 took a more radical stance, urging draft objectors to remain in the United States and engage in resistance, keeping Canada as a haven for deserters and those resisters whose only option was jail. They alerted potential refugees to Canada's subordination to America's economic interests. Subsequently, most of the aid groups dissolved and were replaced by American Exile Associations in the major Canadian cities, dedicated to fighting American imperialism in Canada.

NOTES

1.   *Hansard*, Canadian House of Commons Debates, First Session, 28 Parliament, May 22, 1969, p. 8931. The Minister of Manpower and Immigration is referring to the liberalization in January and July 1968, which eliminated the practice of only processing applications of military servicemen who showed proof of discharge.
2.   "White Paper on Immigration," October 1966, section IV, par. 56.
3.   *Georgia Straight*, March 18–25, 1970.
4.   Brief # 1, "A Note on the Handling of Draft-Age Americans Who Apply for Entry to Canada," 1967, written by Canadian aid groups.
5.   Deputy Minister of Immigration, Tom Kent's letter to the Vancouver Committee, November 22, 1967.
6.   Tom Kent's letter to the Vancouver Committee, February 29, 1968.
7.   Ibid.
8.   Letter from Toronto Anti-Draft Program to the Vancouver Committee, January 1969.
9.   Memo containing immigration guidelines to immigration border officials from the Department of Manpower and Immigration, July 29, 1968.
10.   Letter from TADP to the Vancouver Committee, January 1969.
11.   *Montreal Star*, February 6, 1969.
12.   *Montreal Star*, Ottawa Bureau, February 14 & 18, 1969.
13.   *Vancouver Sun*, February 1, 1969.
14.   *Montreal Star*, February 6, 1969.
15.   *Toronto Globe and Mail*, Spring 1969.
16.   *Toronto Daily Star*, March 8, 1969.
17.   Ibid.
18.   *Montreal Star*, February 10, 1969.
19.   *Montreal Star*, February 18, 1969.
20.   Ibid.
21.   *Hansard*, Canadian House of Common, February 17, 1969, First Session, 28 Parliament, p. 5590.
22.   *Hansard*, Canadian House of Commons, February 24, 1969, First Session, 28 Parliament, p. 5845.
23.   Letter from TADP to the Vancouver Committee, February 25, 1969.
24.   Vancouver Committee leaflet, February 27, 1969.

25. Letter from Vancouver Committee to Yugoslavian Embassy, February 11, 1969.

26. Letter from Ottawa Assistance and Immigration to the Vancouver Committee, March 26, 1969.

27. Brief # 2 from Canadian aid groups to Department of Manpower and Immigration, March 5, 1969.

28. Frank H. Epp, *I Would Like to Dodge the Draft Dodgers, But...* (Waterloo: Conrad Press, 1970); Jim Wilcox, "They Are Up Against the Canadian Border," p. 55.

29. Ibid.

30. Jim Wilcox, "They Are Up Against the Canadian Border," p. 57.

31. Letter from Ottawa AID to Vancouver Committee, March 26, 1969.

32. *Hansard*, Canadian House of Commons, May 1, 1969, First session, 28 Parliament, vol. VIII, p. 8207.

33. Ibid.

34. *Hansard*, Canadian House of Commons, May 5, 1969, First session 28 Parliament, vol. VIII, p. 8304.

35. Frank H. Epp, *I Would Like to Dodge;* Jim Wilcox, "They Are Up Against the Canadian Border," p. 53.

36. Jim Wilcox, "They Are Up Against the Canadian Border," p. 57.

37. *Hansard*, Canadian House of Commons Debates, First session, 28 Parliament, p. 8931.

38. *Vancouver Sun*, December 1, 1970.

39. *American Refugees Newsletter*, June 1969, from Liberation News Service.

40. Vancouver Committee Leaflet, June 5, 1969.

41. Montreal American Deserters' Committee Manifesto, December 1968.

42. Uriah Underwood, "The Political Role of Deserters and Resisters," *Antithesis*, Forum of the American Deserters' Committee, Summer 1970. The name *Antithesis* symbolizes the Hegelian dialectic: the thesis, being the U.S., the antithesis, resistance against U.S., attempts to create a synthesis and new society in Canada.

43. *Antithesis*, 13 (1970).

44. Ibid.

45. "Totality of Desertion in Relation to Deserters and Resisters' Aid Groups," ADC Montreal, undated.

46. Ibid.

47. "History of Montreal ADC," pamphlet, 1970.

48. Roger Williams, "Deserters Gather for Montreal Dinner," *Los Angeles Free Press*, January 30, 1970.

49. "History of Montreal ADC," pamphlet, 1970.

50.   "Weekend Magazine" *Vancouver Sun,* December 5, 1970.
51.   *AMEX* 2 (June 1970).
52.   Ibid.
53.   *The Last Post,* a well-informed Montreal magazine, was one of the few that was critical of the government's response. In its November 1970 issue it takes the establishment media to task: "(It was) the kind of journalism that gives credence to every government rumor, aids the government in perpetrating its mythologies, whips up the appropriate mix of hysteria, anger and revulsion required by the government to launch its legislation. ...Virtually the only kind of jounalism Canadians have been reading throughout the crisis."
54.   Roger N. Williams, "Strong-Arm Rule in Canada; the War Measures Act and its Aftermath," *New Republic,* January 30, 1971, pp. 16, 17.
55.   *Vancouver Sun,* October 16, 1970.
56.   *Toronto Daily Star,* May 26, 1970.
57.   *Vancouver Sun,* July, 1970.
58.   "U.S. Draft Dodger Decline Noted," *Vancouver Sun,* January 7 & 8, 1971.
59.   *AMEX* 4 (1973): 30.
60.   *AMEX* 5 (December, 1974): 32.
61.   *AMEX* 5 (December 1974): 19—20.
62.   *AMEX* 2 (June 1970): p. 24.
63.   *AMEX* 2 (August—September 1970): 8—9.

II

COMMUNITY AND POLARITY NORTH OF THE 49TH PARALLEL

Community and Polarity North of the 49th Parallel*

How have the American refugees fared in Canada? Have they resumed their careers and begun to assimilate into Canadian life? In what directions have they been searching for new meaning in their lives? What kinds of life-styles and relationships with Canadians have they established in their new homeland? Have they made "good immigrants"? How have they earned their daily bread?

Dr. Saul Levine, a Toronto psychiatrist who conducted a study of 60 American refugees, analyzed their adaptation to Canada in terms of a four-stage process of coping with crises that he asserted most refugees went through to varying extents.[1] The first stage he referred to as "disorganization," in which refugees might be unprepared, confused and floundering in their new environment. The second stage described as "acting out," involved a person's dropping out of conventional activity and becoming involved in antisocial behavior such as stealing, pushing drugs, and violence. In the third stage, referred to as "searching," the refugee established positive relationships with new friends, pursued his career and personal interests and searched for meaning to his life. In the final stage, "adaptation and integration," the new immigrant became wholly engaged in being a Canadian and established a new sense of purpose. Although all American refugees did not necessarily experience all of these stages and the intensity with which they experienced each varied enormously, Dr. Levine's analysis does provide a useful focal point for an examination of the refugees' lives in Canada.

Many of these American refugees were "marginal" men and as such were likely to be able to apply a critical perspective to their examination and experience of Canadian society. They were able to do so not only because of their understanding of Canada's colonial position vis-à-vis the American and Canadian complicity in Vietnam, but also because their own cultural background in the United States provided them with a basis for understanding the culture of their new country that immigrants from a more dissimilar culture might not share.

The development of marginal status among American refugees was more acutely felt in the first two stages we have described. The need to negotiate the demands of two distinct value communities within North American culture might render these exiles marginal. According to Robert Park, the marginal man was one whose personal philosophy evidenced consciousness of a

*Notes to this section can be found with those of chapter 6.

conflict in his natural loyalties, of an effort to achieve an inner harmony and consistency and a struggle to maintain his integrity.[2] In this sense, marginality was a sociopsychological problem as well as one of structural integration. The individual involved was to a large degree acculturated to the perspectives of both his membership groups or cultural heritages. Often, despite any possibility for structural integration in either culture, he might have difficulty achieving a state of sociopsychological integration free of conflict. The very ambiguity of his social status as an exile and the consequent difficulty in developing a nonambiguous identification either in the United States or in Canadian culture impeded such integration. Particularly where these individuals were provided with divergent cultural value perspectives as a function of their migration, they were likely to conceive of themselves as "alien" inasmuch as the reaction of Canadians toward them was likely to be ambiguous, if not contradictory. In the view of Robert Park, the personality or social type that would emerge out of this condition would be one that lived in intimate association with the world about him but never so completely identified with it that he was unable to look at it without a certain critical detachment.

The second half of this volume will attempt to describe these stages of the American refugees' acculturation into Canadian society as they experienced it. In chapter 6 we will describe the first stage: the initial reaction of refugees to leaving their family and country, the "searching process" and the seeking out of a new existence in their adopted land. Chapters 7 and 8 will deal in depth with the more problematic aspects of stage two, in which we will describe the subculture of unassimilated refugees and their interaction with the police. These men are seen in more detail than the more assimilated immigrants since they were not only the most visible but they also made the largest impact on the Canadian public and government.

The American refugee reacted to the fact that he had a "marginal" status in Canadian society in two distinctively different ways. The refugee who was able to obtain landed immigrant status but had developed a critical stance to fundamental aspects of North American culture was encouraged to engage in nonconformist behavior. This new immigrant's innovative response to marginality led him to become part of the Canadian youth counterculture. This option was mainly open to middle-class draft dodgers and deserters who felt only temporarily displaced by their forced move to the "North Country Fair." In contrast, the refugee who was not able to obtain landed immigrant status often was the more bitter and alienated young man, usually the working-class deserter. As a result of his exile status and the negative reaction he often encountered in Canada he became only further alienated. He mainly clung to the security of the deserters' hostels that provided him with economic and emotional support. Occasionally his marginal status brought him into confrontation with the law. The immigrant who responded innovatively to his marginal status had the option and chose to remain unadjusted to establishment values and institutions. He sought to build his own community and counterinstitutions, although he could also choose to acculturate and become an "acceptable" immigrant at any time. The nonlanded deserter was forced into further alienation from both cultures. He was considered an unacceptable immigrant by the Canadian government and frequently was pursued by police forces from both sides of the border.

The American exiles' adaptation and acculturation to their new homeland will also be discussed. Whether these American refugees have opted to become new Canadians or have returned to the United States in response to President Ford's conditional clemency program has been dependent on their successful assimilation into Canadian social and economic life. Most of them have assimilated in this respect. Indeed, their "success" has served to reintegrate them into the class-based North American channeling system that continues to provide the manpower for the United States' military economy. The irony of President Ford's clemency program can be seen to lie in the fact that these men need not come home again to return to the control of American capitalism.

6

New Lives in Canada

American refugees came to Canada with the expectation that life there would fulfill all the American ideals and hopes that could not be fulfilled in the United States. They came seeking the Promised Land in the same spirit as the fugitive slaves a century before had hoped to find social freedom and justice. However, as the immediate shock of making the decision to leave their own country and to emigrate to another wore off, they faced another culture shock: they saw American institutions everywhere in their new country. Had they really left the American culture with its values and policies behind? They began to wonder. It seemed that now they were experiencing American policies from the other side, from the viewpoint of the underdog. They were now the Indians experiencing the might and strength of the cowboys.

Pioneers and the American Dream

The American refugees reacted in one of three ways upon realizing that they must still function daily within the sphere of American influence in their newly found status. On one extreme, the minority of activists and political radicals formed American exile groups, like the American Deserters' Committees, that rebelled against the colonial status of Canada and made alliances with the radical Canadian youth and French-Canadian liberation movements. In their publications they revealed the complicity of Canada in the Vietnam War and exposed the continental youth channeling system. These men were even more enraged by the injustices they found in Canada because they had expected an improvement and were disillusioned.

On another extreme were those Americans deeply disappointed in their discovery that Canadians frequently were just as indifferent to the social problems in Canada as Americans had been to the problems in the United States. They felt that the French-Canadians were just as oppressed as the black people in America and that there were just as many "middle Canadians" as there were "middle Americans" who raised their voices for "law and order" whenever a crisis situation threatened to unleash the pent-up anger of minority groups. These refugees were not political activists in the United States and for the most part had not become active in the aid groups and exile groups or Canadian movement activities. They were turned off by all the Canadian nationalistic outpourings and sentiments even if they did have an anti-American imperialism content. They had become deeply suspicious of all solutions through normal political channels. Instead, they believed in the cultural revolution of the Yippies and related to it in a very personal way. They believed only in themselves as the major force for social change and saw the revolution as living an integrated existence themselves. They were part of the "counterculture" that Theodore Roszak wrote about.[3] These individuals reacted to Canadian society by "dropping out" of the conventional institutions altogether. They lived with their friends in communal institutions in immigrant areas of the city, as part of the larger "hip" communities, or left the cities behind and lived in rural communal enclaves as farmers. Their pioneer spirit could not be contained within the framework of Canadian society any more than it could within American social life. Many of these men and women had already begun to consider alternative life-styles and institutions while they were living in the United States, but most of their energies were taken up in fighting the military system there. When the opportunity to experiment was provided, these individuals eagerly took up the challenge. They represented between 20 to 30 percent of the refugee population.

The third reaction was the most common. As patriotic men who were taught to believe in American values of democracy and freedom, they went along with the system as best they could. As educated Americans they aspired to professional careers. They felt it was very unfair and un-American to be forced to interrupt their personal careers to serve in a military that was conducting a war they felt to be illegal and, above all, immoral. They objected to the undemocratic use of the draft and they were happy to find a country of refuge that did not compel them to take part in the military. They were not anxious to leave their country, yet there was no alternative. Many had tried playing the game and following the rules; still there was no reconciliation. They came to Canada hoping to start anew. Although they did not like many aspects of their new country, their struggle was over and they were relieved to be left alone. Most of these men lowered their initial expectations of finding something better and began their educations and careers again, picking up where they had left off in the United States.

All of these refugees felt that they would rather start a new life in another country, knowing they would probably never be free to return to the United States, than serve in the Armed Forces or go to prison. One draft resister described his decision and hopes. "My woman and I came to Canada about a year and a half ago. Immigration provided our only alternative to the draft or jail. For the time being, we have taken the opportunity to begin a family with the natural spaciousness of the Canadian landscape — our hope for a home. As yet, it has not become sufficiently clogged by progressive industrial expansionism to diminish our hopes for a sane environment. We feel lucky. We hope."

Eric Hoffer, in his *Ordeal of Change*, compared such migrant farmers to the American pioneers and found a striking resemblance. He argued that a large portion of America's earlier and later settlers were failures, fugitives and felons, people who were forced to leave their homes or who never had homes. He suggested that a man who was settled, had made good, and was integrated into the established society did not go in search of hardship and privation.[4] Some of the American refugees in Canada resembled these pioneers in many ways and were themselves aware of these similarities.

For refugees, America's war in Vietnam represented the closing of the American frontier and with its closing the loss of all hope of obtaining what had been held out as the American dream. They had been indoctrinated all their lives with the essence of what that dream stood for as it was embodied in the Declaration of Independence, the Bill of Rights and the Constitution. However, American youth experienced daily the contradictions inherent in the gap between the ideals and the realities. Eldridge Cleaver referred to this gap as the "two Americas: the America of the American dream and the America of the American nightmare." He viewed himself and the children of America as the citizens of the dream struggling against the nightmare that constituted the present reality.[5] An American refugee described how his generation lived the dream only to find it transformed into a nightmare:

The American establishment has maintained itself with the fable of the American dream which each succession of fathers was denied, but always told that if they should work just a little harder, then their children would realize it. . . .Our generation was the first one to live the American dream, to grasp it only to find out how hollow a nightmare it is.[6]

Many of the American refugees saw themselves as being similar to the Jews in Germany who felt they had to flee from a corrupt state before it devoured them and all the ideals they stood for. They felt they were leaving behind a "sinking ship" from which they could not bail out since the leak had become overwhelming. They had to abandon ship and flee for the safety of a foreign shore. One draft resister drew the parallel between America's role in Vietnam and the Nazi movement in Europe. "I see the German movement all over Europe as being no more hideous than the American devastation of the Vietnamese because they refuse to let their country be occupied."

Most of the refugees considered themselves patriots. In fact, the ones most disillusioned with the United States were those who had been the most patriotic and believed deeply in the American values of democracy and equality for all. A 21-year-old black elementary schoolteacher from New York City who was drafted into the Army, eventually ended up in the Presidio stockade and escaped to Canada. He looked at his own life in retrospect:

I've completely given up on the U.S. since I went into the Army. Even now, I get a different perspective than being involved in it. . . .I see it from the outside now. And it's much worse than it was when I was there. And how can I go back into the cesspool?. . . Just the whole system is rotten. Who runs the U.S.? It's not the little man like me. I mean, I did my little part in educating the students I had, to what I believed in. As a matter of fact I was *over*-patriotic to my class. I taught them democracy as I believed in it. But it's all a sham. . . .

In citing some of the major factors that were taken into consideration in their decision to leave their country, 62 percent of the men said they were opposed to the imperialist system. As part of the questionnaire described in chapter 1, 64 percent indicated that they were opposed to American culture. They explained that it was a monolithic culture that no longer permitted freedom of expression for unconventional ideas and no longer embodied the values of the country's founders. They pointed to the violence in the cities and racial conflict to substantiate their claims that the American culture was "antipeople," more concerned with property values than with human dignity and life. Thus, over half of these Americans made it clear that it was not the Vietnam War alone that disturbed their sensibilities and ultimately made them refugees. The war simply triggered off their immediate crisis with the draft or military. Most of them saw the war in the context of a larger malaise that was afflicting America.

When asked whom they respected and identified with, most of the refugees I interviewed cited individuals who were also alienated from and repudiated by the mainstream of American society. Their heroes were the spokesmen and singers of the counterculture; singers like Bob Dylan and Phil Ochs and rock stars who described the distortion of the American dream. Young men like themselves, some of the New Left leaders and Yippies who fused New Left politics with the youth culture also rated very highly among those they closely identified with and toward whom they looked for leadership. Since they had turned their backs on almost all of the present adult leadership in the United States, these men were actively engaged in what Keniston, Erikson and others called a quest for identity.[7] They sought role models of people they admired and identified with and past traditions and life-styles that stressed the kinds of goals they were seeking.

John Kreeger, the 22-year-old deserter from the United States Army who was illegally deported from Canada, was very proud of his pioneer background:

I'm the fourth generation. We're the first pioneers in California — my father, his father and his father's father. My great grandfather was one of the first pioneers. He came from North Carolina. He left there sometime around the 1780s and came west to St. Louis. He knew a teacher there and taught school for a while. Then he came on out to California to pan gold, taught school out in California, and was in business as a farmer until he died.

John learned of his pioneer past from a family history book which, he boasted, was the first complete history ever written on California. At a critical time in his life, he was forced to sell this family book in order to raise money for him to come to Canada. He commented: "I got sick of tradition. I got sick of the Army. I didn't want any part of it. I'm still proud of my pioneer tradition but I don't think they'd be proud of the American system right now. They'd probably roll over in their graves." But John felt he was carrying on the tradition in his own right and viewed himself as the new pioneer. "I've got a chance to start over, make a life of my own, start from scratch in a new kind of a young country just like my great uncle, who was a native son of California." John described what he meant by a pioneer:

Pioneers are adventure-seekers. People who like change. They go to a new, prosperous country, where it's rapidly expanding and growing. Constant change. That's the way you'd describe Canada. It's a young country; it's just beginning to grow. And you got to grow with it. Whereas you can't in the U.S. The U.S. is not growing — it's growing old, but it's not growing in that sense. It's not expanding with new horizons, it's just decaying.

Mark Satin, a pioneer of the Toronto Anti-Draft Program, made a similar observation. Upon applying for landed immigrant status, he pointed out that "the U.S. is growing, but has lost its frontiers."

Many other refugees in Canada were interested in pioneering up north and getting some land. The aid groups often received letters requesting information on homesteading and communal farms. I asked a draft resister named Frank why he thought so many young people who had come to Canada from the United States were interested in getting land. He explained:

A lot of people are getting rid of the middle-class, uptight, junior-executive way of life. And the obvious alternative is the commune, or living kind of loose on the streets. And of course there's lots of land in Canada and it's very appealing. You can still feel like a pioneer. Be out where you can be free and do things on your own terms. Easy rider, sort of. Your own thing.

He had first "cut loose" when he went logging and fishing in Alaska during his summer vacation from school. He liked it so much that he dropped out of college for that quarter. While he was in Alaska, he received an induction notice, so he joined the National Guard, when he was promised that he would not have to be on active duty. But after he was in a couple of months, the Guard broke its promise, placed him on active duty and sent him to Fort Ord in California. Disillusioned with the Army and the "rat race" in the United States, he came up to Canada with fresh memories of Alaska. He was attempting to find work in logging in British Columbia when I met him. If he could not obtain landed immigrant status soon, he was considering disappearing in one of these logging camps.

Steve was another young man with the pioneer spirit. He had formerly worked for the Detroit resistance helping to carry resisters and deserters across the border at Windsor, Ontario, opposite Detroit. The resistance movement, according to him, was "splitting up under the attack of the FBI," which was attempting to arrest persons for "aiding and abetting draft resisters." I met Steve at the deserter's hostel in Vancouver in the spring of 1970. For the past two weeks, he had gotten up at dawn to work on the Vancouver waterfront doing booming, part of the logging operation. He heard about his job from another deserter. Steve was working to get some money together, to learn about salvaging operations and to get some general savvy around the waterfront. He was also planning to purchase a 96-foot tugboat for $3,600 when he and a friend had saved enough money. Their goal was to set up a cooperative salvaging operation off the Sunshine Coast near Vancouver and relate to the communes in the area. A large number of American refugees lived in communes and worked in the area of the Sunshine Coast, especially at Gibson's Landing, where he had planned to set up his salvaging operation.

An early draft resister who came to Canada in 1967 was a British subject who had lived in the United States for ten years. He chose to leave America because he did not want to continue in school, was not interested in the military and "felt the need for a clean break with the past. I wanted to live some of Kerouac's adventures. . . .I was beginning to fit too much into a groove. . . .In a strange way I was losing my ability to feel." He was particularly impressed with the attractiveness of Canada as a frontier country:

It isn't just in terms of geography and economy that Canada is a frontier country; it's the men and their experiences. . . .Hitch-hiking in Canada, one is picked up by men who have worked in and who talk of, the mines, the railroad, the sawmills, the oil fields, and the forest....

As for me, the writer, the draft evader, the laborer making $1,000 a month on a dam off the Alaska highway, I am glad I came. It is a time to try new ways of living, to try new faces, to think, to remember. Things are building. It's a good country for young men.[8]

The new Canadians saw their Canadian future as the fulfillment of the dreams they had about America. Charles Campbell, a Toronto draft dodger writing in *AMEX*, explained this transfer of hope:

There is a television commercial for the publically owned Canadian National Railroad which equates something it calls the "Canadian dream" with the service CN provides. This transference of the American dream onto Canada seems at first distasteful but, on reflection, becomes symbolically apt. The American dream of conspicuous consumption and possessive individualism which finds its basic expression in the figure of the ruthless tycoon contrasts revealingly with a Canadian dream of creatively tying the diverse areas of the country together, of communication, of coming to terms with ourselves in the land rather than on it.

This Canadian dream, unlike the American, is not in danger of corruption due to its internal contradictions, but only by ignorance among new and native Canadians of its subtle implications of self-awareness and self-respect through a social pluralism and expansive humanity and through a growth and change from within, leading Canada away from the Faustian nightmare of self-alienated imperialist America.[9]

These Americans were attempting to establish a new frontier across the northern border in Canada.

New Reactions to Canada and Oneself: The Changed American

The frontier spirit was just one of the attractive features of Canada for Americans. According to an early draft resister, "Compared with the United States, most of the draft evaders find Canada a simpler, quieter, saner society." He felt that this was true because of Canada's world role and history as well as her political and social structure.[10] A 24-year-old deserter from the Army Reserves expressed similar sentiments. "Since Canada is not a major power, it does not set itself up as a protector and leader of the 'free world.' Canadian nationalism doesn't have as much to do with blood and steel as does American nationalism." Another characteristic that was attributed to Canada by draft resisters was that Canadians were "more relaxed due to their slower pace of life." Also referred to was the greater cultural differentiation in Canada than in the United States and, at the same time, less pressure to conform, more tolerance, more sanity and in some ways more freedom.[11]

Older American expatriates who moved to Canada because of the repressive atmosphere in the United States found Canada very similar to America in the thirties. Many more immigrants, not yet assimilated, still spoke their native European tongues. According to a Toronto resister, "In Canada there is no big push for everyone to conform to Anglo culture and become part of the melting pot.... Canada doesn't quite melt; everything just kind of sits there."

Other refugees felt relieved when they found out the atmosphere in Canada was less polarized politically. Almost all Americans found Canadians to be more open, friendly and more receptive to new ideas. A draft resister from Toronto, jokingly, but with an air of seriousness, said, "Oh, you miss some things like dirt, crime, and violence. The police are nice and polite. The subways are clean and you walk through the parks all over the city at night without fear. The people here are less paranoid." One resister explained the more open atmosphere by saying, "Canada's still a backwater to a large degree; it's not important that people be uptight."

Other refugees who had spent more time in Canada were more critical and attempted to probe beneath the surface life in Canada. Mike commented:

There's a freer ability to express your opinions — but not to *do* anything about them. You can express any kind of viewpoint. I think the Canadians are freer in one way and more repressed in others. Like in Toronto, you can have long hair and work for a stockbroker. There are people running around here looking like "freaks" who are the straightest people in the world. It's very confusing. Like in the U.S. there are some things you associate. You're going to run into a spectrum of people that take in rock music, drugs, and politics. All that in the same people. Yet here, you'll find people that do one thing and who totally don't do anything about the other. People seem to be progressive in a cultural sense, but not a political sense.

But despite some of these differences, the overwhelming number of refugees found Canadians to be very similar to Americans, with the exception of the French-Canadians. Probably this discovery of similarity more than anything else accounted for their initial culture shock and later their profound disappointment once they had spent some time in Canada.

Two members of the Union of American Exiles in Toronto wrote that "the new immigrant begins to recognize the influence of United States culture, politics, and society everywhere in Canadian life."[12] A leading Canadian columnist, Robert Fulford, wrote:

Canada was a kind of myth to them back in the States, and, when they come here to encounter the reality, they find a myth: Canada looks so much like America that they can't quite believe they've arrived some place else; it's a kind of fairyland. The Canadians they meet aren't quite sure that their own country exists and the newcomers are profoundly confused. It's hard enough growing up with the Great Canadian Identity Crisis; think how much harder it is to be forced to adopt it.[13]

The topography and countryside of Canada looked like that of the United States, depending on what regional area you were in. You could still buy your food at Safeway stores, your gas at Esso, Standard and all the rest of the American-owned petrol stations and you paid your phone bill in British Columbia, albeit at a much higher rate, to the Bell Telephone Company run from New York. It began to occur to many refugees that they had not really arrived at so totally foreign a country as they had anticipated. They had left but they had not left. They still saw America all around them. They still could buy Elton John records and follow the latest on the Watergate scandal on CBC. So as far as most of these men knew they could never go back, yet they could not really leave America behind either. These men were sentenced to a unique limbo characterized by marginal status. According to sociologist Rivka Bar-Yosef, assimilation can be defined as a developmental sequence in which a certain "measurable level of satisfaction is the necessary prerequisite for a certain measurable level of identification." This in turn is necessary for acculturation.[14] In the following case, Tom, a deserter, was dissatisfied by the lack of differentiation between Canada and the United States:

This is Little Brother country. Canadians envy Big Brother to the south, admiringly wish they could conjure such an awesome identity for themselves, but, very small-brotherlike, merely emulate and allow Big Brother to make their decisions for them. They seem to sense that power has its unfortunate obligations, and so try to let Big Brother bear the responsibility while they garnish the rewards of American investment.[15]

Almost all these Americans criticized the increasing Americanization of the Canadian economy and social sphere. One young deserter from the Navy took a strong personal stand on this issue:

Once I get landed I'm going to start a nationwide drive to completely block out all U.S. ties, a boycott of all U.S. goods. So many nations around the world are telling the U.S. to get out, especially with their monopolistic corporations. They don't want any more U.S. control of their government through their economy. And I think Canada should wake up and start doing that, too. The problem is that too many Canadians are convinced that they're just northern U.S. people. And I think *we* have to dispel that notion before *we* can get anywhere.[6]

This man's use of "we" when he referred to Canadians was typical of these refugees' desire to identify with the underdog, which denoted Canada's relationship to the United States in their eyes. Since these men felt they had been "ripped off" from their homeland, their family and friends, they were avidly searching for another country to which to give their commitment. Just as new converts to a particular religion are usually the strongest advocates of their new religious philosophy, so it was with these new immigrants to Canada.

The more politically oriented refugee more readily acknowledged that being in Canada was qualitatively no different than being in the United States. He felt that the major issues continued to be the struggle against imperialism and elites and the liberation of all people from oppression. An exile publication from Vancouver, *Yankee Refugee,* expressed the sentiments of the radical deserters' group:

> Whether we view ourselves as exiles or refugees is irrelevant — particularly if one realizes he is neither — because both connote leaving one's home culture, and we haven't even divorced ourselves from the "system" that rules. We all share the feeling of being unable to cope with what's happened in the U.S. and some are unable to cope with the looming prospect that Canada will, as it is prone to do, soon follow suit.[17]

Some refugees had more optimism about Canada and felt that "while time may be running out, we still have a few more minutes to rectify things than Americans do." One radical resister in Toronto saw the struggle in terms of survival:

> The youth of North America have got to get themselves together to survive. And we know it, and we're getting ourselves together. I don't think it's important that people come up here or not come up here. Really, except psychologically, it doesn't make any difference. The only thing you beat when you cross the border is the Selective Service Act. You come over here to the same bullshit system. And we react to it in the same way.

This gives us an insight into the significance of the move for these Americans, even though the new surroundings they found themselves in were not so new at all. In many respects it was the new psychological freedom that had profound effects upon the lives of many of these men.

The Refugee and His Family

Usually the loneliness of missing one's friends and family were most acutely experienced in the refugees' first few months in Canada and became more bearable as they gained new friends and became more involved in their new environment. For some individuals, coming to Canada meant the permanent rupture of their family life. Almost all of these men, though, felt that leaving the United States was not an easy thing to do. A draft resister from Vancouver said: "I felt that I wasn't allowed to take essential things for granted. For example, that I *belonged* here; that I wasn't a foreigner; that I knew no one. Also I felt rather more keenly than usual that absolutely no one gave a damn what happened to me." A deserter who first went to the prairies and later came out to Vancouver said, "I felt alienated for about two months, like an animal in a zoo, although I had more freedom to move around than in the Marines; but I couldn't because I still had intense feelings of paranoia." Feelings of temporary paranoia and anxiety were very common among refugees during the first few months. This was especially true for those men who had warrants out for their arrest and those who had been "on the run" and had been chased by military police and the FBI.

"I felt cut off from my friends and relatives" was a common reaction. "It was a severing of developing friendships and a temporary break in family ties," said another resister. Those who experienced the most acute feelings of loneliness in Canada came from the country or from small towns and lived the better part of their lives among the people in their immediate hometown vicinity. They placed a large importance on their primary relationships with people there. The larger portion of these men were from lower-middle-class and poorer families who could not afford to send them away to school. For them, going into the service was perceived as an opportunity to obtain more education and training and "see the world." Also, many of the men from middle-class families had lived in two or more large cities away from their families while they were going to college or traveling during the summer months. Many of them were not at all sure what the question "Give the name of your hometown" meant, since they had been away from their families for several years and no longer considered it home. About 10 percent of these men had traveled and lived abroad with the Peace Corps, Fulbright Programs or on their own, in addition to spending time working or going to school in the larger cities in the United States. They more readily accepted the idea of coming to Canada to live and more readily adapted to the change once they were there.

The refugees' families, however, were not all supportive of the actions their sons took.[18] The largest number of parents initially attempted to deny the reality that their sons were forced to leave their country. They would not discuss the matter openly. A number of families pretended that their sons were away on temporary vacations. Anticipating their parents' negative reaction and fearing they might stop them from leaving the country, over half of the deserters in my sample did not inform their families that they were deserting and seeking refuge in Canada. Some feared that their parents would turn them in to the military authorities. In fact, a few of them had already been turned in by their relatives the first time they attempted to come to Canada. Other parents disowned their sons and severed all ties with them. More common was the generally nonsupportive, suspicious attitude that parents communicated to their sons at the time they most needed support and understanding. Doyle, an ex-Army enlistee, said that during his first few months in Toronto he received letters from his parents stating things like, "We're not going to live much longer. Think about what you're doing: you can't run forever. You're killing your father" (or your mother, depending on who was writing the letter). Doyle described his parents as supporters of Governor Wallace. His father sympathized to some extent with his dislike of the military; he had lowered the date on his birth certificate during World War I in order to evade the draft then. Despite this, Doyle felt that his father was "sort of a Fascist and doesn't quite agree with what I'm doing." But he knew his fate could be worse yet. While Doyle was a counselor for the Union of American Exiles, he met many refugees whose parents had turned them in to the authorities. He also mentioned cases where "irate fathers came up to Canada and physically attempted to drag their sons back to the United States."

Many refugees' relationship with their parents underwent a change from initial mistrust and hostility to a gradual acceptance of their decision after they came to Canada. Below is a sequence of letters from a refugee's mother, based upon actual parental correspondence:

April 21

You have disgraced your family and your country. We don't know what possessed you to do what you've done, but we never want to hear from you again except to have the money back we lent you to fly back to your base. If we had known where you were headed. . . .Your Uncle Fred was in for twenty years and says he enjoyed every minute of it. You say to send your birth certificate. Well, we burned your birth certificate and your insurance policy. You are no longer a son of ours.

April 26

We got your letter and are still waiting for the money you owe us. We want nothing to do with you. Uncle Fred is sick at heart and wants to know how you could prefer a foreign country to your native land and isn't Canada the United States' ally? As far as we're concerned, you can do what you like; but whatever you do it's wrong.

May 8

Two and one half years of service is not a lifetime. If you go back now, you will lose some pay and be confined to your base for a few weeks, and that's all. If you don't believe me, why don't you write to your unit chaplain?

May 10

Jimmy, why don't you write or call? You are hurting the parents that raised you. We still have no idea what motivated you in pursuing your course of action. Uncle Fred says those Marine officers can be very mean sometimes. Maybe that was it.

May 22

We got your letter and were glad to hear you got a job. At least you won't starve. We can see in a way what you mean about that My Lai incident. Is it very cold up there this part of the year?

June 3

Daddy is getting his vacation this month and we were going to Atlantic City. Thought we might drive through Toronto on the way, and if you're not busy maybe we could stop and talk for a little while. How are the roads up that far? Uncle Fred says he might come along for the ride. He says he's heard the scenery is nice up there.

September 10

How do you like your new job? What is a "Head Shop"? We hope you like living in your new commune, but be careful getting mixed up with those political groups. The war goes on and on down here, and we, the people, have no say in stopping it. Your youngest brother says he would like to drive up and see you and talk about something. He's never driven so far before, but we guess it will be O.K. Things are so ugly here. The police seem to be going too far when they beat up people for demonstrating. We will all be glad when we come up again at Thanksgiving. Daddy wants to look around at the housing situation there. Is it true that your president is a communist?

Your loving Mother[19]

Most of the individuals I interviewed received some support for their decision to leave from one or two good friends and their wives or girlfriends. Only one resister from Salt Lake City, Utah, had to face the prospect of a divorce from his wife, who would not come to Canada with him. Our findings here seem to concur with those of psychiatrist Saul Levine who pointed out that those who had lived away from home previously had some moral support from their families and those who thought in more ideological terms had an easier time adjusting to their new environment initially.[20] These factors, particularly the continuing identification with primary support systems, were important for the maintenance of the individual's psychological integration. They helped neutralize the effects of marginal status where the possibilities for broader structural integration within the social and cultural institutions of the new country were initially limited.

The negative effects on the refugee's personal life were almost always complemented in part by some positive reactions to being in Canada. A 21-year-old Navy deserter who spent some of this time AWOL in one of the largest sanctuaries for deserters in Honolulu related: " I had an intense feeling of freedom. You know, finally, God, after almost three years. Finally I'm free. I can do what I want. I don't have to shave if I don't want to, and I don't have to cut my hair. There's a lot of petty bullshit that you have to put up with." Many other men alluded to this feeling of exhilaration at their new sense of personal autonomy and power in Canada.

Career Aspirations

Sociologist Henry David has suggested that migration was one of the most obvious instances of complete disorganization of the individual's role system and, because of this, some disturbance of social identity and self-image was to be expected. Migration can thus be seen to have a desocializing effect.[21] In this light, it was interesting to examine the kind of adjustment these refugees made in their new country and how emigrating affected their self-concept, feeling of control over their lives and their life-styles and career goals.

When I asked 123 men if they felt they had more control over their lives since they had made the decision to leave the country, three-quarters of them stated that they did. Eight individuals felt they had always had control over their lives and had never really relinquished it, except for the brief time they had struggled with their draft boards or were in the military. Sixteen men felt they did not gain any more control over their lives. Two persons were not sure.

"I kept myself in control of my situation by coming to Canada. Control would have passed from me to other hands had I stayed in the States," Steve explained to me. Almost all the men felt they had lost control over their lives by letting the military determine what they would be doing during what they considered to be the most important years of their lives. Dealing with an authoritarian draft board made some individuals realize that they never did have any significant say as to how they lived when they were in the United States. One deserter said: "My life was completely controlled there in the U.S. My parents put me through the university, the government wanted two years, then I was supposed to enter a business career. I had no control. Now I do what I really want to do."

A black deserter who had escaped from the Presidio stockade reviewed the events in his life that led him to Canada: "I looked back and kept seeing the things that I went through were unnecessary. For the first time in my life I had the feeling that I had done the right thing fully, wholly, done the right thing with no qualms or guilt feelings whatsoever. The only guilt that I have is for letting myself get shanghaied into the Army in the first place."

All of these comments lent credence to the newly discovered independence that most refugees found to act out their own dreams and their own impulses. It did not seem to be a matter of actually having more power over social or political institutions in Canada than they had had in the United States. Freedom and control over one's life was experienced subjectively. For many of these men, just being released from an all-encompassing restraint system was enough to make them feel freer. And it became a self-fulfilling prophesy, as Robert Merton has suggested,[22] for if one acted as if one had more control over one's life, one actually did gain more control.

How an individual views himself is a function of how others define him and how he is defined by the larger society. The self is a social self that responds to the judgment of "significant others towards oneself."[23] In the United States the majority of others — the law, teacher, parents and other authorities — did not support these young men. In fact, they defined and labeled them in a negative manner. Once in Canada, the overall disapproving climate was no longer evident and those who were not openly sympathetic were indifferent as to why the refugees had come. They were accepted and treated for the most part as new immigrants. This reaction was reassuring to many men who were initially very defensive and who carried their paranoia with them from the United States.

How did these men feel about and handle the fact of their exile status once they were in Canada? Tom, a resister living in Toronto, summed up his and others' feelings toward his exile status; "I wasn't doing anything for a great cause or anything. I just had to do it. I'm a dodger with a capital 'D' — when the train comes in, I get off the tracks." Initially, when he came to Canada, Tom was reluctant to let any Canadians know why he was there. He explained how he dealt with his situation: "I just avoided using any term at all to let people know who I was. I figured most people would disapprove if they knew, so I just kept quiet about it until I got to know how Canadians felt about things. Now I call myself a "draft dodger" — like saying I'm a Democrat or a Republican; I don't even think about it."

Some American refugees mentioned that they revealed their exile status only to their friends. They viewed it as a very personal decision that one only confided to those one knew well. Others felt proud or even heroic about their exile status since it had changed their lives. They therefore mentioned it to everyone who inquired. This differential response toward their exile status largely depended on how "significant others" in Canada reacted to their exile status and on the specific personal meaning that they attached to it. Those men, for example, whose employers were sympathetic and aided them in getting their jobs because they were resisters from the United States, used their exile status quite positively to define themselves with little hesitation, since it had elicited a positive response.

Upon asking a draft dodger working at the Red, White, and Black office how he liked being called a draft dodger, he replied, "I don't know. It doesn't have quite the prestige as saying you deserted." He went on to explain, "It's just like the circle you fall into. Like you go over to visit the American Deserters' Committee hostel and if you say you are a draft dodger, they don't think that much of you." The example cited above was a common reaction of the draft dodger who had come to Canada in 1969 and 1970. If you mistook a dodger for a deserter, he would usually reply apologetically, "No, I'm only a dodger."

This could be explained partly by the fact that many of the Canadian aid groups distinguished earlier between aid to dodgers and to deserters, as we have already noted. It was also due to the fact that many draft dodgers felt guilty that they had a much easier time obtaining landed immigrant status in Canada and obtaining a job, just as in the United States many of them felt guilty when they received student deferrals. Perhaps it also stemmed from a desire to turn the American system of values on its head. Since deserters were labeled more negatively than dodgers in the United States and were more often considered traitors, there was a strong desire on the part of many refugees to neutralize this among themselves and among the Canadians they met. "The higher the risk, the higher the punishment a man would have if he returned to the States, so the more prestige he should have," explained one American refugee.

A number of American refugees, for expediency, attempted to maintain a dual identity. After being a full-time counselor for the Toronto Anti-Draft Program, John decided to return to the University of Toronto. He applied for a scholarship and was fearful that his part-time work with TADP would jeopardize his scholarship opportunity, so he began using an assumed last name. All his new friends called him by his new name and he appeared to be quite comfortable with it.

Over half of the American refugees in my sample stated that their self-images had changed in a positive direction since they made the decision to leave their country. Only one-third stated that they did not experience any change in their self-concept. Another 15 percent of the men were not sure of this type of change or did not answer. To illustrate the direction they felt major changes had occurred, let us consider their own comments.

A draft resister from Salt Lake City who had experienced a separation from his wife over his decision to come to Canada talked in very positive tones about his present life in Canada after two years. "I see myself as better able to calmly and peacefully plan, live and enjoy my life. I also feel a greater sense of personal autonomy and feel I am better able to carry out my life positively."

A deserter who had first felt paranoid and was extremely alienated when he arrived in Canada confided to me eight months later that "I'm more to-gether now than I ever was in the States. I feel I have roots that extend 40 feet deep." He had never had a stable home life and his parents were sepa-rated early. He had grown up in foster homes and enlisted in the Army at the age of 18.

Another deserter who had wandered around in the United States unem-ployed, looking for a job, finally enlisted in the Army under the pressure of the draft. He commented, "I've stopped running from life and now have found the life I want to lead." He was living in a communal arrangement with other friends in Vancouver.

Whether or not these men still had the same kind of goals and career choices that they wanted for themselves in the United States was another im-portant measure of what kind of changes had resulted from their decision to leave the United States. If we look at my sample, we find a pattern that is similar to those responses regarding feelings of control and self-concept. The same men that experienced changes in the above categories almost always ex-perienced changes in their lives and career goals. More than half of the refu-gees said that they had altered their lives or career goals or both and only one-third of them indicated that they experienced no change in either one. Ap-proximately three-quarters of those who indicated that changes took place felt these had been positive changes corresponding with changes in their newly experienced freedom. Approximately 10 percent of these men stated they no longer felt that career goals were relevant to their personal goals and that they were reevaluating their personal goals from scratch. A deserter from Seattle said, "I have no ambitions left as far as a career. I just want a quiet life with few material things, no steady job and just enough money to travel on." A draft resister from Virginia who lived in a commune in Vancouver stated that he had ripped up his career plan. "Que sera, sera." Others felt that their career and personal goals "can now be attained rather than biding my time waiting to be inducted." The draft had prevented them from pursuring their career goals and they intended to follow these in Canada. This group usually consisted of students who were drafted, who fled to Canada and who enrolled in Canadian graduate or professional schools.

Many viewed their life choice as a moral decision similar to the one that brought them to Canada in the first place. Along these lines, a newcomer who had been in Canada only a few days said, "I feel I have to make a choice between a life I believe in and one I don't. Whether this means getting back to nature, I'm not sure. But I think it does." Often this meant that they felt more justified in acting upon their nonconformist views. A draft resister from St. Louis, Missouri, who was an English instructor in Vancouver and had lived there for several years stated, "I no longer attempt to make my personal life goals compatible with general social mores and goals in the community although I am concerned with community mores."

Successful adaptation to migration was often, at least in part, dependent upon the migrant's ability to assume a role and social identity that was meaningful in terms of the new society. When we consider that it was primarily the institutional structure of the United States that caused these men to leave it, it should not be surprising that so many of them attempted to create a role identity for themselves that was more directly related to the people and the community of their new country rather than with its formal institutions. This identification with the problems of the people of their new country involved a process of interpersonal adjustment and attachment which to some extent neutralized the effects of the break they had suffered with primary support systems in the United States. Those who carried this identification into their career aspirations made a further attempt to ameliorate the marginality of their status and the ambivalence of their social situation.

Almost all the refugees who altered their career goals opted for careers in more creative or more person-oriented activities. For example, Kent, an earlier resister who was a vocational counselor aiding the Vancouver Committee and working as a rehabilitation counselor with the handicapped, also devoted time to composing and planned to enter the entertainment and creative arts field once he completed his M.A. at the University of British Columbia. Another individual who was attending graduated school in sociology and was planning on becoming a professional sociologist was now concerned with "less formal, more immediate and personal contact and aid with other people." He was doing social work and was moving into probation work. Joe explained, "Imagine me, a felon from the law, a probation officer; that's a good one." Other individuals who were in the physical sciences changed fields and went into teaching and social work. A very typical response of another draft resister was "I'm concerned more with people problems instead of material problems." Those who had become radicalized by their experiences focused their interests on other "victims of the imperialist system." Comparing his past and present interests, an aid group counselor said, "I used to be very interested in typical middle-class things — more material goods, a career with good job security. Now I'm interested in freeing the oppressed peoples of the world."

Over half of these Americans characterized themselves as "easygoing" rather than "uptight." A majority of them in my sample indicated that they had "hip" or communal life-styles in Canada. Forty-three percent indicated that they had a "straight" middle-class life-style. Some of those who had a "hip" life-style in the United States had merely transplanted it to the hip communities in Canada. Many more of them identified themselves with such communities in Canada for the first time in their lives.

You could often tell how long an American refugee had been in Canada by the length of his hair. Dana, a deserter from the army, reminisced about when he first came to Montreal a year before, and said, "Man, that would make a good movie, *Deserters in Canada*. It would start off showing us when we first deserted to Canada. We all had crew cuts and were frightened, didn't know a soul... just came up cold..." Jimmy, a Toronto resister from New York, confided, "When I got landed at the border, I looked pretty straight. I cut my hair for them and dressed up in my shirt and tie." He showed me a picture of himself at that time and laughed. One year later when I met him at his "head shop" in Toronto he had shoulder-length wavy hair that was held back from his eyes with a headband. "Once you get free and get outside their games, then you can do it any way you want," he explained.

The majority of American refugees, then, altered their social and political views, career goals and life-styles in the direction of less "uptight" and nonconforming modes. They felt that they had gained more control over their lives and had become more self-assertive and fulfilled as human beings. Many came from conservative backgrounds and had rejected their former social and political values in favor of more free-thinking and free-floating life-styles and choices. Yet, a sizable minority of refugees transplanted their previous middle-class life-style to Canada and continued pursuing their former career and life goals.

Emergent Social Types

Several social types, based upon differences in their life-styles, social roles and personal identities, can be found upon examination of the refugees:

1. *Unaltered American.* Those Americans who maintained the same life-style and social and personal identity as before they came to Canada can be viewed as the "unaltered Americans." These represented approximately 37 percent of the refugee population. This includes those who had always felt they had little control over their lives before they joined the military or were drafted. After they came to Canada they continued to feel a loss of control over their lives and did not experience any major changes as a result of their decision. This group also includes those men who had felt they had always exercised some control over their lives. They were confronted by the military or the draft, which temporarily threatened their freedom of choice to guide their own lives, and came to Canada to maintain and assert this choice. The mode of adjustment selected by these men would seem to affirm Henry David's premise that the integrative capacity of an individual was under particular strain when an immigrant started life in a new country away from familiar surroundings which had previously provided some protection or nurture. These individuals faced with situational ambivalence or conflict tended to retain or readopt former patterns of behavior.[24]

2. *Changed American.* The majority of Americans (60 percent of my sample) experienced a profound change in their life-style and social and personal identity as a result of their decision to evade the draft or desert from the military. This type of change usually involved a new personal sense of political involvement and responsibility for one's own actions, together with a greater sense of individual control and competence. Different social roles emerge from the nature of the type of change these men experienced.

a. *Political convert.* This person made a sharp break with his past life, often spontaneously and similar to that of a religious convert. He was an American patriot who became disillusioned with America and became an ardent anti-Yankee. In Canada he shifted his position to that of a Canadian nationalist.

b. *Evolutionist.* This individual gradually developed his new beliefs and values from crucial episodes and ideas that brought him to a greater under-standing of the Vietnam War, American policy and his role vis-à-vis the draft or military. Leaving his country and coming to Canada often repre-sented a culmination of those beliefs.

c. *Radical activist.* This person had not been actively involved in any po-litical or social group in the United States, though he may have generally supported the   goals of the peace movement. As a result of his personal stand against the draft or the military he became politicized and actively involved in Canadian aid and exile groups.

d. *Uncommitted or culturally alienated.*[25]   This refugee usually made a sharp break with his homeland, although not with his personal beliefs and principles. However, these beliefs became strengthened with his ability to act positively upon them. Some expressed their disaffiliation with the United States by coming to Canada, renouncing their American citizen-ship and asserting their right to control their own lives.

What accounted for the major changes that many of these Americans went through in coming to Canada? The explanation did not seem to be directly re-lated to the nature of Canadian society itself, since the youth-channeling system had taken on continental proportions, operating through the Canadian immigration policy and branch plant institutions. Therefore, the changes in life-style and goals of these Americans could best be explained by an exam-ination of the process itself of becoming a refugee.

Being labeled a criminal separated these American exiles from the rest of society into a new class of nonconforming "troublemakers." Forced into exile, they were temporarily disoriented, cut off from their primary ties of family and friends and thrust into an alien environment. This uprootedness created some feelings of identity crisis and marginality in relation to their old homeland as well as their new. According to David the danger to an in-dividual's psychological well-being increased when the period between immi-grant and definitive resettlement was protracted and diffused with uncertain-ty.[26] Thus the refugees, for the sake of their own well-being, selected a radi-cal course of adjustment. Having no reference group to reinforce their own values and behavior, they were more receptive to new ideas and ways of be-having. They were consciously searching for new friends. On their route to Canada, they met many other Americans who, like themselves, were experi-encing the same dilemmas and newfound freedoms. Many quite naturally banded together to liberate themselves and seek more fulfilling life-styles.

Those who brought their wives or girlfriends with them had a distinct advantage in adjusting to their new country. Many of these women played an instrumental role in the men's decision to come to Canada in the first place. While their men were in the service they had explored alternative courses of action and visited GI counseling and resistance centers that aided AWOL soldiers to obtain information about Canada. Once these couples arrived safely in Canada, the women continued to be important sources of encouragement and support. This was particularly crucial to those men who were shunned by their families and friends. It was a little easier to bear the feelings of loneliness and hard times when you had a partner with whom to share your burdens. In my sample, I found that at least one-third of the men were in large measure supported financially by their wives or girlfriends. The work of these women enabled many of their husbands to continue their higher education in Canada. In the first few months in Canada, it was frequently easier for women to find jobs than for men. Women also made major contributions in the refugee aid groups. In almost all the aid groups, women were counselors and aided newcomers in obtaining housing and jobs.

In the process of becoming a landed immigrant the wives of refugees were completely ignored. According to the Canadian immigration laws, married women, like children, were considered as dependents and were landed on the basis of their husbands' applications. Their education and vocational skills were therefore not considered. This example of discrimination against females was a disadvantage to the man who did not have adequate points to obtain landed immigrant status when his wife did. A wife could not sponsor her husband; only a husband could sponsor his wife. Only those women who were not married could obtain landed immigrant status on their own application. Many of the women refugees lobbied for legislation that would change this archaic law.

Many more draft resisters were married or had the support and help of their girlfriends in Canada than did deserters. Those deserters who despaired and eventually returned to the United States usually did not have a companion. A number of them were motivated to return to see their girlfriends in the States; sometimes these turned them in to the military police. Those men who had the economic and emotional support of women were most likely to make a good adjustment to their lives in Canada.

Earning a Living

Over half of the American refugees supported themselves by holding jobs in Canada. The other men depended for their livelihood almost totally on their wives or girlfriends and the hostels run by the aid groups. They were involved in all kinds of work. Since the majority of draft dodgers were college educated, they had skilled work. Most of the deserters predominated in the unskilled jobs (see Table 18, Appendix B for a breakdown of their occupations in Canada). Approximately 22 draft dodgers and 11 deserters in my survey became students in Canada and obtained student loans and fellowships. Most of the professional workers were teachers and social workers. This category also included graduate students working on advanced degrees in the universities. Movement work referred to those individuals who spent more than half of their time working for the aid and exile groups. Most of those individuals in artistic or creative work were self-employed with their own small businesses, in "head shops" catering to the psychedelic consumers, making leather crafts or doing bead work.

Only 35 men stated that they were doing the same work in Canada as they had been doing in the United States. Almost half of these men were involved in different types of work. Ten men reported that their new jobs in Canada had higher status than their previous jobs, usually because this was their first job after college graduation. Fifteen persons reported that their jobs were of lower status than their previous jobs in the United States. But the majority felt that the status rewards were so different and based on such different values that they could not compare them with their previous jobs.

Most reported that they had difficulty finding a job initially. Their jobs were obtained through personal contacts or friends, especially fellow refugees. Twenty-eight persons found jobs in this manner and 14 found jobs through Canadian Manpower, student placement offices or jobs advertised in the newspapers. Six men found jobs through their contact with a Canadian aid group and 23 men obtained employment by going out and looking for it themselves. Often the refugees were either overeducated or underskilled for a particular job. Ten persons cited "negative feelings against Yankees" as the reason they did not get jobs. Almost one-third of these refugees indicated that their exile status did make a difference in obtaining employment, either in a positive or negative direction. This was especially true in their experiences seeking jobs in companies that were American subsidiaries. For example, a number of men who sought publishing jobs were told that they would have to attend job training programs as well as major conferences in the United States. Thus, these jobs were off limits for the refugees.

Many of the American refugees who were students easily transferred their credits to Canadian colleges. Steve, a draft resister who was just beginning graduate school in Boston in mechanical engineering before he was drafted, explained how he got settled and found a teaching job in Montreal:

> I was thinking about what I was going to do, since I came up with about fifty dollars in my pocket. Well, the French University had to be ruled out, because I can't speak French, and Sir George Williams University did not have a graduate program at the time. So, McGill was left, an established and well-known school.
>
> The first weekday after I arrived, I walked over to McGill to the Mechanical Engineering Department and went to the chairman's office. I knocked on his door and sort of announced that I was there. Here I am, a fugitive from American justice. And I was really quite proud. Of course I was 100 percent novelty; nobody had ever seen a real live draft dodger before [1966]. I presented my credentials to the chairman and he had me speak with various people. And within two days, I was a graduate student and bonafide teaching assistant at McGill. It was pretty much the same kind of position I had. . . .I fell right into things here.

Many refugees who could not find work immediately in Canada usually fell back on their student status.

Many jobs were obtained through a sympathetic grapevine, where one resister would tell another about job possibilities. For example, there were six draft resisters who were employed, mostly as guides, at the new Vancouver Planetarium. This was due primarily to a sympathetic employer who was doing the hiring and let a couple of draft dodgers know about the openings. They quickly told their friends.

Another haven for American refugees in British Columbia was the library of the University of British Columbia. MacElrod, the head of the Cataloguing Division, was a Unitarian and an American expatriate himself who moved from Ohio to Canada in July 1967. He worked tirelessly from the outset with the Vancouver aid groups and helped hundreds of young men with housing and jobs. Bob was one of the resisters in the University of British Columbia library. He had come from San Francisco and had worked in the post office there when the hippies took over most of the jobs in 1967. Then, after hassling with his draft board, he came to Montreal. A year later, he came to Vancouver with his Japaneses wife and their young child. He viewed his work in the library as temporary. They were saving money to go to the countryside with two other couples to begin a commune. "I don't want to be in an urban environment in 1980," says Bob, "it won't be healthy." He felt that his chances for survival against pollution and disease were greater in the countryside. He would also have plenty of room for his brother and brother-in-law there, both of whom had just turned 19 and would be coming to Canada shortly.

The majority of men I interviewed and observed had made a successful adjustment in Canada and had managed to find enough employment to keep them alive. In many cases they found more fulfilling and satisfying types of work and life-styles than they had had in the United States. Their ability to become part of the Canadian work force and hence to achieve a certain degree of structural or institutional integration was a prerequisite for becoming culturally integrated. However, the cultural integration of many Americans did not necessarily occur.

Nationalism and Assimilation into Canadian Life

How these American refugees felt about their identity and nationalism and how the two concepts were linked together in their minds would have important consequences for the process of assimilation into Canadian life.

The subject of an individual's national loyalties inevitably came up in a discussion with American exiles. "I don't think I could ever erase being an American. Even if I become a Canadian citizen, I don't think I could. I would still be partially a product of my American experience," said Mark, a deserter who grew up in a patriotic southern California home. Tom, another resister, said, "I'll always be an American. I can't help it. Though I'll become a Canadian legally after my five years are up, I'll still be an American from having grown up and developed and being there for the first 20 years of my life." Tom became very active in exile politics after coming to Canada with the Union of American Exiles in Toronto. The majority of American refugees came from families that were patriotic toward their country and were believers in the patriotic symbols and values that comprise American nationalism. Their parents felt that America was the greatest country in the world and had a lot to offer them. Although many of these men disagreed with their parents' values, many of the men still retained their sense of patriotism and felt America could be a great society if it lived up to its own democratic values. It was very difficult for most of these men to be as indifferent toward America as many Canadians were toward Canada; most Americans have been imbued with patriotic values in the home, school and the church. These nationalistic feelings strongly manifested themselves as part of the "American way of life." American refugees from the Deep South, more so than the others, expressed a particularly strong sense of commitment and duty to their people and their homeland.

Ironically, both the black and the white refugees felt that their identities were molded there and felt an obligation to return to the United States. These men were profoundly influenced by the relationship and social forces that had shaped them in their home communities and felt that as a result of their growing consciousness they had a special responsibility to return and work to enlighten people there. In most outward ways, these Southern refugees had adjusted and attempted to make new lives for themselves in Canada. They obtained landed immigrant status, jobs, and made new friends. Despite this, however, thay still felt a strong pull from south of the border. John, a black draft dodger from Mississippi who had come to Montreal in 1969, traveled to Vancouver after a year and married a Canadian girl. When asked whether he would return to the States in the event of amnesty, he replied, "Certainly! My roots are definitely American because my family is there and that's where my heart is. The ties I feel are family ties more than anything else." According to John, "If there is going to be any erosion of the Southern way of life, it's going to come from people like me." Bill, a white draft dodger also from Mississippi and now living in Toronto, expressed a similar attachment to his Southern roots. "My identity, good and bad, is really tied up in Mississippi, and it feels funny to leave. There your identity is kind of imposed upon you." Bill was active in the civil rights movement and had dropped out of college to work on an underground newspaper. He felt that he could do social work better in Mississippi than anywhere else because he knew how to relate to the people there.

For those refugees who had strong nationalistic feelings, there were generally two outlets in Canada: they could either participate in American exile politics or become involved in the Canadian nationalist movement. Involvement in exile politics usually occurred for most refugees as part of what psychiatrist Saul Levine referred to as the first stage of coping. They relied upon other American exiles for support and found it necessary to collectively articulate their beliefs during this initial period of loneliness and uncertainly. Although they had already come to grips with their "break" from the United States and had formed meaningful relationships, they felt they had a political responsibility to continue to express their anti-Vietnam War and antiimperialistic beliefs collectively as exiles. Some of these individuals had become part of the larger Canadian community through their work and leisure pursuits. However, many could not foresee becoming completely assimilated into the Canadian mosaic and saw themselves as Americans in exile although they had no intention of ever returning to the United States.

American refugees also expressed nationalistic sentiments through activity with the Canadian nationalist movement, such as working with the Committee for an Independent Canada. The majority of Americans who chose this were usually older and were landed immigrants for a number of years or had become Canadian citizens. They were approaching what psychiatrist Levine labeled "adaptation and integration." They were "engaged wholly in being a Canadian," and felt more comfortable with this kind of activity. However, their participation usually involved some ambivalence and uncomfortable feelings at times since a major component of Canadian nationalism was anti-Americanism.

It is important to note, however, that there were significant differences between Canadian and American nationalism, as pointed out by Ron Lambert, a sociologist at the University of Waterloo:

> Exiles should try to understand the peculiar thrust of the nationalist movement in Canada. It should be acknowledged that, whatever nationalism in the U.S. may mean, it does not mean the same thing in Canada. Structurally, the context of nationalism in the two countries is quite different. Canada, for instance, has no worldwide empire to sustain. It is crucial that we adjust our understanding of political phenomena, such as nationalism, to take adequate account of the Canadian experience. It makes little sense to berate Canadians for their complicity in the Indochinese war if, at the same time, we undercut the only vehicle (nationalism) which can sustain an independent Canada capable of confronting American power.[27]

As a result of becoming refugees, however, most of these Americans felt that they no longer looked toward a national entity or nationalistic activities, but instead looked more toward a larger world view. This in fact was close to the *weltanschauung* of a typical Canadian. Anthony Richmond coined the term "translient," meaning to leap across, to pass from one place to another in order to describe this type of immigrant's relationship to his host society.[28] This man could be viewed as part of an internationally mobile labor force characterized by a cosmopolitan outlook, a good education and career mobility. This in turn meant a lack of permanence in any one country or locality.

After many American refugees in Canada became settled, they yearned to travel around the country as well as outside of Canada, a feeling they had not experienced before. One deserter explained his urge to travel in terms of the fact that life was more internationally oriented in Canada than in America. According to Mark:

It's not so ethnocentric here. I am just much more outward looking toward the whole world than before, whereas when I was in the States, I was pretty well satisfied traveling and spending my time there. I wasn't desiring to develop my experience internationally as much as I am now. Given the position of Canada in the community of nations, not being the self-proclaimed leader of the free world, she is able to develop more of a genuine international feeling just being one of the nations, not on top of the world, or the nation.

Mark felt that this reaction was probably a product of his leaving home and coming to Canada. "Once these very strong hometown ties are broken by draft dodging or desertion, most people are going to be freer. The cord is broken and they can explore," Mark commented. This explained why often obtaining a Canadian passport or being able to "clear one's record" and obtain an American one was a high priority, higher even than returning to live in the United States.

Pete, a draft dodger who has lived in Vancouver for a couple of years, felt that whether or not American resisters and deserters assimiliated into Canadian life depended very much upon "how satisfied they are with their life-styles and with their particular decision to come to Canada." He noted:

> You have to assimilate to a degree, unless you ignore the Canadian, his feelings, and his culture. Some people I know have become largely Canadian and don't ever want to go back to the U.S. You can go through the rainbow. Others are dying to go back right now, crying for amnesty. As for me, I feel ambivalent. It can be painful some days, with the constant bombardment with the reality in the States. And you're still a part of it, to a degree, being an American citizen. But today, it's a beautiful day, and it's nice to be here talking with you. If there were an amnesty, I don't know if I would live in the U.S. again. But I certainly would like to have the ability to go there if I wanted to. I'm not pining away the way that some people are, but I miss my family and friends and places.

Many of these Americans have experienced the ambivalent feelings Pete expressed. Yet, the majority of Americans have begun new lives in Canada. At a critical moment in their lives when family and friends often turned their backs, they were forced to rely on their own resources. Many of them became profoundly disillusioned with the "American way of life" and were hopeful that they might fulfill their vision of the American dream on the frontiers of their new land. In some cases, their lives were changed in a positive direction as a result of their decision to leave the United States. Some gained more control over the ways in which they wanted to live. This newfound optimism gave them a sense of themselves as frontiersmen forging new paths. At the very least, the majority of refugees managed to find enough employment to keep them alive and made a relatively successful adjustment to their new country. In the next several chapters, we will explore the lives of those Americans who have changed in more creative directions, as well as the smaller minority of men who were not able to begin their lives anew in Canada.

NOTES

1.　Saul Levine, "Draft Dodgers: Coping with Stress, Adapting to Exile," *American Journal of Orthopsychiatry* 42 (April 3, 1972): 6—8.
2.　Robert Park, *Race and Culture* (Glencoe: Free Press, 1950), p. 374.
3.　Theodore Roszak, *The Making of a Counter-Culture* (New York: Doubleday and Co., 1969).
4.　Eric Hoffer, *The Ordeal of Change* (New York: Harper and Row, 1963), chapter 16.
5.　Lee Lockwood, *Conversation with Eldridge Cleaver: Algiers* (New York: Dell Publishing, 1970), pp. 59-63.
6.　*Yankee Refugee*, Vancouver, British Columbia, American Deserters' Committee.
7.　See Kenneth Keniston, *The Uncommitted* (New York: Dell Publishing Co., 1960), and *Young Radicals* (New York: Harcourt, Brace and World, 1968); Erik H. Erikson, "Identity and the Life Cycle," *Psychological Issues* 1, no. 1 (1969), and *Identity: Youth and Crisis* (New York: W.W. Norton and Co., 1968).
8.　"Emigrants to Canada," in *We Won't Go*, ed. Alice Lynd (Boston: Beacon Press, 1968)
9.　*AMEX*, August—September 1970.
10.　Alice Lynd, *We Won't Go*.
11.　Ibid.
12.　*Manual for Draft-Age Immigrants to Canada*, 4th ed. (Toronto: House of Anansi, 1970).
13.　*Saturday Night*, November 1968.
14.　Rivka Weiss Bar-Yosef, "Desocialization and Resocialization: The Adjustment Process of Immigrants," *International Migration Review* 2 (Spring 1968): 29.
15.　*Yankee Refugee*, pamphlet, Vancouver, British Columbia, American Deserters' Committee, 1969.
16.　*The Rebel* 1 (March—April 1968).
17.　*Yankee Refugee*, Vancouver, British Columbia, 1969.

18.   This point is also emphasized in a study conducted by Katherine Rider and Dr. Carl Kline, who interviewed 30 American resisters, landed immigrants, in Vancouver, B.C. "The Young American Expatriates in Canada: Alienated or Self-Defined?", paper delivered at the American Orthopsychiatric Association convention, San Francisco, Spring 1970.

19.   *AMEX* 2(April—May 1970).

20.   Saul Levine, "Draft Dodgers," p. 4.

21.   Henry P. David, "Involuntary International Migration: Adaptation of Refugees," in *Behavior in New Environments,* ed. Eugene B. Brody (Beverly Hills, Calif.: Sage Publications, 1969), p. 250.

22.   Robert K. Merton, *Social Theory and Social Structure* (Glencoe, III.: The Free Press, 1968), pp. 182—83 and 475—90.

23.   George Herbert Mead, "The Social Self" (Bobbs-Merrill Reprint S-187). For the ideas of Mead, see Anselm Strauss, ed., *The Social Psychology of George Herbert Mead* (Chicago: University of Chicago Press, 1956).

24.   Henry P. David, "Involuntary International Migration," p. 239.

25.   Kenneth Keniston, *The Uncommitted* (New York: Dell Publishing, 1960).

26.   Henry P. David, "Involuntary International Migration."

27.   *AMEX* 2 (August—September 1970): 21.

28.   Anthony H. Richmond, "Immigration and Pluralism in Canada," *International Migration Review* 4, no. 1 (1961): 5—24.

7

The Subcultures of Unassimilated Refugees

American refugees constituted one of the fastest-growing, youthful minority groups in Canada in the early 1970s. The majority of refugees had a relatively easy time becoming new Canadians and adapting their lives to their new country. However, a sizable number of them had difficulties similar to that of other minority groups that had experienced discrimination.

Two distinctive groups of American refugees did not assimilate well into the Canadian setting: the "cultural innovators" and the "underground exiles." The former were, for the most part, some of the middle-class youth that rebelled against the larger North American culture and became part of the counterculture. Many of them became social innovators, forging new lifestyles as well as new counterinstitutions to serve the young people who had dropped out of the established institutional framework. They had become landed immigrants with the right to work and, if they so chose, they could become citizens after five years. This group included representatives from each of the emergent social types in the "changed American" group described in the last chapter.

In contrast, the "underground exiles" were in a disadvantageous position. Most of them were unskilled deserters who were not able to get their feet in the door and who were unable to obtain landed status. By necessity, they were transient and made use of deserters hostels provided by the Canadian aid groups. A number of these men had been in trouble with the law for petty offenses and still felt hunted by both American and Canadian officials. In this group we found representatives of the "unaltered American" social type. We will discuss both of these American refugees, the "cultural innovators" and the "underground exiles," as parts of the subculture of unassimilated Americans.

Cultural Innovators.

In the major Canadian cities — Vancouver, Toronto and Montreal — large youth subcultures were located in certain areas of the city where youths congregated and spent a large portion of their leisure time. Some American refugees formed their own groups within these youth subcultures. In part, they were acting out their aspirations and ideals on a new stage that they felt had been denied them by a repressive America.

Toronto, the second largest Canadian city, quite naturally attracted the largest number of American refugees. It is located in Ontario, one of the wealthiest provinces in Canada accounting for 40 percent of the gross national product. It has the most highly developed industrial and manufacturing sector in Canada. White-collar and service industry employment have been expanding at a faster rate than the blue-collar sector for a long time. Half the provincial budget goes to education, including the network of 14 public universities and smaller community colleges, the most comprehensive system of higher education in Canada.[1] Many American refugees became part of the student culture that formed an important part of the youth and political culture in Toronto. Many students from the University of Toronto were the founders of SUPA, the left-wing community organizing group to originally support and house the first Toronto aid group for American refugees.

In Toronto most of the American communes were in the "lower village" between Spadina and University avenues and College and Huron streets. Within this area were located most of the organizations and groups serving the American refugee community as well as the office of the United States consul general. It contained the University of Toronto campus as well as Rochdale College, the largest free university experiment in North America until it was forced to close its doors in 1972. In this area could also be found the underground presses including *Harbinger, Guerrilla,* and *AMEX* (the *American Expatriate in Canada*). "Head shops" owned by communal families and natural food stores were located in the area. It was rumored that on some blocks apartments and basements were filled only with American refugees.

Jimmy, the social worker who once lived in New York, had been living in Toronto with the rest of his "tribe" since 1968. He and his wife, Anna, came to Canada on his induction day in their yellow Ford truck. Soon the Yellow Ford Truck was a well-known "head shop" selling hip clothes, water pipes and other oddities. It supported a family of seven persons living communally and was intertwined with other shops through tribal friendship networks.

Jimmy started out by living in his truck and doing moving jobs with it in order to raise enough money to open a small shop.

The idea began with three of us initially. One of them dropped out as I took more and more control over the store, which I think is the one drawback. People became alienated more and more, so I finally realized this, and when we had a chance to expand, I said, "OK." I laid a month's rent on that store and another month's rent on this one and they started their own thing. One of them went in with us originally and now they are running their own leather store. We've seven people now, solid. And everyone's living communally. Mine supports three people full time. And we all work on subsistence income. Like rent, food and cigarettes. That's all we get and the rest stays in the store. It's a communal fund that's going to be applied to a communal farm eventually.

Jimmy conceived of the commune on many different levels. He set up a procedure for incorporating people who work in the store as a commune. He explained the importance of his tribal interrelationships as part of his larger family:

There's the commune which is the whole tribal totality. And that could number up to 250 or 300 people. It's kind of a seminationalist type of development. Most of the people are leaning towards communal economy, communal social ethics and everything else. At this point we are two stores in Toronto and a warehouse where a rock group practices, and seven communal houses in the city. Also, we have another store in Stratford, a couple of farms in Stratford and another one further north. And we are expanding as we establish a kind of network.

Each of the seven communal houses in Toronto had its own rules and conceived itself as part of a growing tribe or community. Jimmy explained in more detail how the communal houses were run:

> Whoever wants to set up a commune leases the house and everyone who lives there splits the rent. Each person will take a different responsibility. For example, one person will be in charge of collecting rent, another person will be in charge of collecting electricity, someone else the gas, other people the phone bill. And then everything is distributed so that no one person really controls it. And as for initiation of anybody new into a commune, there has to be unanimous support. And to remove someone, there's nothing hard and fast, but generally you need about two-thirds majority to have someone removed. Usually if people can't stand or dig a particular commune, sometimes they move out into private living arrangements. However, a lot of them will just start another commune with another group of people. One commune usually can't take more than seven people anyway. So we just got our seventh house. They're going to turn that into a restaurant or café.

The houses and stores were linked together as a tribal whole through a common identity and group activities.

The communal dwellers described their tribe as a political and cultural revolution. They used the term political in its broadest sense, describing everything they did as political, in much the same way as the Yippies. They were against segmenting things into narrow compartments like university reform or workers' rights because, according to Jimmy, "you ignore all the other parts of life which are also political." Jimmy and friends viewed themselves as social revolutionaries.

When I asked Jimmy what his goals would be five years hence, he responded:

> My idea would be the education of a lot of people to the fact that they can't depend on the established structure for anything. And if they don't do that, then they'll run into the hassles of the 9 to 5 world. The commune itself is something which says, "O.K., if you don't want to make it the established way, then here's an alternative." And at the same time, we're developing a critique of the established structure we're leaving, so that we don't come out with something like this bullshit "flower power."
>
> Ideally we're working for a totally integrated society that can almost support itself based on communal lives. We will educate ourselves with our own people, learn from each other and build our own counterinstitutions as we need them. One model of educating our kids is right around here, called the Super School. It's completely run by the kids themselves. They

pay their teachers and live together in a communal situation. Aberdale Place is another example of a good school. We can always find teachers. We find a mechanic when we need one. We find a plumber when we need one. On a tribal level, we're trying to incorporate as many skills as possible. All of these skills will be especially useful for our farm.

Before Jimmy came to Toronto he claimed he was more introverted and although he was attracted to the idea of living communally it was not possible because of his fears and paranoia regarding the draft and the uptight atmosphere in New York. He lived in the East Village where he claimed there was "nothing but speed freaks," and the communal scene was under constant harassment from the law. According to Jimmy, "I just decided I was going to have to live somewhere, so it might as well be Toronto. So I came here and got landed. Since then I've started coming out." He elaborated further:

I've gone through a lot of strange changes in my own head, gone to a lot of places since then. I think that's like an important thing because like what that says is one of the truths of today's existence is change. And that exists on every level, in every sphere. It exists even geographically. Like the original commune. . . .By the time 11 Baldwin Street opens, there will not be an original member there. Everybody else has either gone to other communes or has gotten out of the communal thing and gotten into something else. And it has grown from the idea of one store to seven stores and communal houses.

Due to the changes Jimmy has gone through, he seemed more tolerant of people who were not as committed to communal living. He recognized the possibility that some people in the tribe might choose a different life-style for themselves:

Even with the tribal unit, there's probably a good-sized minority that isn't completely communal. But that's their right. If I get tired of communal living, I feel no ethical or religious responsibility to stick to it. If it works you do it. That's the only way to work it; you're not going to force anyone else to do it. There's no restrictions. So it's part utopian and part revolutionary in the sense that, at this point it's just building the structure 'til it gets to the point of strength . . .and at the same time offering people an alternative without actively destroying that system, except for the fact that you are siphoning off their best minds — and their best workers. And then, on the other hand, when it comes to guns, we'll be together.

The strength of the community as a whole, according to theses communitarians, is in the struggle of the people toward a viable community and in their working through their hassles within the group structure.

The first commune in this tribe consisted completely of American refugees. But after one and a half years of living in Toronto, the Yellow Ford Truck's commune had come to be about two-thirds American and one-third Canadian. Jimmy surmised that the ratio of Americans to Canadians would approach half and half as the Americans became "more and more into living here." John, a photographer of the Baldwin St. gallery and a member of the larger tribe, took a series of photographs recording how he, as an American refugee who came to Toronto in 1967, viewed Canadians as well as his own group. Under a photo of the Union of American Exiles his caption read, "This was in Queens Park, Toronto, before a march on the American Consulate over Vietnam, not long after we arrived. When we first came here we naturally felt like strangers and we felt closer to this group than to any other. Now, of course, we know a lot of Canadians."

Peter, who was introduced in chapter 5, when he dropped out of the Peace Corps was drafted and had split to Toronto, also considered himself to be part of the larger tribe that Jimmy described, although he was living in a different commune than those connected with the Yellow Ford Truck. He had been counseling for the Toronto Anti-Draft Program part time for over a year. Although Peter felt, "it's drudgery work," he also felt that somebody had to do it and he knew how. Unlike Jimmy, he did not have any initial ideas as to what he wanted to do when he first got to Toronto. According to Peter, "I fell into immigration counseling and the communal idea." Peter became a convert to the community ideal: "Now I'm more turned on to the community as a thing to do, politically, in terms of its organizing possibilities. It gets kids' heads together — it's really good. I'm excited by the things that happen in communes."

Peter considered his communal house to be more closed than that of some of his friends. All the occupants were Americans who together were saving enough money to buy a farm, but they were not all draft resisters. Peter described them as "just scientists who work at the University of Toronto and are completely fed up with the system. They're past the point of taking traditional political action. So they are going to just disappear out on the farm — and I may go with them."

Peter's feelings about disappearing out on a farm were more ambivalent than those of his friends. He came from a New York State farming family that was very political. He especially admired his father who was an active organizer in the cooperative movement. Because of his father's interest in politics, Peter had always closely followed political movements. He explained why he felt that going along with friends to a communal farm would probably be a "cop-out" for him:

I like the idea of a farm. But for them to leave, it's not a cop-out. But for me it probably would be. I'm more political, maybe. I just know that the thing for me to do if I have the social consciousness that I pretend to have .... Well, it's pretty hypocritical for me to disappear out to a farm somewhere. You know, I don't believe in struggling too hard, but I don't believe in stopping struggle either. In town all the excess energy that I have goes into the things that are socially relevant, that have to do with other people and the way people live. On a farm, all your energy goes into chopping firewood and planting a garden.

Two Mormon deserters, Bryan and Larry, had serious plans to join a rural commune in British Columbia. Upon first coming to Canada, they visited northern British Columbia, explored the area and selected their site. They were both working temporarily as printer apprentices until Larry was able to get landed (Bryan already was) and get enough money together to begin a commune and send for their friends. They were both interested in the occult at that time. Bryan claimed that "a lot of thinking people concur that there's going to be a lot of things happening in the next few years and that British Columbia is going to be a safe place to be, geologically." He substantiated this statement by indicating that the Tibetan Llama had been instructing his people to settle in British Columbia or Switzerland to avoid the oncoming world holocaust.

Louis, a draft resister from New York, was beginning a commune on Vancouver Island with two other draft resister couples that he and his wife had known since they arrived in Vancouver. For the past two years he had been teaching high school in Vancouver while his wife attended Simon Fraser University. Louis looked upon his family's move to the land as a "pioneering and utopian venture for all of us." He explained:

Our generation is at the age where we can start utopian colonies. You know, you have to be at least 18 or 19 before you leave home. And in the U.S. you have to worry about the draft. So you know, this is just the time that our generation can start. People like us have just been waiting for the opportunity to go out and do it. . . .Coming to Canada is the first opportunity we had to plan something like this out and do it.

Louis described himself as an anarchist. "I don't believe in organized government of any kind," he stated. He felt that going off to his commune was a positive retreat in the sense of "creating something new." Although none of them had done any real farming before, they had read books and checked into intensive farming. Louis figured that they could raise 10,000 tomato plants per acre and earn $1,000 to $5,000 on one acre depending on the market prices. They also planned to raise pigs and chickens.

They all accepted the fact that conditions would be rougher than they were used to. But they felt that the luxuries they had had in the city were the "cons of our society." They were in the process of building their houses. Louis explained that when he was teaching it was a 9 to 5 job, "a life of merely existing and then you live after that." He wanted to enjoy working, instead of going to work or hiring someone else to work. "I want to live all the time!" Louis exclaimed. "That's what I really hope for, to live with a community of friends." He rejected the concept of the self-made man in favor of a self-made community:

> My ideal is the idea that friends help me to make myself and I help to make them. It's more like a self-made community. You see, the self-made man image is using someone else's structure and climbing up someone else's ladder. That's kind of a negation of what we're doing. I want to make my own ladder together with my friends and climb up it together. The thing is to help the other people climb it, too. We're not out to get any place. The only thing we want is to *be happy*!

New Canadians also began to set up communal existences outside the Canadian cities from the rolling hills and forests of Georgian Bay, north of Toronto, to the western part of Vancouver Island in British Columbia. They found out about rural communal existences from their friends and from information that was readily available in exile publications, Canadian underground presses and magazines that exclusively dealt with communes, like *Alternative Society*. A 1971 announcement in *AMEX* described the Yukon Valley as a wilderness area that could be utilized for farming and ranching: "The Canadian government has a 'Homestead Act' under which you can purchase up to 160 acres of land for one to five dollars an acre. In addition, you can rent 40 acres of land per head of livestock at the rate of 50 cents per acre per year."[3] A group of Doukhobors, pacifist Russian emigrants, as well as communal Mormon farmers in the prairie province of Saskatchewan aided American deserters to learn farming. Deserters were encouraged to live and work with them for a period of a few years and then were helped in the setting up of their own farms.

Creating Counterinstitutions

The underground press has been an important counterinstitution in North America in creating as well as sustaining a new communications network among the youth culture. It has standardized the youth rock language and has created a feeling of solidarity and strength among the youth. American refugees supported the underground presses in Canada by selling and reading them. A significant number of these Americans also initiated and served as editors of new underground papers in Canada.

Many refugees had their first contact with the underground papers in the United States either as civilians or as soldiers. For many refugees, the underground newspapers both in America and in Canada were crucial in helping them locate counseling aid groups and finding the free "crashpads" and food that enabled them to survive until they got a job.

Most of the men who were active in the GI movement and wrote for the GI underground within the military deserted after the "heat" was put on them from their commanding officers. Many of the deserters who arrived in Montreal after the spring of 1969 attempted to organize within the GI ranks only to be faced with punitive reassignment or a "bust." The original editors of the GI papers *Head On, The Last Harass* and *Gig Line* were in Montreal, as were the co-editors of *Shakedown* and the *Fatigue Press*. Each of these editors had been busted on sedition charges, reassigned and ordered to Vietnam.[4] Sandy Hodge, the young Marine who revealed the conditions in the Camp Pendleton brig to the now-defunct *Life* magazine, was forced to leave the United States soon after *Life* printed his picture and name in an interview, something the magazine had promised it would not do. He then went to Canada to continue the struggle.[5] Walter Pawlowski, a major spokesman of the Presidio "mutiny" in San Francisco, the infamous Presidio 27, together with his friends Keith Mather and Lindy Blake, also veterans of the sit-in, escaped from the stockade and made their way to Canada to begin a new life.[6]

Many of these men carried their struggle against militarism and the experiences they gained in organizing against it with them. Working for an underground paper was a major expression of their antimilitarism in Canada. Laird was a deserter from both the United States Navy and the Marine Corps who worked for an underground press in Montreal. He wrote the following letter to the Vancouver Committee in the spring of 1969:

Dear Friends:

As of May 1969, I have been a resident of Montreal, a fugitive of the

U.S. Navy and U.S. Marine Corps. Stationed at Camp Lajeune, North Carolina, as a Navy medic, I edited an underground newspaper we called *Head On!* Now in Montreal I help edit *Logos* [an underground paper] and write free-lance for the *Montreal Star.* I am presently trying to gather as much information as possible for a complete analysis of the deserter situation in Canada.

Peace,
Laird

In the plains, from Winnipeg, a 19-year-old United States deserter edited the underground paper *Omphalos*. In Regina, a number of deserters were regular contributors to the socialist *Prairie Fire.* Among them was Dick Perrin, one of the original organizers of RITA (Resistance Inside the Army), who deserted to Paris and organized a deserter's group there that published the *Second Front.* In 1969 he was a counselor for the American Deserters' Committee in Regina, Saskatchewan. In Vancouver, the underground press of the Vancouver Liberation Front, *The Yellow Journal,* begun in the spring of 1970, was a joint effort of young Canadians and some American deserters who also worked with the Vancouver ADC. *Georgia Straight,* the largest underground paper in Vancouver, also had contributions from American refugees from time to time.

Because of the American refugees' involvement in the various underground papers in Canada, these papers frequently covered stories on political exile groups. The underground press in Canada closely resembled its American counterparts. Since they were all members of Liberation News Service, Anarchist Press Movement and other underground press syndicates, about half of their stories were reprints from other papers on movement activities in the United States. They contained a mixture of street people news, ecology, American New Left news and Canadian politics. As their American counterparts, they were always under attack and harassment from the establishment press, conservative politicians and others who neither agreed with their viewpoint nor recognized their right to freedom of the press.

In addition to working with the Canadian underground papers, American refugees also published their own news directed to the American exile community. Some deserters also wrote GI newsletters in Canada directed to their friends who remained on military bases. Their function was to make other soldiers aware of desertion and their options in Canada and elsewhere. Lee, a deserter who was active in the GI movement at Fort Jackson, South Carolina, founded *The Alternative* with a fellow deserter. It was a newsletter published in Toronto and sent to the various military bases in the United States. The Ottawa branch of the ADC published *Ambush*, which was also directed toward American military bases. The underground GI paper *Fed-Up*, written by a group of Fort Lewis GI's in Tacoma, Washington, was smuggled across the Canadian border to be printed in Vancouver and then taken back for distribution at the Shelter Half, the underground coffeehouse that was the center of local resistance.

In Toronto, as well as Vancouver and Montreal, the American expatriate community was very much a part of the larger dislocated youth community. The Red, White, and Black in Toronto, an expatriate group that sprang up early in 1970, together with other American expatriates like John Phillips of the Baldwin Art Gallery and Canadian artists and friends, obtained a community hall from the Province of Ontario Council for the Arts. In its brief to the council it announced its intention to serve the "community of the dislocated." This referred to the large numbers of new Canadians from Europe, Africa and the West Indies as well as the United States and the transient youth of Canada, "kids on the move, away from home, exploring their country to find out where it's at and how (if at all) they can fit into it." The brief referred to the fact that the initial dislocation for most of these youth was not geographical but cultural. It therefore argued that any long-range approach to the reasons for dislocation would have to begin with cultural changes.

The hall was helping to build the kind of networks among communal groups in Toronto that Jimmy was talking about. The projects to be run by Red, White, and Black included a free school for new Canadians to learn about Canadian history, politics and current affairs, as well as French; a 24-hour drop-in center for new arrivals with counseling; a 24-hour telephone information center modeled after the "free switchboards" in Los Angeles and San Francisco. Other initial programs included a music hall, a workshop, a studio set up with an emphasis on jazz, a free store, a food-sharing system, a junk retrieval operation run by the Whole Earth Family and a photography gallery and art yard where "novice, student, and master can exchange their views of each other's work and examine their own and each other's visions."

Before its demise in 1972, Rochdale College was another major counter-institution serving the needs of the dislocated youth in Toronto. It was financed by the government in 1968 as an experimental free university. There has been considerable difference of opinion as to how well this experiment had worked. Some claimed that Rochdale turned into nothing more than a "high-rise ghetto for hippies and heads." Others claimed that a good deal of valuable experimentation went on there. Nevertheless it was a major gathering place for youth of the counterculture. Many different communes and tribes worked together out of Rochdale. Many American refugees called Rochdale their new home. It provided easy friendships with other transient youths as well as relatively cheap living accommodations. Since it was so immense, it was also easy to be relatively anonymous when one wanted some privacy. From 1969 to 1970, the president of Rochdale was an American draft resister. Dan, a deserter from the United States Marine Corps, worked out of Rochdale providing odd jobs for American refugees so they could temporarily survive until they became immigrants and found more permanent jobs.

Mike Bilger first started his free medical clinic for transient youth at Rochdale and operated the clinic for one and a half years. Mike came from a broken home in Miami, Florida. He dropped out of high school a few days before he was to graduate, waited until his eighteenth birthday and enlisted in the Army. He did well in basic training and graduated from noncommissioned officers' training with the rank of E-5, in charge of 97 persons in advanced infantry training. Six months later he applied for a 1-AO, conscientious objector status within the military. This was approved. Mike then decided that he would apply for a 1-0, alternative service in civilian life; it was disapproved and he lost his appeal. Consequently, he spent seven months in the military stockade. When his sentence was up, he was reassigned to an armored battalion. Mike could not in good conscience perform these military duties, so he deserted and hitchhiked to Toronto in the winter of 1968, after spending almost two years of his life in the Army.

Mike got some preliminary information about landed immigrant status from the Toronto Anti-Draft Program and was given temporary housing at the Union of American Exiles. He obtained odd jobs through university professors. He wanted to continue his education so he began going to a local "straight college, looking very clean shaven and straight." Here he met a girl who wanted to start a medical clinic. Mike told her his background as a medic in the Army and they started a free medical clinic together at Rochdale. After a few months the girl left and Mike stayed on with the clinic.

The free medical clinic then expanded and was called the Toronto Free Clinic. It was funded through community and provincial grants. When I met Mike at the new clinic in June 1970 it had only been open one month in their new location, an old house rented from Rochdale College. The only identifying symbol was a small sign hanging outside the house saying, "Happiness Is

Helping Others." Mike really typified this motto. He believed in working in a very personal way with other people. In discussing the clinic he stated:

It's the only free youth clinic in Toronto. We're trying to bring medicine back to the people. We get people on the street who don't have any money. We're a community clinic and the community needs us. Although we are not specifically a drug clinic, we have a research program so that we can learn how to deal with addiction to junk, speed and all sorts of different drugs, since we get quite a few drug problems. We are also a community center and we are planning to incorporate a free store and feed-in when we get additional funds.

The free clinic staff consisted of Dr. David Collins, a resident doctor, and six other people. The doctor was also an American expatriate who had had a private practice in the suburbs of Louisville, Kentucky, for 14 years. According to Mike, "He had it with the U.S. culture and all those middle-class housewives he was prescribing headache pills and tranquilizers to." Now Dr. Collins earned $100 a week from the Toronto Free Clinic.

The clinic had treated about 1,400 persons since its opening in May 1970. Most of the patients had everyday illnesses like colds, pneumonia, bronchitis and cuts, as well as drug problems.[7]

Of the other five staff members in addition to Mike, four were American refugees. When I suggested that they might have applied because he was a deserter, he denied this was the reason. Instead Mike suggested an alternative explanation.

Americans are involved in the community, in all the service organizations in town. All of them are staffed mainly by Americans. It's a real phenomenon. Every youth agency in Toronto has quite a number of them. I think that there is a definite evolution which brings people to the point where they start their own programs. And it started happening a few years ago in the States and it's happening everywhere, but it's just beginning to happen here in Canada. So Americans have already gone through it before and know what needs to be done perhaps.

Underground Exiles

We have already indicated that there existed an important minority of American refugees during the Vietnam War era that could not assimilate into the Canadian mainstream for the same reasons that they were not able to adjust and assimilate into the "American way of life." The largest portion of these men were deserters from the United States Armed Forces.

While they were in the United States, both the draft dodger and the deserter were labeled deviants by both lawmakers and the authorities and even by their own friends and relatives. By coming to Canada, many of these Americans hoped to be able to begin a new life where they would no longer be subjected to these negative definitions of themselves and their actions. Most of the draft dodgers had been successful in creating new definitions for their lives by becoming landed immigrants and new Canadians. Yet, the majority of the deserters were not able to become new Canadians. This meant that they could not pass the first step to legal assimilation in Canada, the right to permanent residence.

The class bias of the Immigration Act discriminated against those who were uneducated and unskilled and channeled them out of the system. Thus, most of the estimated 3,000 to 6,000 deserters in Canada before the fall of 1973 were illegally present there.[8] That the deserter had a more difficult time attempting to deal with his deviant label can be partially explained by the significance of his act of desertion, the circumstances surrounding the act and, in part, by his experiences in Canada.

While these men were in the military, they were involved in a tight authoritarian social system that controlled all their actions. The military demanded its right to control these men's lives as long as they were within its jurisdiction. Most of the men accepted the legitimacy of the system's demands initially, with the exception of those men who were drafted against their will. Deserting from this system not only broke one or more of its regulations but also defied and challenged its legitimate control over the individual. Deserters were described as "traitors" who were "unpatriotic" or "disloyal," words indicating a breakdown in the individual commitment to the values of the system. Men who deserted from military life were making a radical break from their pasts in attempting to sever their ties with the military and reenter civilian life. For this reason, deserters in Canada who attempted to analyze the consequences of this act viewed desertion as a "total life commitment and total strategy of psychological survival." One of them wrote:

The physical act of desertion involves an instantaneous severing of nearly all the traditional ties of the individual's former life experience. This usually will at least include government, culture, religion, and family. Desertion involves this instantaneous severing to the extent that a physical act inevitably will be recognized by the individual as a psychological one of such intensity that the deserter soon finds himself set in an alien world, alone, unaided and condemned without any of the social attachments which he could identify with and be strengthened by. The effect of psychological aloneness leaves the individual in a void, in a vacuum, in a world so unreal that desperation, paranoia, and depression become the constant reminders of that world.[9]

The deserters displayed more of a fugitive complex than did the draft dodgers. When the entire power apparatus of a country labels a man a "deserter," a term that is synonymous in the public mind with "coward," "felon" and "criminal," it is a difficult image to shake. Self-doubt is usually the result even for those who had strong convictions. We have already indicated that the deserter was heavily subjected to these charges by his military superiors and by his fellow soldiers, friends and family. Those who had enlisted in the Army and who had patriotic feelings were most affected by this negative labeling process. One American explained his feelings of doubt:

I knew I was right in going to Canada and everything seemed O.K. However, it was still a very scary sort of thing because all the time you are thinking, "Gee, am I doing the right thing?" And I guess because of all the brainwashing you have gotten about patriotism and so forth, and "your country do-or-die," you know, this sort of stuff. . . .Well you feel like you are on shaky ground.

The individuals who had been indicted by the government for draft violation or desertion or who had spent time in a military stockade or brig and had gone underground before coming to Canada were subjected to the greatest degree of harassment and negative labeling. They were also more likely to be most deeply affected and hindered by their exile status even after they left the country. They were truly marginal men who were shunned by the country they left and the country to which they had come.

Many of these men became "secondary deviants," defined by sociologist Edwin Lemert as a "person whose life and identity are organized around the facts of deviance."[10] These men became segregated and isolated from other individuals in society because of the negative societal reaction to their action of desertion or draft resistance. Consequently they received little support for their actions. They experienced a number of "degradation ceremonies" such as military physicals, conscientious objector hearings, inductions and military discipline, which served to further isolate and humiliate them.[11] Once they were in Canada, they were prevented from becoming landed immigrants and were, therefore, prevented from working and making an ordinary citizen's living in their adopted country. As they became more isolated from others in society, they were forced to rely more and more upon others in a situation similar to theirs, namely, fellow deserters. Many of them were forced to go underground even in Canada because they remained in the country illegally. Since they were unable to acquire a positive identity through their work and a new life in Canada, they began to organize their lives around their exile status. These men formed a protective subculture for mutual support and aid.

The channeling system that prevented many deserters from obtaining landed immigrant status up until 1973 also prevented deserters from obtaining employment in Canada (see Tables 19 and 20; Appendix C). Out of a total sample of 59 draft dodgers and 55 deserters, the overall unemployment rate for all deserters was 60 percent, whereas the overall unemployment rate for draft dodgers was 20 percent. Thus, deserters had three times the rate of unemployment as did draft dodgers in Canada.

This high unemployment rate for deserters was directly related to the fact that only half of them had landed immigrant status. Yet even landed deserters had three times more unemployment than landed dodgers. It is apparent, then, that discrimination was stronger against deserters, whether they were landed immigrants or not.

The unemployment rate for refugees not landed should have been 100 percent had they all obeyed the law that made it illegal to work until an individual had landed immigrant status. However, nine unlanded refugees were illegally employed. If caught violating this rule, one could be brought up on deportation charges, as in the case of Jerry Mihn.[12] The jobs generally held illegally by these refugees were of a temporary nature. Still, data show that draft dodgers who were not landed still had a much easier time getting temporary work than did deserters not landed. Clearly, the labor market favored the dodger over the deserter in each category, legal and illegal. Only landed deserters had an easier time finding work than nonlanded dodgers.

The Vietnam War triggered off stagflation in both the United States and Canada. Recession and unemployment were combined with inflation in both countries by the early 1970s. Youth as a class was the hardest hit group, with double the unemployment rate of all other workers. American refugees were thus in competition with young Canadians for scarce resources. In December 1970, the overall unemployment rate in Canada was more than six percent of the labor force, affecting over 481,000 Canadians. The youth population was particularly stricken. Between October and November 1970, it was reported that the number of unemployed youth between the ages of 14 and 24 years increased by 23,000 to 212,000.[13] Inflation had so increased by this time that this was a major factor in discouraging new immigrants to

Canada. By 1973 and 1974 the unemployment rate continued to be high and that of youth (between 14 and 24 years) was double the unemployment rate for the overall population.[14]

We have already seen that most of the deserters came to Canada with very little money. A number of them were lucky enough to obtain a few allotment checks from the military; that is, until the military discovered that they had gone "over the hill" and discontinued its aid. One deserter was bold enough to send the Army his new address in Montreal and he continued to receive a couple of payments there. However, most of the unemployed refugees attempted to obtain odd jobs in order to survive, since they had no savings and had little contact with their families. Odd jobs were sometimes obtained through the aid groups, where sympathetic individuals wanting someone to do repair work and other housekeeping functions requested refugees for these jobs. Other jobs were obtained by walking around town and seeing what other immigrants and jobless men did to earn a day's wage. It was common knowledge among the Americans living at the Vancouver refugee hostel that during the four-month-old newspaper strike in 1970, firms were hiring extra men to deliver advertising circulars door to door for $10 a day. Selling the local underground papers was also a popular way for refugees to make enough money to live.

Refugee Hostels

A large majority of American refugees who were living a marginal existence lived in hostel-type accommodations provided by the aid groups. These hostels had a lifespan of six months to two years. Most of the refugees were referred to a hostel by the aid groups after their first contact with the new arrivals. These aid groups also had lists of private homes that accepted Americans. There was no set procedure to determine what type of temporary accommodations would be assigned to a newcomer. In some cities, like Toronto, there was a decentralization of labor and the newcomer was sent to a service-oriented group like Red, White, and Black or the ADC, which provided housing of all kinds. In other cities, like Vancouver, these decisions were made within the Vancouver Committee by the counselor. Effort was made to match the refugee with sympathetic families who came from similar backgrounds and interests. Consideration was given to job possibilities that might interest the individual concerned. Those who could not be placed with private families because they wanted to stay with their buddies or because they were judged to be "unlandable" were usually sent to the hostels. Informally, then, there existed a type of tracking system in the aid network, a preassessment, taking into account the individual's appearance, desires, ability to get landed and available accommodations at the time. A smaller number of refugees were directed to hostel accommodations through the underground press. In 1970, these newspapers began listing the various youth accommodations available in a city under the headline "Crash Pads." A refugee might also hear about a refugees' hostel at another hostel for Canadian youth in the city. The latter might then refer him directly to the hostel for exile Americans.

There were generally three distinctive populations that stayed in these hostels. The largest one viewed the hostel as a temporary accommodation and spent only a few days to a few weeks living there. A smaller minority usually spent a few months or longer at the hostels. This group, consisting of secondary deviants, developed an exile subculture. The third group was usually responsible for the running of the hostel and making sure the men participated in taking care of the house. It planned group activities, counseled and aided newcomers, collected the rent and maintained liaisons with the aid groups. These men often lived permanently in the hostel.

Although there was rapid and intense communication of deep feelings, individuals only got to know each other on a rather superficial level. Both the transient nature of the population and the forced, rather than chosen, communal arrangements were in large part responsible for the nature of these relations. One deserter summed up his feelings about the others by saying, "I really don't know too much about my other friends. Among deserters and dodgers, you learn just not to ask about background unless they volunteer because it's really not important."

There were many discussions about military life; much bitterness was expressed. The situations where GI's told off their superior officers and other assertive reactions were emphasized in their conversations. There was also much fantasy, in which the tables were turned on their military superiors. For example, a deserter would meet a despised officer in an unlikely situation in Canada. In this fantasy, the deserter would give the orders and the officer would be "bootlicking" and catering to his wishes. These discussions served an important tension-releasing function and helped the individual cope with some of his strong resentments against the military.

Friendships were often formed from brief but intense relationships based on their past. For example, three deserters in a Vancouver hostel first met each other for a week while they were AWOL at a sanctuary in a church in Honolulu, Hawaii. They all decided to desert and to go to Canada, but they all went at different times and used different routes via the underground. They maintained contact with each other and eventually reunited at the hostel in Vancouver. They hung around together, looked for jobs together and stayed together for their first few months in Vancouver. Other individuals sought each other out on the basis of the proximity of their hometowns in the United States. Others had been at the same military bases or had been confined in the same stockades and had swapped stories and names. Some men, having no point of contact or mutuality with their past, formed relationships on the basis of common interests.

Mainly the hostel served as a place to rest. Here they did not have to explain why they had come to Canada or why they did not work. Nor did they need to account for their time spent in the service if they did not want to. In the company of others, their loneliness was a little easier to bear. Their similar experiences created a sense of camaraderie and moral support.

The refugees living in the hostel celebrated their rites de passage together. One of the most important was the day they conducted their immigration interview for landed immigrant status. Every detail of the procedure and conversation was shared information. Another occasion for celebration was their first anniversary in going AWOL from the military. Reunions with old friends from the service or friends who had deserted together were also celebrated. Sad occasions were shared when a deserter did not obtain his landed immigrant status, when an individual lost out on a job or was discriminated against in other ways because of his exile status. All kinds of tidbits of information useful to an American exile were exchanged, from sources of free food or good drugs to useful job tips. Although this information was sometimes misleading (inaccurate immigration counseling from hearsay) much of it could be extremely valuable in helping a man survive during this difficult period. Information concerning which employers were sympathetic and which ones did not care whether or not you were an American refugee was particularly useful.

The majority of individuals stayed at a hostel during their first few weeks in Canada. As soon as they were able to get landed, they usually moved out. Most of these men had grown tired of living with other military men even if they were ex-military men. They wanted to build relationships with women and other people and try to forget about their past.

The men who stayed the longest in the hostels were those who were not able to get landed and did not have regular work. Some of them attempted to get temporary jobs and to look for job offers the first few weeks after

they arrived but had been discouraged. Others spent many months constantly on the verge of being picked up by the authorities. They grew mentally
and physically exhausted and felt like doing nothing but sleeping and eat-
ing for the first few months. They needed to unwind and recover from
the shell-shock type of existence they had led and the strong feelings of
paranoia that accompanied it. They rarely ventured far from the hostel.
Most of these men were not used to looking for work since they had never
held jobs before they entered the service and grew used to the social welfare of military life. It was the course of least resistance for them to live in-
definitely in the hostel and accept welfare in the form of housing and food.
Many of them were in need of mental counseling and medical services. They
had grown so used to an authoritarian system, where someone was always
ordering them around and planning their lives for them, that they could
not cope with a less structured situation. They were not able to assume
complete responsibility for their lives, so they fell back on the protective
hostel environment.

Many of the men who stayed in the hostel for long periods of time
considered themselves to be living "underground" in Canada. They had not
been able to become settled in Canada, and had adopted a drifter's life-style.
They retained their fugitive existences. Many of them continued to make use
of the aliases they adopted in Canada.

Fred, a black deserter who was underground in Canada for over a year,
described his existence:

Being underground in Canada is worse than being underground in the
States. There are little or no jobs. You have to stay with your own group.
You don't dare extend yourself outside your group, fearing that you will
be busted, deported and sent back to the States to serve time. Most of the
time I went from the hostel to the bar; from the bar to home. The same
little triangle for over a year.

During this time, Fred met at least 20 other American refugees who also
were not landed in Canada. These men had precarious futures and depended
greatly upon each other for aid. Lacking money and resources, they learned
various techniques of survival that sometimes led them into illegal activities.

Steve Trimm was another resister who lived for four years underground in
Montreal, Quebec, and in Dundas and Hamilton, Ontario. He told the following story of his experience underground:

Four years in prison would have destroyed me. Rather than submit to
imprisonment, rather than acquiesce and go off to that obscene war, I

went underground. Ironically I was underground exactly four years.

Existence underground turned out not be be a complete nightmare. I was a fugitive, true, but not a fugitive as one sees in the movies. I literally could not go to the corner store without first scanning the blocks up and down for policemen. I was looking over my shoulder every day. Truly every day, wherever I went. The tension was there, every day, in greater or lesser degrees, for four solid years.

I could confide to no one — it takes so little for that grapevine to start growing. I made up a fake personal history, and juggled it when I had to. That was one of the worst aspects of it: not being able to tell the truth to people I had come to respect and care for. I simply did not dare.

I had to repress all memory of family and friends. If I started to think and wonder about them, I knew it would drive me mad. So I broke up my past and buried it. Family, girls I had loved, guys I had once regarded as brothers. All gone, put out of mind. To let their images into my consciousness would have broken me, made me crack. And I wouldn't let that occur.

I froze my memory, froze my emotions. In many respects I became an automaton. I had to surrender the humane side of my life to retain life. It wasn't as bad as prison — quite.

Jobs: low paying. Fake I.D. would go only so far. The fewer forms to be filled out the better. A literate society traces its fugitives by the pieces of paper left behind. I got by on an income of about $25 per week. That wasn't too rough. Material things never mattered to me much.

Keeping the lies straight, developing an iron self-control, neutralizing memory and emotions. And blending in, always blending into the crowds. A hundred small tricks and deceptions. That was my way of "life" for four years.

There were chance encounters with the police. They scared me but I always managed to brazen my way out. The FBI and RCMP were looking for me. The RCMP made a near miss once, but I kept my head.

The pressure was there constantly, but it wasn't nearly so intense as the pressure I'd known prior to dropping out of sight.

Vietnam had always been a part of my life. Since the sixth grade, when I was 12 or 13, I'd been aware of it. I'd grown up with it. It had been hovering there at the edge of my vision through high school, and it was at the center of my consciousness well before the day I registered for the draft and requested classification   as a conscientious objector at age 18. After high school, for three years, I had worked to end that damned war. My whole life had been bound up with that atrocious battleground in Southeast Asia.

Now I could know nothing about it. All I could do was keep my head down and my mouth shut. Yet there was something else. For the first time I had the opportunity to think deeply about myself as a person. Up to my period as a fugitive — my 21st through 25th years — I simply had not had a breathing space; a space of tranquility in which I might look into myself. I had been too busy trying to stop the killing in Vietnam and reducing my complicity in it.

The war had alienated me from myself. Now — for the first time — I could look at the pieces of my life and try to fit them together. It was no easy task after being a stranger to myself, some of it positive, some of it negative, but all of it good and important to know, however difficult it was to face.

So these four years underground were neither wholly bad nor wholly good. I survived them, that's all I can say. I survived, after a fashion.

I am now out of hiding and midway through the processing for landed immigrant status. The odds are hopeful that I will be allowed to stay in Canada — a country which I have come to love — with my own name and identity and with a real life which I can go about constructing.

I tried to reestablish contact with old friends. Many are scattered to the winds. I will never see them again. Others are married and have kids and have evolved in directions which make genuine communication impossible now. Others are dead, victims of cancer and car crashes. A few, here and there, are eager to keep in touch again and do not care that four years have gone by. But the truth is that most of the threads cannot be picked up again. They had been unraveled even before I went underground, when the mad storm of Vietnam hit us and, reeling from the blow, we had to pick among impossible and insane alternatives.[15]

Immigration Adjustment of Status Program

After three and a half years of an underground existence as an illegal visitor, Dan was able to make his existence in Canada legal in 1973. Dan was an Army deserter who made his decision to desert in opposition to the war when he was to be sent to Vietnam. He came to Vancouver and initially stayed in the refugees' hostel for a month. He was advised not to apply for landed status since he could not qualify under the point system, even if he had a job offer in hand. So Dan lived the life of an underground deserter for the next several years. Most of this time he lived on Quadra Island near Vancouver Island working in the sawmills under a false I.D. A number of his friends lived similar existences. He was not too conspicuous, although he never felt terribly secure, and had some close calls with the police. In the fall of 1973, Larry Martin, a counselor working for the Vancouver Committee, informed him that he would be able to become landed under the new Adjustment Act. Although he had read some ads about this from the Department of Manpower and Immigration, he felt that he might place himself in jeopardy. However, the aid counselor, who was being paid indirectly by the Canadian government, convinced him to apply for landed status. Now that he was landed, his future plans included obtaining a better job and using his own name.

Dan had surfaced in Canada to apply for landed immigrant status under the Canadian government's Immigration Adjustment of Status program, an amendment to the Immigration Appeal Board Act.[16] This was designed to legalize the status of illegal visitors to Canada by granting them landed immigrant status and thus eliminating the backlog of appeal cases. It was also designed to clear the deck for a new look at immigration policy that was unveiled two years later in the government's green paper in 1975. Under these suggested policy alternatives it would become more difficult for unskilled immigrants from India, the West Indies and other Third World countries to become landed in Canada.[17]

Under the 1973 Immigration Adjustment of Status program, a special 60-day "amnesty" adjustment period was declared between August 15 and October 15, 1973, for all those illegal immigrants, either underground or appealing their cases who could prove their entry into Canada before November 20, 1972. The adjustment was designed to enable them to become legal immigrants under relaxed immigration criteria. Although this policy was not specifically directed toward Dan's special problems as an underground resister in Canada, or to the problems of other American draft dodgers and deserters in Canada, it did have major consequences for American underground exiles. Ultimately it changed their fugitive existence in Canada and thus dampened their desire to return to the United States.

According to Larry Martin, a counselor with the Vancouver Committee to Aid American War Objectors, the Department of Manpower and Immigration enlisted their aid as well as that of other immigrant groups during the last five weeks of the campaign. It also contributed financially to step up their operation. This grant-in-aid from the government enabled them to hire an additional four counselors during this period.

Prior to this new policy, a number of other revised immigration regulations had attempted to deal with illegal visitors. Still, the growing underground of visitors not landed was an increasing embarrassment to the Immigration Department and indicative of a dysfunctional policy that allowed lax control of visitors, most of whom were illegally in the country, in a time of growing unemployment. In addition, the Immigration Appeal Boards were also becoming dysfunctional. Over the few preceding years they had become increasingly bogged down by these same visitors who attempted to seek landed immigrant status while in Canada. As early as the fall of 1970, outgoing Minister of Immigration MacEachen initiated a study headed by Toronto civil rights lawyer Joseph Sedgewick, which was concerned with illegal visitors who did not qualify for landed status. At that time 66 percent of the appeals being handled were launched by rejected applicants, 22 percent involved persons ordered deported for being illegally in Canada and only 12 percent were launched by landed immigrants ordered deported for illegal acts committed in Canada.[18] According to Canadian immigration expert Anthony Richmond, "The backlog of appeals in 1973 was so long that a visitor or illegal immigrant launching an appeal against deportation could theoretically have remained in Canada for ten years awaiting his appeal board."[19]

The new minister, Robert Andras, described the 60-day amnesty as follows:

It is a *final chance* to apply for adjustment of their status to that of landed immigrant, with full appeal rights if their application is refused. I am inviting them, urging them to take advantage of this *last opportunity* to come out of the shadows and put their presence in Canada on a legal footing. I can assure them that they need fear no prosecution for the manner in which they either entered this country, or remained here after they should legally have left.[20]

The legislation that made this offer possible also prevented future backlogs. After the adjustment deadline casual visitors and illegal immigrants would no longer have the right to delay their deportation by an appeal to the Immigration Appeal Board. It was estimated by the aid groups that there were approximately 100,000 illegal immigrants in Canada who could potentially benefit from this program. Approximately 10,000 of these were American exiles. An earlier attempt to deal with the illegal visitor by an adjustment to the immigration policy was presented in June 1972. However, this complete policy turnaround brought forth few of the thousands of underground visitors. It was viewed with such skepticism and paranoia that it proved to be a dismal failure. The second attempt in the fall of 1973, done in a high-profile 60-day blitz and promoted by a $1.4 million advertising campaign, guaranteed a higher success rate.[21] As many groups as possible were enlisted in the Immigration Department's campaign to transform illegal visitors into landed immigrants, including the Canadian aid groups helping American refugees. All the illegal visitor had to do was present evidence for his self-reliance during his illegal stay in Canada. Thus, ironically, comments indicating that he had held several jobs that previously would have consituted *prima facie* evidence of his illegal status without a work permit now constituted grounds for granting him landed immigrant status under the Adjustment of Status Program.

After a two-year period of relatively decreased activity from 1971 to 1973 with the end of the draft, the Immigration Adjustment Program in 1973 spurred the aid groups to renew work throughout Canada. Their usual sphere of activity was now enlarged to include "visitors" from all quarters of the world as well as thousands of underground deserters and holdover draft dodgers. A grant of $110,000 was donated by the Emergency Ministries Concerning the War of the National Council of Churches to increase their staff and reach the underground people during this 60-day period. This was the largest grant they had received from the churches. The Department of Manpower and Immigration likewise gave them a grant to carry on these operations. A Canadian Coalition of War Resisters, an umbrella organization of aid groups, was set up. The coalition financed a mobile information center in the form of a multicolored school bus and sent it out to spread the word of the adjustment program. It traveled into the rural communes and subcultures of the underground deserters. The goal was to convince them of the government's sincerity in wanting to grant them landed status under relaxed criteria and freedom from prosecution for having entered or stayed in Canada illegally or for having worked without a permit under false identification.

The Adjustment Program was highly successful by the Immigration Department's standards, as it registered approximately 50,000[22] illegal visitors. Nevertheless, estimates of the number who did not take advantage of the campaign ranged from 50,000 to 200,000. According to the Minister of Immigration there were no truly reliable estimates.[23] The Canadian aid groups felt that 60 days proved too short a notice to bring forward a large proportion of those Americans existing underground in Canada. According to Dick Brown of the Toronto Anti-Draft Program, fewer Americans took advantage of the grace period than were expected. According to *AMEX* magazine, "At the half-way point reports from 6 to 10 counseling groups disclosed that they had counseled about 1,500 Americans of whom about 700 were war resisters."[24] Of the total number of 49,416 applications made for the legalization of status, "an estimated ten percent were American, of which about half (approximately 2,500) were war resisters, according to the estimates of counselors at some of the major war resister aid centers across Canada. However, precise figures were not available."[25] Although the majority of the underground exiles probably came forward to legalize their status in Canada, it was still felt by some exile counselors that there might be 500 to 1,000 exiles who had been underground for a few years that were not reached. The aid groups petitioned on behalf of this population along with members of Toronto's black and Portuguese communities for an extension of the 60-day "grace period" but this was denied by the minister of immigration.

During the Adjustment Program, some American exiles feared that there would be a "witchhunt" for illegal immigrants after the 60-day deadline, especially since it was clear in the government advertisements that this was an offer never to be repeated. Three months after the deadline had passed, Larry Kearley, a lawyer on the staff of the Parkdale Community Legal Services in Toronto and himself a long-term AWOL from the United States Army, wrote an article confirming this fear. He indicated that the thrust of the program had been against blacks and Indians rather than American exiles. He wrote:

> In February of this year [1974] it became increasingly obvious that despite government statements to the contrary, a crackdown was underway. A series of late night–early morning raids on homes were conducted by the RCMP. Further, raids have also been made at factories and other places where immigrants have been working. The common factor in their raids seems to be color and national origin in that in almost all cases the immigrants are either black or Indian.[26]

Upon termination of the Immigration Adjustment of Status Program, the right of appeal against deportation was curtailed. Thus, approximately 5,000 underground American exiles, most of whom were deserters, obtained immigrant status despite the fact that they could not meet the point system or had engaged in petty illegal activity in Canada. In addition, the exile aid groups in 1973 had come full circle in implementing this program. From disreputable groups that were viewed suspiciously by many Canadian officials in the early years of 1966–69 as being part of the American antiwar protest movement rather than indigenous to Canada, the Canadian government now relied heavily upon the work of the counseling groups in legitimizing the swelling illegal immigrant problem. In the process, the aid groups succeeded in legitimizing their own status. They were viewed as part of the Department of Immigration's established network. Although the Canadian aid groups had more financial resources and status during this brief period of the adjustment program than ever before, they did not utilize these resources to educate American refugees and other "illegal visitors" of the implications of continental channeling for their new lives in Canada. In particular, they did not inform these refugees that their landed status and acquisition of employment in Canada would reintegrate them into a North American economy dominated by multinational corporations headquartered in the United States. This had been a major position of the aid groups at the 1970 pan-Canadian conference in Montreal. Instead, the aid groups acted as if channeling did not exist in Canada. During the period of the Adjustment Program they once again cooperated with the channeling system to trade off their political independence for the sake of integrating the underground exiles.

For Canada, it was a case of letting a few working-class American deserters through the immigration barrier, despite their lack of qualifications, in order to revamp the overall immigration program. The irony of the situation was that the Canadian Immigration Act and thus the channeling system was suspended temporarily so that in future years large numbers of poor, unskilled immigrants from the Third World would no longer be eligible for entrance to Canada as permanent residents.

Marginality and Assimilation

The critical social disposition of the refugees sometimes made Canadians react negatively toward them further impeding assimilation into mainstream Canadian society. Like any host, Canada at the time found herself troubled or defensive in her interaction with these Americans who tended to be critical of her provisions and facilities. These Americans often identified more with other American refugees than with other Canadians in their earlier stages of adjustment. During this initial period, these residents did not feel any vested interest in the maintenance of the Canadian social order because they were only on the fringes of it. Their exile status, initially their only unambiguous identity, made them very conscious of their marginality while enabling them to maintain a critical perspective. For some, particularly those who chose alternative life-styles in communes, this helped them to evolve a more innovative response to their new environment. These men had reached what psychiatrist Levine referred to as the "searching" process (stage 3) in their adaptation to the host society. They were able to respond to the option for structural integration within the mainstream of Canadian society. At the same time, they maintained their own sociopsychological integrity by sustaining their primary identification with the counterculture.

In response to marginality, these "cultural innovators" translated the value perspective of American life into that of the Canadian perspective. This was likely to occur where the refugee ascribed to the established value system of North American society but perceived an inconsistency between these democratic and egalitarian values and the practices and social policies of his country. They were likely to abandon the decaying and contradictory culture of America as they perceived it and attempted to reaffirm these same values in their lives in their new Canadian localities. Thus, a significant minority of these refugees adopted a frontier ethic and attempted to translate the American dream into reality in Canada. Some of the draft dodgers initiated their first communal experiments, serving their fellow American exiles who needed their support and setting up refugee hostels, aid depots and community switchboards for transient youth.

Unlike the "cultural innovators" who were mostly middle-class draft dodgers, the "underground refugees," mainly deserters, did not have the option of structurally integrating themselves into Canadian society. They continued to. live underground by necessity rather than by a deliberate choice. Most had never advanced beyond psychiatrist Levine's "disorganization" (stage 1) and "acting out" (stage 2) stages of the adaptation process. Many had special problems with antisocial activities that brought them into trouble with the police.

In 1973 most of the deserters who had remained in Canada and were still not landed took advantage of the Immigration Adjustment of Status Program. These deserters renewed hope in starting their lives afresh in Canada. However, being given the permission to live and work in Canada was not the same as being assimilated there. Unemployment was still high in a Canadian economy entering recession along with the rest of the Western world. This meant that the deserters' status was now legal but still marginal. Hence, the channeling system that had been temporarily suspended at the level of the Immigration Act once more was seen to be acting at the economic level to exclude the unskilled, working-class new Canadian from fully integrating into his adopted country. This marginal status left the deserters prey to the machinations, both legal and illegal, of various police and military forces in North America. In some cases where the Royal Canadian Mounted Police was involved, there was collusion with the American Federal Bureau of Investigation in the continued harassment of American refugees north of the 49th parallel.

NOTES

1.   Philip Resnick, "The New Left in Ontario," in *The New Left in Canada*, ed. Dimitrios Roussopoulos (Our Generation Press, 1970), p. 92.
2.   *AMEX*, 1970.
3.   *AMEX* 2, no.7: 11.
4.   Roger Williams, "U.S. Deserters Safe in Canada," *Los Angeles Free Press*, January 30, 1970.
5.   *AMEX* 2 (April—May 1970): 19.
6.   An account of the Presidio "Mutiny" is written in a moving book by an organizer of the early coffeehouse movement among GI's, *The Unlawful Concert* by Fred Gardner (New York: Viking Press, 1970).
7.   "MD Wants to Doctor as Plumber Plumbs," *Vancouver Sun*, CP Toronto, October 7, 1970.
8.   There is a wide range of doubt as to the exact number of deserters in Canada because before 1973 almost 50 percent of them entered the country illegally, not being landed immigrants. I have accepted the estimate of the American Deserters' Committees and other Canadian aid groups that come in contact with the largest number of these men.
9.   Montreal American Deserters' Committee, "Totality of Desertion," 1970.
10.   Edwin M. Lemert, *Human Deviance, Social Problems, and Social Control* (Englewood Cliffs, N.J.: Prentice—Hall, 1967), pp.40—41.
11.   Harold Garfinkel, "Conditions of Successful Degradation Ceremonies," *American Journal of Sociology* LXI (January 1956): 420—24.
12.   Jerry Mihm was a U.S. Army deserter who lived in Toronto with his wife and child. On November 1967 the Canadian Immigration Department refused him permission to remain in Canada because he worked in Toronto before applying for landed immigrant status. *Toronto Globe*, March 10, 1970.
13.   *Statistics Canada*, November 1970.
14.   Ibid., 1973, 1974.
15.   *AMEX* 4 (January—March 1974): 38.
16.   Immigration Appeals Board Act Bill and C-197, passed by the Canadian House of Commons, July 10, 1973, and July 12, 1973. Consult *Han-*

sard, Commons Debates, pp. 4952—54, 4958, 4960, 5026—27, 5031, 5035.

17. A report of the Canadian Immigration and Population Study, "Immigration Policy Perspectives," Manpower and Immigration Information Canada (Ottawa, 1974). Also, W.A. Wilson, "Green Paper Is Trying to Mold Form of Debate," *Vancouver Sun,* February 6, 1975.

18. Joseph Sedgewick, Q.C., "Report on Applicants In Canada," October 1970, Dept. of Manpower and Immigration. Also see background by Freda Hawkins, *Canada and Immigration* (Montreal: McGill—Queen's Press, 1972), pp.145—50.

19. Personal Correspondence from Anthony Richmond, spring 1974.

20. *Vancouver Sun,* Letter to the Editor, July 5, 1973.

21. Ibid.

22. A Report of the Canadian Immigration and Population Study, "Immigration Policy Perspective."

23. *Vancouver Sun,* October 16, 1973.

24. *AMEX* 4, no.5: 32.

25. Ibid., p.24.

26. Ibid. 4, no.7: 14.

8

The Long Arm
of the Law

In 1970 Canadian press headlines revealing an illegal deportation of three American deserters caused such an outcry on the part of the Canadian public that the solicitor general, who is also commander of the Royal Canadian Mounted Police, found it necessary to conduct a government inquiry into the case. Similar incidents raised serious questions regarding the police powers of the RCMP and the type of cooperation that existed between it and the FBI.

There had always been active cooperation between the RCMP and the FBI in the handling of criminal investigations, just as Canadian and American military forces cooperated as part of the defense-sharing treaties linking the two countries. However, the harassment of deserters by the RCMP and the role of the RCMP as an intelligence-gathering agency to assist American authorities in the channeling of American youth was not included in their legal duties as understood by the Canadian government. As noted in chapter 5, by 1969 American exiles could not be deported simply for being deserters. Also, there was no Canadian law prohibiting individuals from living in hostels. Yet, the RCMP assumed the right to interpret and enforce its own laws on a number of occasions that came to the public's attention. Furthermore, the collusion between Canadian and American police authorities was the norm rather than the exception. Such collusion eventually raised nationalistic qualms among other Canadian authorities; questions of Canadian sovereignty in Parliament temporarily squelched RCMP zealousness in acting as a watchdog of American refugees for the FBI. However, the autonomous nature of the RCMP enabled it to pursue its own justice towards new visitors from south of the border.[1]

Run-Ins with Canadian Law Authorities

Refugee hostels in Canadian cities became prime targets of police harassment. They were usually located in run-down houses in lower-income, working-class or student neighborhoods where there already existed a differential law enforcement policy of heavy surveillance throughout the area. Large numbers of deserters were concentrated so that their visibility as a group was known to both their neighbors and to the law enforcement officials. The intervention of the city police and the RCMP in the affairs of these hostels was responsible for the antagonistic attitude many American refugees had toward these Canadian officials.

During my period of observation in Vancouver, two hostels were under constant police surveillance. One, which was supervised by the American Deserters' Committee, had been visited by the police seven times in the nine-month period from April to December 1969. Many of the ADC members had been individually harassed during the same period. According to the ADC members, there was always a police car five blocks from the house. The police were familiar with the individuals who came in and out and with the cars of some men who supervised the hostel. Dennis, an ex-Marine, told me that "they know mine and other cars and constantly stop and search and harass us." He described an incident during which he was pulled over on the road by an RCMP officer who identified himself by his badge. The officer searched his car and examined his personal ID. Dennis explained that he went through a similar experience with the RCMP on the average of once every other week.

The ADC hostel on Second Avenue was raided by the police early one morning. Six Americans, all deserters, were rudely awakened at 9:00 A.M. by nine plain-clothed policemen, later identified by their badge numbers as RCMP and one city police officer. They had kicked their way in at this hour, damaging the door. They claimed that they had a Writ of Assistance and that they were there to search for drugs, but the Americans living at the hostel were convinced that it was a political investigation. According to Steve, a resident ADC member:

They entered our home under the pretext of searching for drugs and they began investigating everyone and asking for IDs. They spent most of their time not searching for drugs, but going through personal documents, correspondence, files on certain organizations and people whom we have contact with in the U.S. and Europe. They kept stressing the fact that they weren't after any personal information. But when they began questioning me as to who was the editor of a local newspaper we put out [*Yankee Refugee*] and searching my private bank account slips, then I began to wonder as to what the nature of the raid really was.

Another deserter in the house at the time of the raid verified Steve's story:

They took down every name they could find. They spent most of their time going through files, personal letters and wallets. We were running a raffle, and they even took the names of all the people who had bought raffle tickets, about 60 of them. They really messed up the place.

They tried to keep us all seated during the whole time. One cop said if we didn't sit he'd handcuff us to our chairs. I needed to go to the can really badly because I'd just got up and they wouldn't let me for a long while. Then when I went anyway, one guy followed me into the can and watched.

Ray, another ex-Army deserter, testified that he was questioned by the police as to where he had been stationed in the United States, his Army number and what he thought would happen to him if he was caught and sent back. He felt that he was being intimidated. Other deserters present testified that harsh words were used and that they were pushed around by the officers.

All the Americans present unanimously agreed on the overall purpose of the raid. Dennis, a leader of the Vancouver ADC who had come to Canada two years earlier, felt it was "a political type of harassment." On a Canadian Broadcasting Corporation TV program he revealed why this was so.

I feel the RCMP are getting information not only for some organization in the U.S., most likely the FBI, but also information for the Canadian Immigration Department. This seems true because the raids tend to fall on one day and then, a few days later, an RCMP officer will come around the hostel with an Immigration Officer, seeking out people who have been identified through the previous raid.

Dennis's observation of the RCMP closely cooperating with the Immigration Department has been borne out in a number of incidents.

During my period of observation in 1970, two immigration officers visited the Vancouver hostel. According to the refugees present, two men knocked at the front door, and Mark let them in after they flashed their badges and identified themselves as immigration officials. Word of the visitors traveled instantaneously to the approximately 15 deserters who were in the house at the time. One of the officers inquired about Joe, a deserter he claimed had gone back and forth from the United States, delivering luggage for a couple of men staying at the hostel. As this conversation was going on, all but six of the deserters left the house. Duffy, an Army deserter who was in the sanctuary in Honolulu before he came to the hostel, said, "As soon as I saw them coming in, I headed out the front door right past them and didn't stop to answer any questions." Most of the deserters panicked and ran for the basement door. None of them could afford to get "busted," as they put it, since they were in the country illegally. They had all entered the country on visitor's visas and had not obtained landed immigrant status. Those six men who remained in the house after most people cleared out felt that they had no choice but to stay and face the music. They were given pink visitor's slips by the officers that specified a date, two weeks hence, for the termination of their visit to Canada. After that date, their presence in the country would be illegal and they could be issued a deportation notice. Under some circumstances it could be renewed if the visitor could show $10 for each day he was present in the country.

Later in the evening, when most of the deserters had returned to the hostel, the unanticipated visit by Canadian immigration officials was discussed. The majority of the men were quite shaken about the visit and referred to the officers as the "Immigration pigs who busted into our home." Most of them agreed that its purpose was mainly harassment and an attempt to put pressure on them to get landed or leave the country. One of the deserters explained to me, "The deserter in Canada is always taking the risk of being questioned as to his identity and how long he has been in the country. If he can't produce a justifiable story his name is turned over to immigration and the RCMP locates him and tells him he must get landed within a short period of time, or else he is deported." In January 1970 the following article appeared in the *Vancouver Sun* under the headline " Immigration Charge Jails Deserters":

Four young Americans, three of them described by the RCMP as U.S. Armed Forces deserters, have been arrested here and the three given jail terms for unlawfully remaining in Canada by overstaying their visitors permits. The fourth was turned over to Canadian immigration authorities. Jack and Greg, both 18 from Camp Pendleton, California, were given seven days each, and William of Ft. Lewis, Washington, was sentenced to 14 days.[2]

I followed up this story, a search which led me to the Lower Mainland Correctional Centre in British Columbia where young offenders were kept. William entered Canada approximately eight months before my interview with him through a small Quebec border town. He had then hitchhiked across Canada. In his search for work he wandered up to Prince George in the interior of British Columbia and had obtained a job as a carpenter and lumberjack even though he was not landed. "I didn't have any difficulties with this," he explained, "since I looked like one of the boys with my big boots and lumberjack pants. With my Social Insurance card I had gotten under another name, I looked like a Canadian. I was able to make $800 this way." He then came down to Vancouver and stayed in a cheap room in Kitsilano, where a large portion of the youth subculture lived. On January 5, 1970, William was going for a drive near Squamish, an hour out of Vancouver, with four other deserters he had met. Their car had American license plates. They were speeding, they jumped a stop light and were stopped by Canadian police. The officer asked for identification. The driver, an American deserter, showed him the Canadian ID he had acquired in Canada. Another deserter in the car supplied the police with the location of the nearby hotel where they and their friends were staying. The police then drove over to the hotel and all 11 deserter friends were taken into custody. At the police station it was discovered that William also had been using a fake Canadian ID, which was a criminal offense. He received a sentence of 14 days. According to William, "They gave me 14 days because they were pissed off that I had made $800 working illegally and they wanted to punish me for that. I had spent most of the money and sent the rest out of the country."

William had just about finished his 14-day sentence when I visited him. He was faced with two options: either he could stay in prison until he could have an immigration hearing, which probably would not take place before eight months, or he could turn himself in to the United States Army base at Fort Lewis, Washington, and serve out his remaining six months in the stockade until he was discharged. He felt he would probably take the latter option since he could always come back to Canada.

While William was in Oakalla prison, he met another seven deserters who had been "busted" on petty charges. After they had served the sentences for which they were charged, the Immigration Department often issued holding charges so that they could be held on different, more serious charges. Eventually many American refugees, originally arrested and jailed for petty theft or violation of their visitor's passes, found themselves deported to the United States in this manner. Most of these cases were unknown to the Canadian public.

Only a small proportion of the American refugees had run-ins with Canadian law enforcement authorities. According to my sample, out of a total of 123 refugees, approximately one-fifth of them had trouble with Canadian authorities. This did not include routine questioning by the RCMP. Of these 23 men, 9 were draft dodgers and 14 were deserters. A Vancouver lawyer who handled legal aid for refugees estimated that not more than one percent of the total number of refugees in Canada had trouble with the law. Often they were involved in a minor infraction that brought attention to their exile status. In a smaller number of cases, these men were involved in more serious offenses that could lead to their deportation. In my sample of 123, two dodgers and seven deserters were arrested and jailed for an offense. The majority of them were charged for drug-related offenses or violations of the Immigration Act. The Canadian mass media sensationalized these few incidents with headlines such as "Draft-dodger in Pot-Weapons Case" and "Some U.S. Draft Dodgers Turning to Crime." They were labeled as a group, and frequently associated with the larger Canadian "youth problem."

RCMP and FBI Collusion

The Canadian government and public in recent years have been wary of their "friendly" neighbor to the south. Due to growing Canadian nationalism, Canadians have become particularly sensitive to issues that hint of the United States dictating policy in Canada's internal affairs. Canadian religious and political groups successfully pressured to eliminate the discriminatory policies practiced by Canadian immigration officials. The Canadian government itself had by and large ignored pleas by the American government to return deserters. There were strong feelings among the Members of Parliament of all parties against American agents operating in Canada. In the recent years that American refugees emigrated to Canada, this suspicion was raised over and over again. John Diefenbaker, former prime minister of Canada, raised this concern in the House of Commons and came out strongly in opposition to American agents in Canada:

Mr. Speaker, I wish to ask the Solicitor General if he will have an investigation made into allegations that has appeared in several press reports, in particular in the Vancouver *Sun* to the effect that U.S. Service police in civilian clothes and carrying warrants are making the rounds of various places in Vancouver that the Minister and I do not frequent, looking for U.S. Armed Forces deserters, and that to all outward appearances there were no members of the RCMP accompanying these individuals? This is a serious matter that should be looked into. We should not have police officers from a foreign country trying to find malefactors of their country.[3]

Diefenbaker suggested that the solicitor general directly contact the FBI in Washington and ask them, "Are any of your officers snooping about in Canada?"

Actually, FBI and other American agents did not have to be physically present in Canada because they had the complete cooperation of the RCMP, which does all the federal police work in Canada and maintains a large security and intelligence department. The comparison with the FBI ends here, however, for in many ways the RCMP has a larger jurisdiction and more powerful position in Canadian society than does the FBI in American society. The RCMP, for example, performs the provincial police function in eight of the ten Canadian provinces.[4] On the whole, the Canadian public accords the RCMP a large amount of respect. This accounts in large part for the large areas of discretion the police are permitted in dealing with lawful as well as unlawful activity. There are very little scrutiny and very few checks on their activities.

I queried those American refugees in Canada who responded to my questionnaire about their possible contacts with the FBI and RCMP and the nature of these contacts. Out of the 113 men who answered these questions, 43 persons had at least one contact with the RCMP. Over 90 percent of them had been questioned by the RCMP as to the length of their stay in Canada, whether they were landed immigrants and whether they had any intentions of returning to the United States. These visits, usually to the homes of American refugees, were conducted after the individual had applied for landed immigrant status. They were conducted in a "matter-of-fact routine manner," according to the Americans. A few of the bolder men asked why this information was needed, as it was not part of the normal procedure for obtaining landed immigrant status. The answer in unabashed tones from the RCMP was that it needed this information for the FBI, which had requested it. Twenty draft dodgers and 23 deserters had been questioned by the RCMP in my sample, so there did not seem to be any apparent discrimination between these two groups (see Table 21; Appendix B).

Since almost all those individuals immigrating during the period up until 1968 were draft dodgers, a much higher percentage of those men interviewed by the RCMP during this early period were draft dodgers. More than one-third of my sample of 62 deserters who entered the country during 1969 were questioned. In the same period, the number of contacts between draft dodgers and the RCMP were reduced by more than half. In November 1969, the RCMP reported that it had interviewed 2,250 Americans during the year to determine whether they were present in Canada illegally.[5] If the ratio between dodgers and deserters in my sample was representative of those who were questioned by the RCMP, almost 1,000 of those men were probably deserters, even though deserters made up less than three-tenths of the total American exile population at the time. Peter Maley, a deserter from the Army who spent more than one year as a counselor at the Vancouver Committee, verified that known deserters were contacted by the RCMP as a matter of routine. He said that "they ask questions on behalf of the FBI and forward the answers back to the FBI."

Occasionally the Vancouver Committee was questioned by the RCMP about the whereabouts of a particular deserter. In the following letter that was sent to the Montreal Council to Aid War Resisters in 1968, the Vancouver Committee described how it handled these requests:

> One interesting thing to note is that the RCMP in making their checks for the FBI have found it easier if they contacted us when looking for someone rather than spending some two or three months in trying to find him in all of Canada. We've had very good talks with a Sergeant Knight who is the head of this branch of the RCMP, whereby it was decided that we would cooperate with them if they wouldn't give any undue hassles to the guys in Vancouver. So far our relationship with them has been beneficial on both sides, with the understanding that if they shit on us we are going to shit on them and vice versa.

The aid group had worked out a *modus vivendi* with the RCMP at the time that involved a compromise of aiding the police only in those things that were "routine" if they agreed to limit their contacts with American refugees in all other areas. This compromise solution proved unworkable because the RCMP never kept its side of the bargain.

Kidnapping and Deportation of American Deserters From Canada

Collusion between the Canadian police and the American FBI did not begin in the sixties. Clive Cocking reports that there was an FBI man stationed permanently in Vancouver during the fifties, securing the return of deserters as well as performing other duties. He quotes a former Vancouver policeman as saying, "We used to ship deserters back regularly. We'd pick them up, throw them in jail, and notify the U.S. authorities. The U.S. Army would send up a special paddy wagon to take them back."[6]

This account has been confirmed by former FBI agent William Turner, who describes himself as "having been in a junior executive role in the Federal Bureau of Investigation,"[7] and then a contributing editor to *Ramparts* magazine. Turner appeared on CBC television in early 1971. In response to a suggestion by a reporter that the RCMP cooperated with FBI in order to deport deserters from Canada, he replied, "That's been going on a long time." He testified that while he was an agent, he regularly went to Vancouver to trace down AWOL soldiers. Due to the 72-hour limit restricting foreign agents, he used to return to Seattle for a short time and immediately return to these duties in Vancouver. He worked closely with the RCMP and Vancouver city police. When he was not able to locate these American refugees, the Canadian police would track them down and "shove them across the border." "Once we deported a deserter who turned out to be a British national who was drafted into the American Army," Turner confessed.

The deportation of American deserters by Canadian immigration and RCMP officials had intensified and probably reached an all-time high in the late 1960s and early 1970s.[8] There were no official figures for the number of American refugees who had been deported without the benefit of a deportation hearing[9] or kidnapped illegally and handed over to the American authorities. However, we can examine some cases that burst from obscurity into the Canadian media and others with which I became familiar during this period.

Deserter Dennis Seaman was deported from Canada with the cooperation of the immigration officials and the RCMP. In the early hours of April 29, 1969, his ADC hostel was raided by RCMP officers who produced no warrants, explaining that "we're doing an immigration check." This young, 17-year-old deserter was ordered to come with them. He had been ordered to go with the officers in such a manner as his lawyer believed constituted arrest. He was then turned over to immigration officials, who shortly deported Dennis to the United States. They later explained that he had returned voluntarily to America. Dennis, however, deserted again and returned to Canada to tell a somewhat different story. He had been under the impression that he was arrested for illegally entering Canada and that he had been deported for the same reason. Dennis did not have a legal deportation hearing.

His Vancouver lawyer, Gary Lauk, who subsequently became a minister in the British Columbia government, offered free legal aid to American refugees for four years. He strongly suspected collusion between Canadian and American authorities in the kidnapping of Dennis Seaman. He maintained that Dennis had not voluntarily returned to the United States but had been forced to return by Canadian immigration and RCMP working closely with the American immigration and military authorities. Although he urged Justice Minister John Turner to investigate the case, his request was rejected.

In 1970 two bizarre cases of deserters being kidnapped came to my attention, one through an interview and the other through Canadian press headlines revealing the illegal deportation of three American deserters. The former case, never made public, involved a deserter named Bob who did not even know who the authorities were who kidnapped him; they never identified themselves despite his repeated requests. He was an Army deserter living in Toronto in 1970 when he experienced his "Kafkaesque nightmare" as he put it.

After several years of college in the New York City area Bob quit because he was not learning very much. Under pressure from his draft board in May 1967, he enlisted in the Army in the Special Language Program and learned Russian for two years. During this time he had a top secret security clearance. Then Bob became disillusioned with the Army Security Agency and left.

During the time he was in the Army, his brother-in-law and sister were fleeing the draft and made their new home in Toronto. Although Bob had originally thought about going to Canada before he had enlisted, he decided at that time that he was "psychologically and emotionally unprepared to leave the States." Two years later, with the help of the Army, he had become quite ready psychologically and he made his decision to join his sister's family in Toronto. Having very little money and knowing no one in Toronto except his sister, Bob decided that he would share a small flat on the third story of an old building in Toronto with his sister and her husband. He got landed with no difficulty and had even obtained a job as a research assistant where his boss, an American, was quite sympathetic. In fact, the company he worked for was owned by four American partners. After a few months, when the business folded, Bob obtained another job as a stage manager with a studio lab theater. At Christmas time, his sister and brother-in-law went on vacation and Bob was left in the apartment alone. It was during this period that the episode occurred.

BOB: I was going to work Sunday morning, and I guess it was about 8:30 A.M. and a car was driving slowly down the street. I didn't pay any attention to it, just a car with four people. And the car stopped. It had Ontario plates. And one fellow got out. He had plain clothes and black, lace-up oxfords. And they were pretty well shined. I kept walking. And this car kind of pulled up alongside me. And this arm came flying around my face. I guess it was a handkerchief. It was white. He slapped it over my face and knocked me out. It was chloroform.

When I woke up, we were on the Queen Elizabeth Highway, heading for the border. And I was scared shitless. It was like a dream. I couldn't believe it was really happening. And like, thoughts were absolutely racing through my mind. Mainly, "Get out of here, man, this is unhealthy!" I wasn't thinking too coherently. I was in the back seat with one of these dudes, handcuffed and the other cat was driving. And I didn't know where they were taking me, like what was the ultimate destination — just to Buffalo — or where? They didn't say a word. All I could get from them was "O.K.," "No," or "Uh."

So we got to the border and the guy in the driver's seat flashed something to the man in the booth and we went through with no questions asked. I was in plain view, with the handcuffs, the whole trip, zap, right through. So we were driving along, I don't even know where we were, I just know we had crossed the border. And I told them, "Hey, look, man, I really have to pee." Because I really did. Whew! They stopped at this little place. I guess it was a restaurant. And we bopped in. One of these dudes came with me. They took the handcuffs off me before we got out.

And we went to the john, the two of us. My shadow and me. And I went into the booth. And when I heard him using the urinal I took my boot off. I was wearing boots with hard leather heels. And I just jumped out and smashed him in the head. Ironically, the Army taught me how to hit him so he would go down the first time. And I took off. I didn't wait. I didn't know where the other guy was. Anyway, I high-tailed it out to the parking lot, and luckily, I mean, very luckily there were a couple of freaks and I ran up to them and I gave them a quick rundown, and they said, "Come on," and they threw me into the back of the VW van and we got away.

They left me just outside of the border. I was around Buffalo somewhere. They stopped, and waited with me while I hitched a ride. And I got a ride with a family. They were coming back after the Christmas holiday. And they drove me right to my door. I had crossed the border as a member of the family. Then Dan came back. . . .

Bob's brother-in-law, Dan, continued the story:

DAN:. . .to find that he had disappeared from the theater where he worked and no one knew where he was. Wow! And I finally came back and there he is, sleeping. So Bob tells me this science fiction thriller. I said, "Wait, try that again!" So he started in all over again. He was like freaked out. He was afraid to go out in the street again. And he was living in the top of this house, you know. Like I escorted him everywhere he went for awhile. The strong-arm thing. If they come, we'll both fall down.

Bob observed that the day before the incident occurred their phone had "gone out of whack," there were no calls coming in and there was no dial tone. Because he had a top clearance while he was in the Army he suspected that his kidnappers might have been United States Central Intelligence Agency (CIA) agents, though he had no proof.

Also in 1970, Canadians were exposed to the kidnapping case involving three deserters in British Columbia that was described in chapter 1. Of all the alleged and actual cases of deserters being "shanghaied" across the border by Canadian officials cooperating with their American counterparts, this case alone has been publicly documented. The president of the British Columbia Civil Liberties Association, John Stanton, welcomed this case. He commented at the time: "There had been enough smoke previously to say there was fire, but where the fire was burning and who had kindled it and just what the whole situation was, we didn't know. It's thus gratifying that with the most publicly glaring case the government did appoint a commissioner to conduct an inquiry."[10]

The three protagonists in this case were Army deserters who had enlisted under the pressure of the draft. None had completed high school or were over 21 years old. In almost all ways they were typical of the backgrounds of most deserters in Canada.

It is interesting how the case became so public at all. By a fluke, one of the deserters was able to make a phone call at the border crossing before the actual deportation occurred. He called a Vancouver minister who in turn notified a Vancouver lawyer of the impending events. The lawyer, Don Rosenbloom, was able to verify the events right after they had occurred by returning the call to John Kreeger, who had just been deported with his two friends to the American side of the border. Both the lawyer and the minister were interviewed on CBC's *Weekend* television program. David Lewis, leader

of the New Democratic party, raised the issue in Parliament and stated that
"it seems clear that whoever is responsible [for the deportation] has acted
entirely illegally and reprehensibly." His account of the kidnapping, as trans-
mitted from the Vancouver lawyer, made news across Canada. In addition to
the NDP's pressure on the federal government to investigate the incident,
other citizens' groups also began pressuring the government. The president of
the British Columbia Civil Liberties Association accused RCMP officers of
an "outrageous kidnapping" and called for an impartial investigation. Thus,
despite the fact that both the immigration and RCMP had denied that they
were involved in illegal actions and that the deserters were deported legally,
public pressure demanded a judicial inquiry.

A step-by-step recounting of the events that led to the deportation,
based on the testimonies presented at the judicial inquiry[11] provides us with
an insight into the bureaucratic functionings of the RCMP and the Immigration Department as well as the exact nature of the cooperation and complicity of Canadian officials with their American counterparts.

The three deserters started eastward on January 25, 1970. They were
offered a ride to Bridal Falls, British Columbia, by a sympathetic Vancouver
family. There they had dinner at a café and met one of the waitresses, who
offered to give them a lift to a nearby town, Chilliwack. While they were
waiting at the café, an RCMP officer entered for his evening meal. He was
on duty, in uniform and had observed the three hitchhikers. One of the
deserters asked the RCMP constable for information on hitchhiking. The
police officer explained the laws as requested and in turn told them it was his
duty to question them as hitchhikers. They provided identification with
American addresses, which prompted the officer to ask if they were draft
dodgers. In the course of the questioning the three men disclosed that they
were, in fact, deserters from the United States Army. Constable Dyck then
informed the deserters that he was going to check their police records by
radio and asked them to wait. He returned and told them they were free to
go. The incident might have ended there, however, the constable had
instigated an inquiry that went beyond checking their records. He had instructed the Chilliwack RCMP's civilian radio operator to check with the
American authorities through Blaine, Washington, informing them that the
men were from Fort Ord military. Thus, even though the men were told by
Constable Dyck they could leave, the RCMP officer continued to check on
their backgrounds in the United States.

The message that the three men were deserters and that the FBI had a warrant out for the arrest of one, John Kreeger, did not come back to the radio operator until two and a half hours after Constable Dyck had first entered the restaurant. Although this information was irrelevant to John's legal status in Canada, the constable went back to the café where the three deserters were waiting and told them to accompany him to Chilliwack for further investigations.

Important events were happening at the same time on the American side of the border. In Blaine, a United States Navy Shore Patrol officer had arrived after driving from Bellingham, Washington, to pick up an AWOL soldier. Before leaving Bellingham, he heard that the three deserters, now in Chilliwack, would be coming through Blaine and he would be required to meet them. Though the source of this information was not disclosed, he expected to take custody of the three deserters. Note that although the three deserters were legally in Canada and had done nothing to warrant deportation, they were now in the custody of the RCMP and a Shore Patrol officer was waiting in Blaine to take them into custody.

Meanwhile in Chilliwack, the three Americans were waiting in the police station as Constable Dyck attempted to decide what to do with them. He asked other officers and checked the RCMP manual on instructions regarding deserters. The document contained the following words: "If located, there is no authority for the arrest of such persons in Canada and the only action required is to verify their presence, ascertain their intentions if requested; and report accordingly."[12] While at the police station John Kreeger made several unsuccessful attempts to place a phone call. He was told by the radio operator that he would be deported and was cited a Serviceman's Act whereby deserters could be returned to the United States. All three deserters were subjected to a search of their belongings. After many radio discussions, Constable Dyck made the decision to take the deserters to the Sumas immigration office. He informed a senior officer that immigration officers stated that they wished to interview the deserters and that the deserters desired a meeting with immigration officials. No facts were presented to support his statement. All deserters denied they wished such a meeting.

At this time, another significant message was relayed by an RCMP radio operator and passed by an immigration official to American authorities. The message indicated the RCMP was bringing the deserters to the Sumas border crossing. American officials informed Blaine officials and as a result Shore Patrol Officer Baty started the 24-mile trip to Sumas in his patrol wagon. Why an RCMP officer should have instructed a Canadian official to carry such a message to American authorities is a question that disturbed the judge conducting the inquiry.

At the Sumas immigration station, the deserters were interviewed by Canadian immigration officer Smith. While immigration officer Smith was interviewing the other two deserters, John, by a fluke, managed to make the phone call to a Vancouver minister that initiated public concern over their eventual deportation. Reverend Phillip Hewett, a Unitarian minister, told John on the phone that "they could not be deported without a proper hearing." Then the immigration officer interrogated him about his manner of entry into Canada, their destinations, identification, etc. According to John Kreeger's testimony, he asked Smith why he was being sent back to the United States and was told by him that the matter had been determined by the RCMP.

At this point there were crucial discrepancies in the testimonies as to whether the RCMP or immigration officer Smith took the initiative in indicating that the three deserters would be turned over to the American officials. Both the RCMP and immigration officers testified that the other agency took the initiative. The judge accepted the version that immigration officer Smith merely called the RCMP to take the deserters away. In any event, the deserters were returned to the custody of two different RCMP constables.

On the circumstances directly leading up to the illegal deportation the judge wrote in his final judgment:

They [RCMP constables] were responding to a call for their attendance; they found an Immigration Officer waiting, also the Complainants whom they had heard mentioned over the air several times as American deserters. There was a border a few yards away and on the other side a waiting military van. These circumstances formed a trap into which these two officers promptly walked.

This sequence of events, including the completion of the interviews of the Complainants, the discovery by Immigration Officer Smith that all RCMP officers had disappeared, the telephone call to RCMP Radio Operator, the exit from the building, the perfectly timed arrival of the police and the commencement of the last act in the play, the walk to the border, was continuous, with an amazing lack of any delay.[13]

During the slow walk across the border the deserters made it quite clear to the RCMP officers that they considered their treatment wholly illegal. On the American side of the border, the Shore Patrol officer immediately took custody of the men and placed them in handcuffs in his van. The transfer of the deserters into American hands ended Judge Stewart's investigation. However, his commission report contains three more important pieces of evidence which he rejected as "irrelevant or unhelpful." According to the judge, "One was capable of interpretation adverse to the RCMP and the other two capable of interpretation adverse to Immigration Officer Smith."[14] Two pieces of omitted information involved important evidence of collusion between the Canadian and American officials and the routine way it is covered up for the records afterwards.

The most important piece of evidence was the testimony of a University of British Columbia student, Mr. Cannon, who happened to be sitting in a police car in the university area on January 25 when he overheard a transmission on its radio that attracted his attention. He testified:

> There was a voice that said they have three deserters in custody and he was asking information as to what to do with them and then there was another voice that came over the radio saying that a rendezvous had been arranged with the FBI and they were to take them over to the immigration officials who would escort them to the border and turn them over to the FBI.[15]

This message had originated from Chilliwack area, undoubtedly relayed by an RCMP radio operator who was in custody of the three deserters. The evidence dealt with a message telephoned to the Douglas border point on the Canadian side by immigration officer Smith within the hour after the return of the three deserters to the United States. The message was recorded by a special inquiry officer in charge of conducting deportation hearings. It read, "RCMP from Chilliwac returned three young U.S. lads back to U.S.A. — illegal entry."[16]

The judge in his report noted that neither immigration officer Smith nor special inquiry officer Booker expressed any surprise that the RCMP should return someone to the United States for illegal entry, and had treated the matter as routine. This was true despite the fact that Smith, after interviewing the deserters, had determined that their entry into Canada had been legal.

However, the rest of the testimony given by officer Booker was omitted from the judge's report. Booker testified to the inquiry that it was a "well-known fact" that Americans had been taken back to the United States, occasionally without having been through the procedures required by law. He said, "I can't name names, but I know it has happened on one or more occasions." He was not surprised when Smith telephoned him and gave him particulars regarding the three Americans so they could be stopped at the Douglas border point if they attempted to reenter Canada. Questioned by the commission counsel, Vancouver lawyer MacEachern, Booker said he gained the impression from Smith that the Americans had entered Canada illegally and therefore were being sent back.

MacEachern: Did you consider this illegal?

Booker: Not particularly.

MacEachern: Why not particularly?

Booker: I believe people have been returned before for illegal entry without going through the formalities of a special inquiry.[17]

Judge Stewart came to the conclusion that the three deserters were unlawfully returned to the United States by RCMP constables in the presence of immigration officer Smith. He exonerated both the RCMP constables and the immigration officer involved by claiming that the constables were under the mistaken impression that they were carrying out an order of the immigration officer. He claimed the immigration officer also was under a mistaken impression that the deserters were under the direction of the RCMP. This conclusion follwed the lines of argument during the testimony; each department tried to prove the other was solely responsible for the removal of the Americans. Don Rosenbloom, lawyer for the deserters, suggested that his case for the deserters could suffice with the sentence, "I accept the RCMP's lawyer's statements when he refers to the role of the Immigration and the Immigration's lawyer when he refers to the role of the RCMP." When the play was fouled up, each department attempted to squirm off the hook by blaming the other, although before they were "caught" in this particular case they had cooperated routinely.

The most important questions remained unanswered by the inquiry. What about the collusion between the American and the Canadian authorities to which all evidence pointed? The judge, by excluding as "irrelevant" the most important piece of evidence concerning the arranged rendezvous with the FBI by the Canadian RCMP and other contributory evidence, concluded that "no Canadian police officer or Immigration official was a party, directly or indirectly, to an arrangement of any kind with the Federal Bureau of Investigation or other American authority relating to the deserters."[18] This was a misleading statement in light of the testimony presented, in my opinion. The judge argued that ignorance, misunderstanding, confusion and coincidence were the reasons for the illegal deportation and that it was all an unfortunate mistake. In his words, it was "an isolated and unplanned incident. . . .The possibility of any combination of events similar to those outlined in this report ever reoccurring to result in a similar or other unlawful act is so remote that it need not be considered."[19] No special recommendations were mentioned in the report. All the officials involved in this incident continued with their regular work with no official censure.

The lawyer for the deserters, the Vancouver Committee, Canadian journalist Clive Cocking and other sympathetic Canadians who followed the events in the newspapers, all have indicated that the inquiry's conclusions were an attempt to whitewash the incident and remove the blame from all Canadian officials and the Canadian government.[20] No one was held accountable for his actions and many of the officials involved in the deportation were portrayed as "victims of circumstances." The inquiry completely ignored any of the established precedents of international law that made it illegal to return political refugees to their country of origin if punishment awaited them there.

After this illegal deportation, all three deserters subsequently escaped from the Navy patrol van a couple of hours after they had been deported. Two of them were recaptured and sent to the military stockade at Fort Ord, California. The third deserter, John Kreeger, managed to evade law enforcement authorities in the United States with support from friends and the underground. Eventually he was helped to return to Canada legally a month later and he testified at the judicial inquiry. Toward the end of the inquiry in March 1970 one of the deserters, Charles Leonard, had gone AWOL again and also had come back to Vancouver to testify at the inquiry and to corroborate Kreeger's testimony. The outcome was a happy one for John after five long years of an underground existence both in the United States and Canada. In the fall of 1973 John was on his way with his other compatriates toward becoming a new Canadian after obtaining landed status under the Immigration Adjustment of Status program.

The importance of the three deserters' case was its public demonstration that in addition to overall surveillance, there was active collusion between the RCMP and low-level officials in the Immigration Department to return refugees, especially deserters, to the American military. Since they did this without legal authority and without approval of higher levels of the Canadian government, explanatory theories to account for these actions must rest largely on the nature of the RCMP and the personal rewards individual officials might have obtained for such acts.

The RCMP is a quasi-military organization, having more authority in certain matters and fewer governmental checks on its actions than its American

FBI counterpart.[21] It has an enormous range of discretion in legal as well as illegal matters, as we have just noted in the deportation case under review. Since the RCMP is a well-disciplined, well-trained organization, the illegal events described could only have taken place under two sets of circumstances: There was either a serious slackness among the senior officers of the force, permitting undisciplined men to take improper action on their own; or there was a climate within the force, for which the senior officers were responsible, which permitted actions outside the policies laid down by the government. The latter explanation seems to be the most likely one.

Journalist Clive Cocking made a strong indictment of both the RCMP and the Canadian Immigration Department. He concluded that arbitrary power was being used against American refugees in Canada in the enforcement of American laws for political crimes.

> The fact that the same policies are employed today against American war protesters without government sanction (if we are to believe Immigration Minister Allan MacEachen) suggests that the RCMP and the Immigration Department have grown accustomed to the exercise of arbitrary power.
>
> What is even worse is that these agencies often seem to be working not for the Canadian government but for Washington. Everyone expects Canadian agencies to cooperate with their U.S. counterparts in normal matters, like the apprehension of criminals but sometimes, consciously or unconsciously, they become Canadian agents enforcing American laws for political crimes.[22]

In these cases the RCMP, in fact, established its own policy on deserters, since the government did not give it any mandate to deport deserters unless it had gone through the established procedures of the deportation hearing and the deserters were found to be present in Canada illegally. In this respect, the RCMP was taking on a political role that displayed greater loyalty to the American FBI than to the formal policy of the Canadian government. The politicization of the RCMP in these matters directly contradicted Canadian government policy that accepted American refugees as ordinary immigrants.

Given this picture of international police collusion to harass them on a continental basis, it is no surprise to learn that many of the deserters returned to the United States rather than stay underground in Canada and continue their fight for landed immigrant status.

Back and Forth Across the Forty-Ninth Parallel

By grouping together answers from my questionnaire it was possible to gain an indication of whether or not an individual successfully adjusted to

Canadian life and intended to remain in Canada. The questions included how a refugee regarded his future and whether or not he was hassled or arrested by Canadian officials. Other factors included whether or not he wanted to return permanently to the United States in the event of amnesty, whether he saw his future plans being carried out in the United States or whether he considered turning himself in to the American authorities.

Only a small minority of men, 17 percent of the total queried, looked toward the United States for their future and also felt they would be likely to return to America in the event of an amnesty. We have already seen that many more deserters were hassled and arrested in Canada than dodgers. Of the 19 men out of 123 who considered turning themselves in to American authorities, all but two were deserters. It was not surprising, therefore, that we found three times as many deserters as draft dodgers unsuccessfully adjusted to Canadian life. Let us look more closely at those refugees who returned to the United States.

It is impossible to estimate the exact number of refugees who returned to the United States; no statistics were kept by either the Canadian or American governments. It could be as many as a few thousand men, many of whom had not been able to obtain landed immigrant status and thus were unable to eke out a living without a work permit. There were also some draft dodgers who came to Canada in 1966 to 1968, before the full development of the resistance movement, who were politically oriented. A small number of them returned to the United States to work in the movement. Some deserters who had become politicized as a result of their desertion experiences and felt that they would prefer to stay in the military to organize from within if they could make their decision over again. They wanted to go back to the United States to help their brothers.

It was the class of downtrodden deserters who were begging an existence and drifting along in Canada who decided to return to the United States and accept their punishment. They became lonely, especially those who were unsuccessful in making contact with the aid groups. They longed for a familiar environment and hoped they would receive minimal sentences. A number of men became disoriented in Canada because they were not used to making decisions for themselves. They were quite young and became involved in situations they were not able to handle. Most of these refugees returned during the first and second coping stages of their adjustment. In Toronto psychiatrist Levine's sample of 24 refugee patients who were having adjustment difficulties, the outcome in three of the cases was a return to the

United States.[23]

Gordon was an 18-year-old Army deserter who gave himself up to immigration authorities in Canada in 1970. He had been in Canada about four months since he had deserted from Fort Riley, Kansas. He told the Canadian police that since he had been in Winnipeg, he had used various drugs, including "speed" and heroin, until he "felt there was no future for him."[24]

Kenny was another deserter who returned to the United States early in 1969. However, unlike Gordon, he escaped once in the United States and decided that however difficult his underground existence in Canada, it was better than a military prison. Kenny came to Canada directly from Fort Dix, New Jersey. He had dropped out of high school after the ninth grade and enlisted in the Army. He first came to Toronto after spending eight months in the military. He was unemployed his first four months in Toronto and then hitchhiked to Vancouver hoping his luck would improve. The Vancouver Committee sent him to one of the deserters' hostels. Kenny could not obtain landed immigrant status because of his low educational level and lack of job skills, so he stayed at the hostel five months. During this time in Canada, he was in communication with his fiancée who was pregnant with his child. Months later, when she had the baby, she pleaded with him to come down to Seattle to marry her. "For awhile I seriously considered coming," Kenny said. "Then I'd think of the risks and thought I'd better save my skin." When the hostel in Vancouver was on the verge of closing down in 1970 and Kenny had no plans and no place to go, his thoughts turned to his fiancée and his child.

> One day I decided that I'd make my way down to Seattle to see my fiancée. She was surprised to see me, as I told her I wasn't going down to see her. It was the middle of April. After we chatted awhile, she said she had to do some shopping and took off to the store. I was sitting in the kitchen having some beer. My fiancée, meanwhile, had left the house and instead of going to the store had gone to a public telephone booth and notified the police that I was a deserter. There was a heavy knock on the door. The police came to take me away. I hadn't been at her place more than an hour and she called the police on me. They took me and booked me into the Fort Lewis, Washington, stockade.

> I played real straight for four days and they eventually gave me a liberty pass. Within the next week and a half I headed north for good this time.

Kenny came back to Vancouver where I interviewed him a second time. He was staying at another refugee hostel that was opened up while he was in the United States. Although his underground existence in Canada continued to be a meager one, at least he was not behind bars.

The newly "politicized refugee" also felt a strong pull from south of the border. These men had become active in exile politics and were dissatisfied with the growing realization that the main political struggle against the war was in the United States. Steve, an Army deserter, became politicized by his act of desertion and was active in the Vancouver American Deserters' Committee. After almost two years in Canada he confessed, "If I had it to do over again and knew what I know now, I think I would stay in the Army and organize GI's." This attitude was also expressed in some of the exile publications that focused on the antiimperialist struggles in America.

This minority of Americans in Canada identified more with other revolutionaries in exile, particularly those South Vietnamese who had also sought sanctuary in Canada, than with their fellow Americans. They referred to themselves as "exiles" and "political refugees." Like their comrades, the South Vietnamese dodgers and deserters, they did not think in terms of becoming Canadians. Just as the Vietnamese deserters said, "We hope that somehow, someday, there will be a Vietnam we can safely go home to," so too this category of American exile was hoping that he could be able to participate in the second American revolution in the motherland.

Doyle was an Army deserter who came to Toronto and then decided to turn himself in to American authorities for what he felt were political reasons. Although his career pattern with the military was atypical, his attitudes and behavior reflected the feelings of many such politicized deserters. He came from a small Midwestern town where his parents were Wallace supporters. When he was 18 he refused to register for the Army on the grounds that "the draft was unconstitutional and illegal." Two and one-half years later when Doyle was 20, a neighbor turned him in for being unregistered. Between the time that he was arraigned and the time of his trial, he joined the Army, but remained unregistered for the draft. Doyle explained his actions.

> My opposition at the time wasn't necessarily to the military. I was opposed to the draft and thought it might be interesting to play a game with them and stay unregistered and still be in the Army. It took me about three days in the army to realize that it would drive me out of my head. So after eight weeks and two days I left.

After he left the military he came to Toronto. Doyle slept in a park for a week before he noticed a sign on a wooden fence by the Vietnam Mobilization Committee. His contact with it led him to obtain aid from the Toronto

Anti-Draft Program. Doyle then became active in the Union of American Exiles. After a number of months working with this group, Doyle made the decision to turn himself in to the military authorities at the Presidio and hitch-hiked to San Francisco. He explained his actions in political terms, "I felt that perhaps I had rendered myself impotent to do anything for the movement. . . by coming to Canada. In this sense, I felt guilty."

Doyle, however, needed only 24 hours of military treatment at the Presidio to decide to escape again:

I was in the Special Processing Detachment at the Presidio. It's limited security there; I walked into the FBI office and turned myself in. I was sitting in their reception room for about half an hour while they checked me out and found out there was a warrant on me. So they came out, told me to stand up, turn around and put handcuffs on me. And I started laughing. It was totally ridiculous. I was turning myself in and they still wanted me handcuffed. And I said, "Wait a minute, fellows," and I decided by that time to leave again.

It seemed to be the height of irony to Doyle that the military would not even allow him to exercise his act of will in making the decision to "return to the fold." This snapped him out of his fantasy that it was possible to bring change from within the military. "I realized that there was really very little one could do from inside the service. As soon as you'd start doing something, they'd put you away." Doyle spent a couple of months wandering around Berkeley, California, at the time of the People's Park controversy there and obtained enough money to return to Toronto. When I met him, he had returned to his organizing and counseling work with the Union of American Exiles and had rationalized that "denying the military the use of bodies" was an important function indeed.

These exiles, like Doyle, felt a strong sense of commitment to the movement in the United States that was working toward revolutionary social changes in the society. They felt a strong sense of guilt that they had "copped out" of the movement and gone to Canada. However, they were not, for the most part, willing to return and quietly accept their jail sentences.

These Americans were sentenced to a unique limbo. They could never become "complete" Canadians in the sense that Canadians who moved to the United States could become "complete" Americans. For what every Canadian possessed and what these refugees lacked was the ability to freely enter the United States at will as visitors. However, many of these refugees who had family and friends in the United States took the risk of returning to celebrate births or mourn deaths for brief visits. Some of these visits ended unfortunately with their arrest by the FBI. The much-publicized case of Ronald Anderson in 1974 was a return that began with calamity, but because of a technicality had a happy ending.

Ronald Anderson deserted the Army in 1968 because of his opposition to the war in Vietnam. After being sent to the Fort Lewis stockade in Washington he escaped and sought refuge in Vancouver. He became a landed immigrant in September 1969. Five years later in August 1974, only a month away from the date he would be eligible to apply for his Canadian citizenship, Ron took a chance and returned to Seattle where his mother lived in order to take care of family business. He had returned to the United States previously with no problems. However, on this occasion a computer check on his British Columbia license by the American customs officials set off a chain of reactions. Ron was arrested by the FBI, transported to the Bellingham jail and then to the Fort Lewis stockade once again. In an investigation of this case, Vancouver lawyer Don Rosenbloom was able to present conclusive evidence that Anderson had in fact been arrested on the Canadian side of the Peace Arch, which sits exactly on the 49th parallel. In the present case he was lucky enough to secure a photo of American customs officials dragging Ron Anderson across the Canadian border into the United States. This picture was snapped by a Vancouver reporter who was off duty and relaxing with his family at the park near the Peace Arch.[25]

The simple fact that Anderson had been removed from Canadian soil mobilized Canadian government officials in Ottawa to request the return of Anderson back to Canada. To them, the issue was one of Canadian sovereignty, which had to be defended. The consul general remarked that this decision had been made "because of the invasion of Canadian sovereignty. We were concerned there had been pursuit of an individual on Canadian soil."[26] Reluctantly, the U. S. State Department ordered the release of Anderson to the custody of Canadian officials and he was returned to his home and family in Mission, British Columbia.

In this particular case the issue of Canadian sovereignty enabled the Canadian government to assert its will successfully. However, an important question in Anderson's case remained unanswered. Why should a military "wanted" notice have appeared when United States officials ran a British Columbia license number through a computer hookup with the United States National Crime Information Center? How did an American computer program get Canadian license numbers in the first place? A British Columbia motor vehicle branch official acknowledged that it was possible there was co-operation in this field of police surveillance between the American FBI and the Canadian RCMP of both countries.[27] The RCMP verified this supposition in a letter to the Britisch Columbia Civil Liberties Association regarding the Anderson case. Mr. Marcus, head of the criminal investigation branch wrote, "In response to your first question, then, 'whether it is the practice of the RCMP to provide United States authorities with information concerning a resident of Canada for any nonextraditable offence,' the answer is clearly: 'yes.' We enquire for the American agenies — and the American agencies enquire for us. The issue of extraditable and nonextraditable, does not enter into either's determination."[28]

The picture that emerges from this consideration of police harassment of American refugees on both sides of the 49th parallel is one of a network of cooperation between American and Canadian authorities, sometimes legal and sometimes not. The importance of this network becomes apparent when we recognize that the police agencies helped to maintain the channeling system whereby dissident American youth opposed to the Vietnam War were allowed to seek exile in Canada. This acted as a safety valve to restrain dissent within the United States. However, Canadian authorities were concerned by the arrival of such volatile youth that added to their already growing concerns with the Canadian youth counterculture. Thus they willingly assisted American authorities in spying on these youth, especially since the functioning of the channeling system required proper information on how many youths were being channeled up to Canada and who they were.

American draft dodgers were relatively less harassed by the RCMP as many had assimilated into Canadian middle-class life-styles. As in many Western countries, the police were primarily utilized by the state to socially control the working class and ignore the crimes of the middle and upper classes.[29] Hence, the very process of differential law enforcement was itself part of the larger channeling pattern that worked to the disadvantage of the poor and working-class youth. By remaining on the fringes of Canadian life until the Immigration Adjustment Act of 1973 and by being forced underground, the deserter would have exposed himself to a greater degree of police harassment. The active collusion between the RCMP and the FBI simply aggravated, often to intolerable levels, what was the normal mode of harassment of the powerless in North American police practices. It was only the fear of endangering Canadian security by infringing on Canadian sovereignty (as in Anderson's case) that made government officials urge restraint on the RCMP's collusion with the American authorities. As the network of collusion also included Canadian and American immigration officials, however, the bureaucracies involved were too cumbersome to properly direct the lower layer of officials. As long as there existed a small minority of American refugees still underground, the probability of abusive practices by the police would remain an issue, surfacing to public view on an intermittent basis. Given these conditions of marginality and harassment, many unassimilated deserters continued to look to some sort of amnesty offering from the United States. They hoped that former President Nixon's "never!" stand on amnesty might give way to a more conciliatory attitude as the American troops pulled out of Vietnam. Yet in 1974, when the new President Gerald Ford was to replace a disgraced President Nixon and grant him unconditional amnesty, he would offer American exiles in Canada only a "conditional clemency." This offer proved to be too meager and too unjust not only for the assimilated dodgers but also for the American deserters who preferred the marginal but legal life in Canada to the punishment that still awaited them in the United States under President Ford's so-called "clemency" program.

NOTES

1.   Lorne Brown and Caroline Brown, *The Unauthorized History of the RCMP* (Toronto: James Lewis and Samuel, 1973).
2.   " Immigration Charge Jails Deserters," *Vancouver Sun,* January 1970.
3.   *Hansard,* Canadian House of Commons Debate, November 23, 1966. First Session, 27 Parliament, pp. 10251–2.
4.   Lorne Brown and Caroline Brown, *Unauthorized History of the RCMP.* More conventional books on this topic include: E. Cloutier, *Law and Order in Canadian Democracy: Crime and Police Work in Canada* (Ottawa: Queen's Printer, 1952); Kenneth McNaught, *The Pelican History of Canada* (Baltimore, Md.: Penquin Books, 1969), see index Canadian Mounted Police.
5.   RCMP Statistics Press Release, November 1969. Reported in *Fellowship Newsletter* (November–December 1969).
6.   Clive Cocking, "How Did the Canadian Mounties Develop Their Unfortunate Habit of Deporting People They Don't Happen to Like?" *Saturday Night,* June 1970.
7.   CBC "Weekend" program January 3, 1971, and "Ex-Agent Alleges Deal on Dodgers," *Vancouver Sun,* January 4, 1971.
8.   Other documented cases are included in an article "RCMP Harassment of U.S. Deserters: A Three Year History," *AMEX* (October–November 1970): pp. 18–19.

9.   The person served with a deportation order has the right to appeal to the Immigration Appeal Board. The Appeal Board Act created an independent board with broader powers in November 1967. It has exclusive appealing jurisdiction and all the protections of a court of record. See Freda Hawkins, *Canada and Immigration*, Immigration Appeal Board — Index, pp. 164—5. After the Adjustment of Status Program (fall 1973), the right of appeal against deportation was curtailed.

10.   *Vancouver Sun*, February 6, 1970.

11.   Judge E.J.C. Stewart, Commissioner of Inquiry, "Report of the Commission of Investigation Relating to Charles Allen Leonard, Earl Hockett, and John Kreeger," submitted to the Solicitor General, Minister of Manpower and Immigration and Minister of National Revenue Customs and Excise, June 1970.

12.   Ibid., p.58.

13.   Ibid., p.34.

14.   Ibid., p.36.

15.   Ibid., p.36—37.

16.   Ibid., p.39.

17.   Testimony of Mr. Booker for the Inquiry, Vancouver, B.C., April 14, 1970.

18.   Judge E.J.C. Stewart, "Report of the Commission," p. 41.

19.   Ibid., pp.42—43.

20.   Clive Cocking, "How Did the Canadian Mounties?" The following newspaper articles appeared on the three deserters' case: "Gov't Probing Deserters' Story," *Vancouver Province*, February 6, 1970; "RCMP Fetch Deserters for Americans," *Georgia Straight*, February 18—25, 1970; "Commission to Probe Case of U.S. Deserters," *Vancouver Express*, February 21, 1970; the *Express* was a temporary newspaper put out by the employees of the *Vancouver Sun* while they were on strike February—April 1970. "RCMP Kidnapping," *"Georgia Straight*, February 25—March 4, 1970; "AWOL Pair Jailed, Third Still Loose," *Express Times*, February 26, 1970; "American Deserter 'Safe' in Canada. 'I Couldn't Stand the Army,' Says 'Kidnap' Victim," *Georgia Straight*, March 4—11, 1970; "Judge Probes Deserters' Case," *Vancouver Express*, March 10, 1970; "U.S. Deserter Testifies: 'Face Deportation, RCMP Man Said',", *Vancouver Express*, "Forgot Deporting Rule,' RCMP Officer Says," *Toronto Globe and Mail*, March 26, 1970; "Officer Says Immigration Man Not Concerned about Deserters," *Toronto Globe and Mail*, March 27, 1970.

21.   Lorne Brown and Caroline Brown, *The Unauthorized History of the RCMP*, chapter 8, pp. 112—19.

22.   Clive Cocking, "How Did the Canadian Mounties?"
23.   Saul Levine, "Draft Dodgers: Coping with Stress, Adapting to Exile,"
American Journal of Orthopsychiatry 42 (April 1972).
24.   *Vancouver Sun,* November 21, 1970.
25.   *Vancouver Sun,* August 24, 1974.
26.   *Vancouver Sun,* August 31, 1974.
27.   *Vancouver Sun,* August 28, 1974.
28.   RCMP letter to B.C. Civil Liberties Association, November 5, 1974
(E 380—2—4).
29.   See Steven Box, *Deviance, Reality and Society* (New York: Holt,
Rinehart and Winston, 1971), pp. 83—91; see references, pp. 91—97.
Donald R. Cressey, *Delinquency, Crime and Differential Association*
(The Hague, Netherlands: Martinus Nijhoff, 1964), p. 50. William J. Cham-
bliss, *Crime and the Legal Process* (New York: McGraw—Hill, 1969),
chapter 6, pp. 84—86. Robert H. Hardt, "Delinquency and Social Class:
Bad Kids or Good Cops;" in *Among the People,* ed. I. Deutscher and E.J.
Thompson (New York: Basic Books, 1968), pp. 132—43.

Amnesty or Exile?: American Refugees Choose Canada

A cartoon by Conrad of the *Los Angeles Times* showed a brass band and assorted government officials standing beside the gate of a United States Army stockade. The caption read: "What if we gave an amnesty and nobody came?"[1] Why, indeed, did only a handful of the estimated 40,000 American exiles in Canada take up President Ford's offer of "conditional clemency"?[2]

Most American exiles remaining in Canada had already obtained landed immigrant status, deserters as well as dodgers, because of the Canadian Immigration Adjustment of Status Program in 1973. The bulk of these young men, in addition, had made successful adaptations to Canada and had assimilated into Canadian social and economic life. The audience that should have been most responsive to the clemency program was the subculture of deserters, most of whom were landed but many of whom were still unassimilated into the Canadian economy. This group was completely disinterested in the punishment awaiting it under "earned reentry." They were also turned off by the lack of clear vindication of the morality of their position taken in opposition to the Vietnam War. In short, they wanted President Ford to do unto

them as he had done unto his predecessor, former President Nixon, no more
and certainly no less.

Undoubtedly under a program of unconditional amnesty more American
exiles would have returned to the United States in 1975, yet probably not as
many as support groups in the United States would like to think. Many
Americans interviewed at the height of the immigration to Canada in 1970,
before amnesty became a political issue, favored such a program in order to
visit their friends and relatives and to travel in the United States, but not to
return to live. This remained the predominant view five years later in 1975
at the height of the amnesty debate after America had suffered a major
political and military defeat in Indochina.

In addition to their interest in seeking justice and the right to travel,
American exiles in Canada supported the movement for unconditional
amnesty in generous support of the many young men living in the United
States whose lives had also suffered from the war when they had agreed to
fight in it. Refugee groups, such as the Toronto and Vancouver exile associations, pointed out that the need for unconditional amnesty actually was
greatest among the hundreds of thousands of men who received less-than-
honorable discharges from the Armed Forces and thus were condemned to a
handicap in their search to obtain a job, veterans benefits and to start their
lives anew in the United States. Thus, as *AMEX* magazine headlined in 1973,
"Amnesty Is not Primarily an Issue of Exile."[3] A global view of those needing unconditional amnesty included: first, the half-million Vietnam veterans
in the United States with less-than-honorable discharges; second, the 200,000
young men estimated to still be living underground in the United States and
third, the exile community of some 40,000 American refugees in Canada.[4]
The wheel had come full circle. It was now the exiles who offered their
support to those who had not fled but had chosen to participate in the war
and who had been burned by their participation in it. This support was indicative of the position that American refugees had carved out for themselves
in Canada by the end of the Vietnam War era, a base secure enough to offer
assistance to their less fortunate compatriots in the United States.

Still, the very assimilation of American refugees into the Canadian economy signified their reintegration into North American capitalism. Clemency
could be identified as yet another example of the channeling process directed
by the state that shaped the lives of draft-age Americans during the Vietnam
War era. The support of unconditional amnesty was seen by American
refugees as the first step in a movement to put an end to this channeling

based on class and to restore full economic and civil rights to the majority of the population in both Canada and the United States. In order to understand this movement, the background of the fight for unconditional amnesty in the Vietnam War era and its antecedents in American history should be known.

Amnesty Precedents in American History

When President Ford unveiled his program of "conditional clemency" for opponents of the Vietnam War and earned reentry for those dodgers and deserters in exile, he did so after granting an unconditional amnesty to former President Nixon for his participation in the crimes related to the Watergate scandal. What was unusual here was not only the political timing of these two announcements, one following on the heels of the other, but also the fact that amnesty for the crimes of a president while in office was unprecedented and thus a radical step for an otherwise conservative politician to undertake. Casting a brief look back at earlier amnesties in American history for deserters and dodgers indicates that President Ford had much more precedent to grant an unconditional amnesty to deserters than to a former president.

The word amnesty comes from the Greek word *amnestia,* meaning "a general overlooking or pardon of past offenses by the ruling authority."[5] It differs from a typical pardon in that it involves a whole class of offenders, in this case draft resisters and deserters already convicted for their actions, as well as a pardon for those men who exiled themselves in other countries before they could be brought to trial.

Amnesty is generally granted only for political or military-related offenses against the state. Political crime is reserved for those violations of the law occurring "when an individual protests the existing social structure."[6] Thus, violation of the conscription system was a political offense by this definition in that it challenged the political actions of the United States government. Draft objectors viewed the Selective Service System as an illegitimately constituted authority whose rules they did not accept. Those men who resisted conscription constituted the largest category of political offenders in the United States during the Vietnam War era.

The purpose of granting amnesty is to promote a reconciliation between the state and its dissidents. According to Arlie Schardt, associate director of the American Civil Liberties Union, amnesty is a discretionary act of a sovereign state and a "decision not to prosecute a class of citizens who may be in conflict with the law for political reasons." This is "the law's way of undoing what the law has done. Unlike a pardon — which applies to an individual who

has been tried and found guilty and thus implies forgiveness rather than forgetting — amnesty relates to an entire class of people."[7]

Thus, in testimony before the Kastenmeier Hearings in the House of Representatives in the spring of 1974, Democratic Congresswoman Bella Abzug
of New York declared: "I submit that a broad amnesty measure would honor
us as a nation and serve our most vital interests. It would heal at least some of
the wounds remaining from this immoral war and would enable us — as a
nation — to utilize one of our most valuable resources, the thousands of
young men and women lost to self-imposed exile."[8]

Amnesty would thus integrate both draft dodgers and deserters back into
the American society. The latter group is of special concern to the state as
it constitutes not just a large group of dissidents but of militarily trained
ones. Hence the alienation of deserters from American society could pose
a threat to the security of the United States.

Such a special threat was foremost in the minds of a number of American
Presidents like Jefferson, Madison, Lincoln, Roosevelt and Truman, each of
whom extended unconditional amnesties during their terms of office to
deserters from a number of American wars, beginning with the Revolutionary
War and continuing through the Civil War and World War II.[9] It is apparent
that the tradition of granting amnesty to American deserters is deeply in-
grained in America's development as a nation.

Amnesty is not unprecedented. It has a long and distinguished tradition in
American history. After almost every military engagement in our history,
whether at home or abroad, this country has extended amnesty to those
who found themselves in conflict with national authority over these wars.
Amnesties can be declared in the United States by Congress, by the President acting with the authorization of Congress, or by the President alone.
Thirty-four amnesties have been proclaimed to date by thirteen American
presidents.[10]

President Ford's amnesty was the thirty-eighth offered by the chief
executive or Congress since the founding of the republic, defining amnesty in
the broadest sense to include several executive pardons as well as legislative
actions by Congress. The first one was proclaimed on July 10, 1795, when
George Washington granted "a full, free, and entire pardon" to those involved
in an insurrection in Pennsylvania against the United States. In explaining this
to Congress Washington said:

For though I shall always think it a sacred duty to exercise with firmness
and energy the Constitutional powers with which I am vested, yet it

appears to me no less consistent with the public good than it is with my personal feelings to mingle in the operations of Government every degree of moderation and tenderness which the national justice, dignity, and safety may permit.[11]

The first amnesty for deserters goes back to 1807 under Jefferson's administration. Almost half of the 38 amnesties proclaimed in American history dealt with rebels from the Civil War and were designed to return full civil and legal rights to former opponents of the United States. As Representative Abzug noted: "When the Civil War ended, America tried no Confederate soldiers for treason, sent no one who had opposed the Union into exile, sent none of the officers and officials of the Confederacy to prison."[12]

The first presidential pardon of violators of the Selective Service Act was by Franklin Roosevelt, who in 1933 granted clemency to some draft dodgers of World War I. This was followed by Harry Truman's pardon of particular draft violators of World War II. However, there is no pardon on record for draft dodgers of the Korean War. Unlike the amnesty for deserters, which tended to be for a general class of persons — not subject to conditions — draft dodgers were subjected to conditional amnesty in the two instances when it was proclaimed.

Thus in 1974 President Ford could look back on two precedents for conditional amnesty of draft dodgers and 10 precedents for both general and conditional amnesties of deserters. President Ford could have cited ample precedent in American history for unconditional amnesty to Vietnam era draft dodgers and deserters had he chosen to do so. Instead, he opted for "conditional clemency" whose main outlines had been foreshadowed in several Congressional bills on amnesty proposed during the five years preceding the presidential proclamation of 1974.

Amnesty in the Early Period (1969–1972): Call for Restoration of Civil Liberties

During the early period the media exaggerated the visibility of those few exiles who took public stands on amnesty. This will become apparent upon examining the initiation of the debate on amnesty in Congress and the reaction of American exiles to this debate.

The Congressional debate on amnesty was part of the larger struggle between the president and the antiwar faction in the House and the Senate that had sought an early end to American military involvement in Vietnam. Early debates, such as Senator Edward Kennedy's hearings in the Senate in 1972, emphasized the right of Congress to grant amnesty, a right recognized since the Civil War because of several congressional pardons exercised during this period. The amnesty bills offered as a result of such hearings were largely seen as devices to educate both the president and the public to the need for ultimate reconciliation with those who violated the law out of moral opposition to the war. Before American prisoners of war could be exchanged there was little prospect of raising the amnesty issue as an immediately serious one. Indeed, the resolution of this issue had to await the end of American military intervention in Vietnam in 1973 and the inauguration of a new president in 1974. It is questionable whether former president Nixon would ever have issued any clemency on the issue of Selective Service and military code violations, let alone amnesty, had he remained in office to complete his second term as president. In his 1972 presidential race against the Democratic opponent, Senator George McGovern of South Dakota, Nixon declared, "The few hundred that deserted this country, the draft dodgers, are never going to get amnesty when boys like yours died. Never!"[13] This statement was representative of his general view on the amnesty question throughout his tenure in the White House. It was against this backdrop of a hard-line executive position that early efforts by moderate congressmen to raise even the question of amnesty seemed quite radical at the time. Such was the public view of the 1969 visit by Congressman Koch to eastern Canada in order to speak personally with American dodgers and deserters. Congressman Koch, Democrat from New York, an opponent of the Vietnam War, was among the vocal minority to raise amnesty as a political demand in the House of Representatives. He was the first United States congressman to visit American refugees in Canada. He wanted to find out who these young people were, why they had emigrated and how they were adjusting to their new lives in Canada. After interviewing men in Toronto, Ottawa and Montreal, Representative Koch concluded:

> For the most part they are sensitive and mature young people who have emigrated from every section of the United States. They have been outraged by our prosecution of the Vietnam War; they have been victimized by the brutality of military training; and they have been alienated by what they see as intolerance and hypocrisy in American society. . . .They feel that America has deserted them by forsaking its own heritage and ideals.[14]

He felt that it was a "shame and disgrace" that America was driving out "its own young men and women of conscience." In a news conference following his return from Canada, Representative Koch commented that "strangely these men are not as concerned with eventual amnesty as I am. It is possible that many, given the option, will never come back."[15]

Despite these misgivings, Representative Koch introduced one of the first amnesty-type bills to the Congress in 1971. The bill sought to broaden the definition of "conscientious objector" to cover opposition to fighting a particular war, rather than all wars in general. This would have given both draft dodgers and deserters a chance to apply for such status, in effect a granting of conditional amnesty.[16]

Senator Edward Kennedy, Democrat from Massachusetts, also was active in this period, urging exploration of the amnesty question in 1969 and holding hearings on the issue in the Senate in 1972.[17] These hearings explored the possibility of a legislative rather than executive amnesty, although the Senate committee was not granted the authority to propose new amnesty legislation. The public input to the hearings was equally balanced between the pros and cons of amnesty, adding to the growing international debate on this question.

The 1972 proposals of Koch and Kennedy were augmented by the bill of Senator Robert Taft, Jr., Republican from Ohio, asking the 92nd Congress to grant conditional amnesty to dodgers but not to deserters.[18] Along with the bill introduced by Representative Bella Abzug, Democrat from New York, to this Congress proposing that American opponents of the Vietnam War be granted unconditional, universal amnesty, the full range of positions on amnesty that would emerge in the 93rd and 94th Congresses was already on the table.

A few prominent individuals in the United States also initiated the amnesty debate with American exiles in this early period. As we mentioned in chapter 5, Tom Hayden, a leading spokesman for the New Left and one of the Chicago Ten Conspiracy, was invited to Montreal by the American Deserters' Committee to be a keynote speaker at the pan-Canadian Conference of Exiles in 1970. Hayden, rather than the exiles, first raised the amnesty issue in Canada. He suggested to these Americans:

> The only way you can be a political force against the U.S. government is to announce that all 70,000 [sic] of you plan to return by whatever means necessary. You must oppose the U.S. as American exiles, not as Canadians or expatriates. You could be 70,000 Eldridge Cleavers. Either you will come home with an amnesty or you'll... return as revolutionaries.

His remarks were intended seriously but were met with complete silence, followed by annoyance by many of those Americans present. Dee Knight, an early draft dodger on the staff of *AMEX* magazine, expressed the political

exiles' opinion at this time, disagreeing with Hayden's analysis that a demand
for amnesty had a "powerful propaganda value." On the contrary, he felt
that "the sickness in the States is evident enough without more propaganda"
and argued against organizing around amnesty as the central issue. It was
foolish to ask for sympathy from a "criminal state." Dee wrote:

> Like other liberal issues, it [amnesty] asks for sympathy and trustworthi-
> ness from the world's most visciously heavy-handed and conniving regime.
> Worse yet, it gives the impression to the *enemy* that the Movement is run-
> ning on nothing more threatening than simpering warmheartedness by
> people who are not capable of shaping their lives themselves. This is ob-
> viously not true, and must never by implied: imperialism must be defeated
> by our strength, not our weakness![19]

Dee also considered it a mistake tactically to make amnesty the central
goal. "What good is it to fight for something we know we can't get?"[20]

Despite lack of support among exile groups, 1970 marked the beginning of
an embryonic but broadly based amnesty movement in the United States
itself. The main proponents were religious groups such as the Fellowship of
Reconciliation, parents groups for amnesty and Reverend Richard Killmer
of the Clergy and Laymen Concerned about Vietnam, which had aided
American refugees both in Canada and Sweden. In the next few years, these
liberal groups focused public opinion on amnesty and made a general call
to the president for "Amnesty and Reconciliation."[21]

Many of these liberal religious groups displayed some optimism that
President Nixon's programed troop withdrawals in 1971 and 1972 were
signs that the war was definitely "winding down." They also threw their
weight behind Senator George McGovern who challenged President Nixon
in the 1972 presidental race. The McGovern campaign raised the amnesty
issue nationally. In the early stages of his campaign he looked favorably
upon amnesty for draft resisters on a case-by-case basis and favored alternative service. However, he did not include deserters in his amnesty proposals.
McGovern attempted to use amnesty to consolidate the grassroots and liberal
opposition to the Vietnam War and was somewhat successful in his efforts.
Later on, as the campaign grew more serious, the amnesty issue was placed
on the back burner as being too controversial.

Refugee scepticism with regard to liberal support for amnesty was expressed in a Toronto conference in January 1972. The press release clearly
enunciated the view that amnesty was premature while the war raged on; in
this context the conference felt it was a misdirected effort.

In a presidential election year, the emotionally charged "amnesty" issue appears to be becoming a political football tossed about among candidates searching for votes. We reject this kind of political smokescreen of the main issue before the American people — an escalated war, not a war allegedly "winding down."[22]

The Conference also made it clear that the terms in which amnesty was being discussed both in the Congress and by McGovern were punitive and therefore morally unacceptable. In the same press release it stated:

We reject the current"amnesty" proposals because they do not include the same provisions for deserters from the Armed Forces as they do for draft dodgers, they all have a punitive string attached called "alternative service" and they all imply guilt on our part when we were the ones who have refused to commit the crime.

The alternative that was proposed was the "restoration of civil liberties" for all those persons charged and convicted who incurred penalties as a result of the Vietnam War. The Conference put together a position paper analyzing the class distinctions between draft dodgers and deserters. It stated that "all deserters must be included in any restoration of civil liberties. . . . In terms of social class, deserters have the justifiable claim to a full restoration of civil liberties as they have carried the worst part of the load."[23] The Conference concluded by refusing to accept the criminal label and pointed the finger at the real criminals "who perpetrated the crime called the Indochinese War." This position of restoration of civil liberties was an embryonic version of what in the later period became the position for "universal and unconditional amnesty."

Amnesty in the Later Period (1973—1976): Call for Amnesty with No Strings Attached

In the later period of the development of the amnesty movement, Congress played a prominent role. By the beginning of 1973 American troops were on their way home. The amnesty issue thus took on a seriousness that had been lacking in its earlier more educative phase. Now the emphasis was on how to offer a means for resocializing the dissident young men. As might be expected, opinion on this question ran the full gamut from unconditional amnesty on the Left to punishment without mercy on the Right.

The bills offered in the 93rd Congress in 1973—74 showed this diversity of opinion.[24] Representatives Abzug of New York and Ron Dellums, Democrat from California, presented bills to the House that would have recognized the need for an unconditional amnesty, pardoning not only American exiles abroad but also the half million men of largely working-class origin that had received less-than-honorable discharges during the Vietnam War era. The intent of the bill was to "bring them home."[25] It was felt by the sponsors that nothing short of general amnesty would recognize the justice of the exiles' antiwar posture.

Many congressmen representing largely middle-class constituencies took the middle-of-the-road position. This was a call for conditional amnesty for draft dodgers with up to two years of alternative service, generally recognizing that a short term would do, even as short as three months. Deserters would not be included, as their "crime" was deemed to be far more serious; their abdication of the pledge to fight for their country seemed somewhat more reprehensible. In the Senate, Robert Taft, Jr., of Ohio offered the only Senate bill on amnesty supporting this position of conditional amnesty. In the House such a position was supported by bills sponsored by Representatives Koch of New York and McCloskey, Republican from California.

Finally, some Congressmen felt that no amnesty should be offered at all. The Veterans of Foreign Wars (VFW) supported this position, presenting a critique of amnesty from a right-wing populist view.[26] They recognized that "sons of the poor fight wars for the rich" and that it was an "elitist war," but they felt that the commitment to the nation had to be honored. Such a position garnered more respect among the Canadian exile community than did the liberal conditional amnesty position, a stance the exiles viewed as being a typical liberal "cop-out." In their turn, the VFW indicated that they held in greater respect those antiwar protestors who went to jail in defense of their beliefs rather than the dodgers and deserters who fled the country in opposition to the war.

The various congressional initiatives during the 93rd Congress culminated in the Kastenmeier hearings. Representative Robert Kastenmeier, Democrat from Wisconsin, presided over the subcommittee on Courts, Civil Liberties and the Administration of Justice of the House Judiciary Committee. In the spring of 1974 this subcommittee heard testimony from congressmen who had introduced bills on amnesty, the Departments of Justice and Defense, the Selective Service establishment and spokesmen of the amnesty movement in the United States and abroad. This movement contained a diverse number of political views under its banner from the radical antiwar GI's to the religious groups, staunch liberal civil libertarians and even a few political conservatives. Unlike the earlier hearings of Senator Kennedy's subcommittee, the 900-page document reporting the House hearings[27] indicated that they were clearly slanted in favor of granting amnesty. The issue in 1973–74 no longer was amnesty, yes or no, but what the nature of the amnesty should be and for whom it should be offered.

Much of this continuing congressional debate and pending legislation was subsequently preempted by President Ford's proclamation in September 1974. However, the poor response to this offer of "conditional clemency" indicated that further hearings by the Kastenmeier committee were necessary in the 94th Congress in 1975/76 to reconsider alternative approaches to the problem of reconciling all Americans to the end of the war. President Ford's approach was generally similar to the Taft–Koch proposals calling for conditional amnesty for dodgers, except that the president broadened the scope to include deserters as well. The inadequacy of this approach was revealed by the small number of young Americans affording themselves of its opportunity. Despite the lengthy discussion of the amnesty issue by Congress and the adoption by the president of the moderate proposal with the broadest base of support in the nation at the time, the congressional effort in this sphere did not meet with success when implemented by the president. The best that could be claimed by Congress was that it had educated the public and the president to the critical issues of amnesty. The one audience that conditional clemency did not reach was that of the exiles themselves and their supporters in the United States.

After the Paris accord of January 1973 membership in the religious, civil libertarian and other new groups focusing on the amnesty issue swelled into a new movement. It incorporated the remnants of the sagging antiwar movement and many new persons who had never been part of that movement. Individuals and groups joined for universal and unconditional amnesty. Those who raised their voices the loudest and carried the most respect and influence had arrived at their position in close interaction with young men who were in exile in foreign countries or were war objectors at home. Reverend Richard Killmer, director of the Special Ministry, pressured the National Council of Churches into adopting a policy statement in December 1972 which allowed that "genuine reconciliation demands that amnesty be granted to all who are in legal jeopardy because of the war in Indochina." The National Council of Churches, representing 31 Christian communities with a membership of 42 million in the United States, went on record as supporting "a universal and unconditional amnesty for draft resisters and deserters in exile and underground, those in prison or military stockade and those who were subject to prosecution for violation of the draft or military law."[28] In addition, the National Council of Churches indicated its support of Vietnam era veterans with less-than-honorable discharges and those who had committed civilian acts of resistance to the war. "We view amnesty not as a matter of forgiveness, pardon, or clemency, but as a 'blessed act of oblivion'. Reconciliation further requires creating the possibility of new lives for those Americans hurt by the war in Indochina." Another key constituency in the amnesty movement consisted of the civil libertarians. Under the direction of Henry Schwarzchild, Project Amnesty, initiated early in 1973, was one of the major projects of the American Civil Liberties Union (ACLU) in favor of universal and unconditional amnesty.[29] Direct action and conferences were major strategies of the ACLU to publicize its position on amnesty.

By the beginning of 1973 Canadian exile groups had reversed their earlier 1970 position and joined forces with this growing American movement. In the early spring of 1973, ACLU's Project Amnesty sponsored a conference in Washington, D.C., together with the National Council of Churches, the Vietnam Veterans Against the War/Winter Soldier Organization (VVAW/ WSO) and the National Students Association, to gain a wider public following and pressure congressmen. All of the groups across the country working for a universal and unconditional amnesty were invited. However, the Americans in exile were conspicuously absent since they could not travel in the United States without courting possible arrest.

These exiles decided to sponsor their own International Conference of Exiles complementary to that of the ACLU in order to publicly establish their position on amnesty. Paris was selected as a suitable location by American exiles in Europe. It was considered a good site to hold an open conference to define the state of exile within the context of the demand for a lasting peace in Indochina as the conference would be held simultaneously with the Paris peace negotiations. The sponsoring groups consisted of *AMEX* magazine from Toronto, *Up From Exile* based in Stockholm and *Safe Return*, a New York-based group working for unconditional amnesty. The exiles were naive enough to think they would receive good media coverage as a result of the Paris peace negotiations and the significance of the amnesty issue. However, it turned out by necessity to be a clandestine meeting with little publicity; the French government banned any type of public meeting at the insistence of American government officials present in Paris.[30]

The delegation from Canada consisted of Dee Knight, Jack Colhoun and Bill Singer on the staff of *AMEX* and Larry Svirchev, an original member of the Montreal ADC. They met with the representatives of the European amnesty groups despite their disappointment with the official harassment that necessitated a major reshaping of their original plans. French philosopher Jean Paul Sartre declared his support of the exiles' goals in an open letter to the American press.[31] A group of French citizens supported the aims of the exile groups and managed to hold a press conference attended by French lawyers, the president of the League for the Rights of Man and an American GI on active duty. Steve Rothstein, a captain in the United States Air Force stationed in Germany, publicly declared his support for the exiles' demand for amnesty. Captain Rothstein's presence was especially significant in that it highlighted the alliance shared by exiles with the GI movement both in their earlier contacts and in their present movement. On the amnesty issue the exiles and GIs joined ranks and were considered the "radical wing" of the movement that took a strong antiimperialist position.

Although their public conference did not materialize, the exiles drafted their first statement in support of universal and unconditional amnesty. This resolution was passed at a World Conference on Vietnam held in Rome a few days later. The Resolution on American War Objectors of this conference concluded:

> Therefore, the World Conference on Vietnam reminds the President of the United States not to ignore the spirit of the cease-fire treaty and to grant UNIVERSAL AND UNCONDITIONAL AMNESTY for all Americans suffering a loss of their rights as citizens because of their resistance to participation in this war.
>
> Secondly, the conference appeals to all democratic organizations and all personalities to continue to press for POLITICAL ASYLUM for American war resisters until such time as they may live freely in the United States.[32]

Thus the Paris resolution adopted in Rome publicly reversed the exiles' earlier position not to speak directly to the question of amnesty. It also placed the issue at the outset in an antiimperialist perspective, recognizing the class implications that amnesty raised. At subsequent conferences the American refugees in Canada formed a Coalition of American War Resisters, consisting of former aid and exile groups. This coalition adopted "Unity Statements" in December 1973 and the fall of 1974, reasserting the earlier position enunciated first in Paris.[33]

The individual exiles and exile groups in Canada publicly articulating statements on amnesty were even a smaller minority of the entire American refugee community than those persons active during 1970 at the height of the American emigration. Only nine aid groups were functioning in this late period, and with a much reduced staff.

In May 1973, a new peak was reached in the movement for unconditional amnesty. At a conference held in early May in Washington, D.C., a new umbrella coalition of all amnesty groups, under the banner of the National Council for Universal Unconditional Amnesty (NCUUA) was formed. This national organization soon acted as the central liaison for more than 50 groups in the United States and abroad. Its statement of purpose read:

> The purpose of the NCUUA is to mobilize the American people to work for a universal and unconditional amnesty and to educate them concerning the structures and institutions that created the war in Southeast Asia. The Council is committed to working for universal and unconditional amnesty for all persons suffering disabilities because of opposition to the United States involvement in the war in Southeast Asia, to the draft, and to the military.[34]

NCUUA was run by a 12-person steering committee made up of six representatives of those in need of amnesty (veterans with less-than-honorable discharges, GIs, civilian resisters, exiles, draft resisters in prison, families of all these) and six representatives of organizations supporting amnesty. Its major functions were to establish a national clearinghouse and a network of information-sharing about amnesty activities through its bimonthly publication *Amnesty Update*.[35] It also served as a coordinating center for its member groups by developing a speakers bureau, regional conferences, a funding clearinghouse and, most importantly, building nationwide mobilizations on the issue through devices like Veterans' Week. It set up most of these functions in the first year of the operation.

Conferences held in the formative stages of NCUUA established its priorities and the strategies necessary to implement them. The Amnesty Action Conference held in Toronto was a significant meeting in which 125 delegates representing all the 50 national, regional and local organizations participated in the shaping of strategies toward reaching their shared perspectives. It was felt that the amnesty movement should emphasize the political issues of amnesty and related war issues rather than morality. This followed logically from the position that amnesty was not a pardon and that no crime had been committed in resisting United States aggression in Indochina. Another important strategy was that the struggle should be focused in the United States and not abroad, since the majority of people in need of amnesty were still in the motherland. Stemming from this recognition, it was strongly emphasized that minority and working-class people be at the center of the struggle. This meant involving the 560,000 vets with less-than-honorable discharges from the military as well as the 13,000 deserters and AWOLs still at large underground in the United States.[36] This position also reflected the fact that the VVAW/WSO had the largest delegation, including 30 GIs from 15 regions of the United States, at this conference. The overall strategy placed the amnesty proponents within the context of an antiimperialist movement in the United States. They were fighting against racism and unemployment, both of which accompanied the less-than-honorable discharge held by many minority veterans who had borne the brunt of the war.[37]

In addition, NCUUA decided to focus on mass organizing at the community level and was adverse to proposals and strategies that would split the various groups along class and racial lines. It was clear that universal, unconditional amnesty would come from the American people exerting pressure on the government.

At these NCUUA conferences, American refugees in Canada represented only a handful of the political activists who were involved in the amnesty campaign. It was clear in both numerical and social terms that amnesty was not a high priority for the majority of American exiles in Canada. The political exiles in their conferences and interviews with the media repeatedly stressed the higher priority of amnesty for the over half a million Vietnam veterans with less-than-honorable discharges and the large number of war resisters still living underground in the United States.

How did the majority of the refugees in Canada view the amnesty debate in the United States and how did it relate to their lives? At the height of the American immigration to Canada in 1970, I asked 123 refugees about their feelings regarding amnesty. An overwhelming majority, 86 percent of the men, wanted to see amnesty granted, although the same men stated that they would not consider returning to the United States to live if amnesty were granted. What were some of the reasons these men gave for not wanting to return?

In a letter to the editor of the liberal Canadian magazine *Saturday Night*, a draft dodger living in Toronto in 1970 wrote:

It's a relief to live in a country where the people, on the whole, have a sane attitude on world affairs. While living in California, I sometimes had the feeling that I was surrounded with mass insanity. I believe Canada to be the best of all countries to live in. Even if amnesty were granted to draft dodgers, I would never return.[38]

Vance Gardner, an Army deserter who was a counselor for the Montreal Council to Aid Resisters, commented, "There have been guys I knew who were granted deferments or conscientious objectors status while up here, but they found Canada a much better place to be, for themselves and their politics." Many Americans like Vance made new lives for themselves in Canada, experimenting with their new found freedom in life-styles. They were most reluctant to relinquish these freedoms. Ed Miller, from New York City, came to Montreal 18 months before he received his draft notice to report for induction. He was working in a hospital and doing volunteer work with the Montreal office of the War Resisters' League when I interviewed him. He declared emphatically, "I don't think I'd want to go back. Not to live there. I've settled in here and I just wouldn't want to face that New York treadmill again. A lot of guys have married Canadian girls and have no intention of ever leaving." Eric Harms, a Navy deserter who spent a couple of weeks in one of the largest sanctuaries in Honolulu with other AWOLs before coming to Canada, concurred with Ed's opinion, although he had only been in Canada for a few months. "Amnesty would be nice," Eric said, "but I have absolutely no intention of going back to the States to live, amnesty or no. You know, it'd be cool to go down and visit. But as far as permanent residence, I consider myself a Canadian. I want to be a Canadian. I think it's one of the few places where there's any hope."

During the early period (1969–72), the majority of the refugees did not consider amnesty a realistic possibility and could not see themselves returning south of the 49th parallel to resume their lives in the United States. After America signed the Paris peace agreement in January 1973, amnesty proposals were on the congressional drawing boards. Yet, despite a movement for unconditional amnesty in the United States, most refugees in Canada had not changed their feelings on amnesty from that of the early period.

The issue of amnesty did cause some unsettled pressures and strains to surface in the lives of American refugees in Canada. Psychiatrist Saul Levine cited the case of an American student who had completed his studies in Canada, married a Canadian, became a professor at a Canadian university and considered his future to lie wholly in Canada. With the return of American troops from Vietnam his family and professional colleagues in the United States began to call upon him to return as well. Second thoughts about his apparently firm decision to make a life in Canada placed a great strain on his marriage. Dr. Levine also observed in his relations with American refugees an increased sense of anger in 1973, directly related to their realization of an enhanced possibility of returning to America in the amnesty route. It was

anger at Canada for its often indifferent or even hostile reactions, anger at themselves for the original refusal or for current regret, or anger at fellow exiles who promoted amnesty or who returned to the U.S. under other conditions. He observed that the anger was related to the attitude of the American public that everything connected with the "ended" war should be forgotten coupled with an implicit denial of the meaning of refusal to serve in a war that supposedly was no longer being fought.[39]

After the Vietnam peace agreements were signed, most of the American refugees continued their lives in Canada as before, not anticipating any major interruptions. Even Ron Anderson, who became publically known as a result of his kidnapping by American officials, resumed his life where he had left off upon his release in August 1974. He returned to his wife and son in Mission, British Columbia, where he had spent the last five years. He resumed his job as a carpenter with a construction company working on a senior citizens' housing project. He applied for Canadian citizenship about the time President Ford announced his amnesty program and had no plans to move back to the United States. According to Ron:

I'm a felon in the eyes of the American government, but even if I weren't I wouldn't go back. If they granted total, unconditional amnesty, gave me a free ticket home and threw in five hundred bucks, I'd find some excuse not to go back. I can't think of a single inducement to return.... The U.S.A. is renowned for its mouthings of being the greatest, the freest, the most totally integrated, and the richest in the world. But I've encountered more freedom in this country than in the U.S.A. I don't think of myself as an exile. I am home. I think of the U.S. as something I've outgrown.[40]

A reporter for the *Los Angeles Times* came north to Canada in the spring of 1973 expecting to find American exiles anxious to come home. Instead he was forced to write a story entitled "Not Many Care About Amnesty." He reported that in the ten days he spent in Vancouver there was only one of nearly three dozen refugees he interviewed who admitted any "fleeting wish to go home permanently."[41] Typical of most comments were those of Marshall Van Duesen, who used to counsel refugees for the Vancouver Committee. He was a draft dodger who came to Vancouver in April 1969. He stated:

I'm not opposed to an amnesty, of course, but I'm not asking for one either. Personally, I just don't give a damn. Vancouver is home to me now and I don't even want to visit the States. I'm not interested in any kind of amnesty but an unconditional one, and I'm not very interested in that. What burns me is the attitude that we're criminal. That's the attitude of people who have no principles themselves. . . .[42]

Most of the refugees were not quite as bitter as Marshall. Those who still had close ties with family and friends in the United States mainly wanted to see an unconditional, universal amnesty so that they could have free access to both sides of the border. In addition they felt that amnesty would vindicate the justice of their opposition to the Vietnam War.

Foremost in these individuals' desires not to return to the United States to live was their involvement in their new lives in Canada. Three-fourths of the refugees in my own questionnaire sample looked toward Canada in terms of their future plans. All of these men felt very positive and optimistic toward their future plans. Mark, a deserter who had been in Vancouver for over a year, said, "The longer I'm here, the more my friends are here. And the more I become involved and identify with here, the more the United States fades from my memory."

The image of the United States as seen through the eyes of these young men was bitter, however. While they felt optimistic regarding their own futures, most were very pessimistic about the future of the United States. Bob Farrell, a 22-year-old who deserted from the Army in 1969 indeed had reason to feel bitter. Both of his brothers had fought in Vietnam and were medically discharged. He deserted after receiving an order to fight there. "I'd go back to visit my brothers and my mother," Bob said. He quickly added, "But I don't think I'd want to raise a family there. There's no freedom. My country has not lived up to its Constitution. I wouldn't go back to live."

An overall view of the American refugee community in the fall of 1974, before the clemency offer of President Ford, would be largely one of well-adapted immigrants, most of whom were on their way to becoming or had just become new Canadians. In addition, there were a handful of political exiles, actively organizing around the issue of amnesty. These refugees were in favor of unconditional amnesty in order to restore their own civil liberties by ending their fugitive status and to see justice upheld. Upon this rather complacent and assimilated community of American refugees in Canada, President Ford's offer of "earned reentry" fell largely on deaf ears.

President Ford Proclaims "Conditional Clemency"

As might have been expected from such a consummate politician, when President Ford chose to act on the amnesty issue he did so in the grand political manner. Unfortunately the results were less than a lesson in political savoir faire. President Ford linked the issue in the public mind closely with the unconditional amnesty of former President Nixon so that most Americans saw it as a political quid pro quo, perhaps a payment for having been selected for vice-president by Nixon. This apparent link eventually disturbed President Ford himself, for he found it necessary to go before the House to absolve his actions of such intentions.

The program for amnesty President Ford settled on was largely a version of the moderate proposals Senator Taft and Representative Koch had been making for several years. The president chose to call it "conditional clemency." It provided an "earned reentry" back into American life for the dissidents of the Vietnam War era and it was designed to appeal to middle Americans. It required service by those who had denied their service to the state and it required a "reaffirmation of allegiance" to the United States.

The program envisioned five categories of persons who qualified.[43]

1. Persons convicted by federal courts of violating the selective service laws by refusing induction and the like.
2. Persons convicted by military courts of desertion, absence without leave or missing a military movement.
3. Veterans who hold certain kinds of less-than-honorable discharges because of desertion, absence without leave or missing a military movement.
4. Persons who have (or may have) violated the selective service laws but have not been convicted, whether or not they are fugitives.
5. Persons who have (or may have) violated the military laws against desertion, absence without leave or missing a military movement but have not been convicted, whether or not they are fugitives.

The clemency program was organized into a Presidential Clemency Board to service the convicted felons and veterans with less-than-honorable discharges in the first three categories. However, out of more than half a million men receiving such discharges, the board was set up in such a way that only 100,000 were eligible to apply.[44] The Department of Justice took care of the draft dodgers and others in the fourth category and the Department of Defense dealt with deserters and others in the fifth category. The Selective Service System implemented the "alternative service" for all five groups of qualified applicants.

Under the program, the draft dodger applied for conditional clemency and then put in his alternative service under the supervision of the Selective Service System. He waived all his Constitutional rights after surrendering to a United States attorney. Hardships were to be taken into account, but in the words of the American Civil Liberties Union, the categories of "mitigating factors...emphatically appeared not to include sincere antiwar sentiments."

The deserter who wished to qualify for clemency also had to sign a "reaffirmation of allegiance" when he surrendered to the military base at Fort Benjamin Harrison in Indiana. He had to pledge a maximum of two years of alternative service. He was then processed out of the Army in about a day and given an "undesirable discharge." He then had to report to the Selective Service and perform his alternative service before he could obtain a special "clemency discharge." Such a discharge was also obtained by the Vietnam veteran who petitioned the Presidential Clemency Board. The proclamation was worded in such a way as to offer the possibility of a "deserters' loophole" whereby the deserter would declare his intent to do alternative service. He could then decide to retain the undesirable discharge from the Army without actually doing the alternative service to obtain the clemency discharge. However, in the ACLU's opinion, legal prosecution of those deserters who wanted to live in the United States might still be possible despite the so-called loophole. The Defense Department acknowledged that the military used "narrower standards" than the Justice Department or Presidential Clemency Board in the determination of length of alternate service a man would serve to win a clemency discharge. The ACLU filed a lawsuit on behalf of five deserters in Canada. They charged that the clemency program denied the deserter the right to appear before the review board and forced him to sign a confession.[45] With three departments handling cases under totally different criteria, the program was bound to be fraught with bureaucratic inequalities.

Both the draft dodger and deserter who had landed immigrant status or Canadian citizenship possibly were excluded from the clemency program, which specifically prohibited aliens and Americans naturalized in another country from taking advantage of the program. In addition, those refugees who had become Canadian citizens were further penalized by being denied visitors entry into the United States as "undesirable aliens" under the American Immigration Act.[46]

In the opinion of the ACLU another problematic aspect of the clemency program was that it would actually entail more hardship for many exiles than was legally necessary for them to obtain their civil rights. The ACLU attempted to alert exiles to that fact through their repatriation counseling.

Many men who think they have violated the law did not actually do so;

the violations of others were never formally noticed by the draft system; among those whom the draft system considered delinquent and referred to the Justice System for prosecution, nine out of ten were never indicated by the federal authorities because of violations of laws and regulations on the part of the selective service system that would have made a conviction impossible; of those indicted, as many as two-thirds had their indictments dismissed by the courts or were acquitted. The likelihood is substantial, therefore, that persons who think they are in category 4 may have legal defenses to the draft violation charges that can be successfully advanced by their attorney and that would make their submission to the clemency program, with its punitive conditions, unnecessary.[47]

In January 1975 the Justice Department published a list of approximately 6,000 draft evaders still under indictment, under the pressure of ACLU demands.[48]

In summary, then, the main legal organization advising American exiles on President Ford's clemency program, the ACLU, counseled exiles and others eligible for the program not to accept it. The ACLU stated:

We consider the "clemency program"... offensive in its moral and political assumptions and outrageous in its implementation. The Ford "clemency" program is worse than no amnesty at all. It is punitive and demeaning. Most of those who fall under the provisions of the "clemency" have better legal options outside the program than within it.[49]

It is not surprising in light of these comments that the exile community in Canada would respond to President Ford's offer mainly with hostility.

The Exile Community Responds

American refugees in Canada responded on three fronts to President Ford's clemency program: by collective boycott, legalistic subversion and by personal protest. Immediately following the announcement of the program in September 1974 an International Conference of Exiled Americans was held in Toronto. This was the largest gathering of exiles since the pan-Canadian conference of 1970. Over 200 exiles, mainly from Ontario and Quebec, attended in addition to delegates from exile groups in Sweden, France and England. They unanimously called for a boycott of President Ford's "earned reentry" plan in order to subvert politically a program that they regarded as "punitive repatriation." They also reiterated their demand for a universal, unconditional amnesty for all classes of persons affected adversely by the Vietnam War. Their boycott was supported by NCUUA south of the border. Gerry Condon, editor of *AMEX* in 1974, was a deserter from the Green Berets, a

Special Forces unit of the United States Army. He spent his first two years of exile in Sweden and came to Toronto in 1972. His response to President Ford's announcement was representative of many refugees' comments at this time. Writing for the *Los Angeles Times*, Gerry said:

> I am not the only exile already on record as believing that the very reason the question of amnesty was raised so early in the Ford administration was precisely to set the stage for an early, full pardon for Mr. Nixon. This cynical attempt to play off Mr. Nixon's very real criminality against our conscientiously caused legal jeopardy is just one more attempt at cover-up —and not a very good one.
>
> Though we generally reject the concept of "earned reentry" to the U.S., the revival of nationwide discussion of amnesty has aroused in us both hope and anxiety.[50]

Speaking in Toronto, Gerry stated that President Ford's statement was "no way to establish a reconciliation" with the Canadian refugees.[51]

Dee Knight was a representative for the refugees on the NCUUA board. He declared that the presidential statement "is not what we've been looking for....This is what we refused in January 1972...." He felt, "It won't be of interest to many war resisters in Canada," and declared that acceptance of President Ford's offer "would divide the forces of amnesty and disconnect them from the question of the criminality of the Vietnam War."[52]

The boycott of the clemency program promoted by the exiles was successful. The overwhelming majority, more than 80 percent of both American refugees in Canada and eligible persons in the United States rejected the clemency offer. President Ford's "conditional clemency" clearly was a "dismal failure."[53]

According to Larry Martin, counselor for the Vancouver Committee, only 34 American refugees from British Columbia registered with the clemency program. Thirty of them were deserters who were processed at Fort Benjamin Harrison in Indiana. Only four draft dodgers who had been indicted applied to Goodell's Clemency Board. This number was practically insignificant for British Columbia, a province with a considerable exile population, estimated at about 7,000. The number of exiles who took advantage of President Ford's program from other parts of Canada was equally low. According to Larry, even those 34 American refugees from British Columbia who had returned had no intention of reestablishing roots in the United States. They all wanted to come back and resume their lives in Canada. Thus, whether the exile chose to respond or to ignore President Ford's clemency program, he intended to remain permanently in Canada. This was due in part to the shabbiness of the alternate service part of the clemency program. Because of the recession in the United States in 1975, jobs were hard to find. The Selective Service System could not secure any reasonably decent work for the returnees to perform for their alternative service. Describing the job of one American exile who returned to the United States from British Columbia, Larry explained:

> He called me recently and said he just couldn't stand it. He was working for $2 an hour as an orderly and couldn't support his family.

> And with this economic situation there aren't many jobs that fit the category of alternative service, so it has got to the stage where the draft boards are saying, "Don't call us, we'll call you," when people turn themselves in.[54]

Furthermore, according to Larry, most refugees could clear up their cases through legal means, even if they had been indicted since "the government is so willing to rid itself of us dissidents." Larry used himself as a case in point:

> I was issued an indictment for draft evasion back in 1969, which is when I headed for Vancouver. However, due to Supreme Court decisions and other technicalities it is possible that a large portion of our cases can be cleared. Just last week [January 15, 1975] my Los Angeles lawyer informed me he cleared my case, so I can't even speak publicly again as a *bona fide* exile.

In January 1975 President Ford decided to extend the deadline for his clemency offer due to the poor response. He attempted to reach the war objectors through a massive advertising campaign in order to increase the number of returnees. Letters from Goodell's Clemency Board were sent to those resisters who had been indicted by the government, emphasizing the leniency with which the board had handled the first 12 men who took advantage of "earned reentry."

Michael received such a personal letter from Goodell. He was from Seattle, Washington, and had come to Vancouver in 1970 after his third indictment. He had been an activist in the antiwar movement. After his appeal to the United States Supreme Court was rejected, he went underground for a few months in California and then decided to go to Canada. Of President Ford's program he commented, "I don't want to submit to this board as I consider it to be illegitimate in that it represents a criminal government. I don't consider my actions to be criminal."

Even the American public at large was not satisfied with President Ford's program. In a national Gallup Poll taken in November 1974, 41 percent of the polled population indicated its support for unconditional amnesty for Vietnam draft resisters and deserters.

Some members of the exile community in Canada used the 15-day grace period allowed by the clemency program to return to the United States without fear of arrest and obtain an undesirable discharge outside of the program. This enabled them to regularize their status in the United States without adding to the number of returnees, thus subverting the clemency program by a legalistic dodge. As Larry Martin explained it, an American deserter who wanted to obtain an undesirable discharge in the United States could do so under the "deserters' loophole" in the clemency program and then return to Canada. However, he might be jeopardizing himself, according to ACLU legal opinion, by promising that he would perform alternative service to obtain the clemency discharge and then not doing so. A legalistic dodge that would be safer for him would be to return to an American Army base known to give a quick, undesirable discharge to returning deserters and thus avoid the necessity of alternate service. Such an Army base was in Fort Dix, New Jersey. Unfortunately, the deserter who returned to the United States was subject to immediate arrest if recognized as such. However, the 15-day grace period under the clemency program offered an opening analogous to the "deserters' loophole." The deserter in Canada could register his intention to surrender under the terms of the clemency program. Armed with his orders from the Army to report to Fort Benjamin Harrison in Indiana where all the deserters were being processed under the program, he would enter the United States for his 15-day grace period. Instead of going to Indiana, however, he would go to New York City to receive the latest legal advice from the ACLU. Then he would report to Fort Dix where he received his undesirable discharge without being asked whether he had returned to the United States under the clemency program. Larry Martin indicated that in the few months since September 1974 and the initiation of the clemency program, he had been working 10 hours a day processing 150 American deserters in British Columbia through the Fort Dix shuttle. "Those ones [deserters] didn't have to do any clemency stockade time, alternative service or take a loyalty oath. . . Just three days being processed and that was it."[55]

The next step in most cases was to return to Canada where the economic handicap of having an undesirable discharge from the United States Army would not be as severe as in America itself. This was quite satisfactory for most of them. According to Larry, "since just about all of them plan to return to Canada to live, they are landed immigrants but want to obtain visiting privileges and reunite with their families in the United States from time to time." Still other American exiles used the 15-day-grace period to return to the United States and visit their lawyers and their families. A few individuals also returned to the United States for 15 days in order to confront the amnesty issue and personally protest President Ford's program. They also were interested in politically subverting it. One such person was Bill Meis, a draft evader living in Canada who was originally from Decatur, Illinois. He returned with his wife and two children with the aid of the Safe Return Amnesty Committee, the same group that assisted other exiles like the American deserter in Sweden, John David Herndon.[56] Bill traveled to Washington despite the possibility of his arrest to confront the bureaucracy and refuse alternative service. He publicly called for total, unconditional and universal amnesty and declared: "I have never been disloyal. The President demands that I perform involuntary servitude, even though the Constitution clearly forbids such treatment. I cannot accept these proposals."[57]

Steve Grossman was another draft resister who temporarily came back to the United States to challenge President Ford's "earned reentry" program. After refusing induction into the Army he was indicted and headed for Canada. He had spent two years in exile in Toronto and risked arrest in returning to the United States. Ironically, Steve had already served more than two years of the public service required by the earned reentry program. Three of them he had spent in the Peace Corps on a draft deferment in Malaysia, where he became acquainted first hand with American brutality in Southeast Asia. Another year he spent working at a rural community center while awaiting indictment. While in the United States he spent 14 days taking his case to the police before he was supposed to surrender under President Ford's program. He successfully debated former New York Senator Charles Goodell, now chairman of the Clemency Board, on live television in Washington, D.C. He also spoke at the annual convention of NCUUA held in Louisville, Kentucky.[58]

Individually, then, the exiles efforts to normalize their status outside of President Ford's clemency program and their efforts to personally or collectively call for its boycott in Canada and the United States succeeded in subverting the political intent of the program: to reduce the number of Vietnam War era dissidents before the presidential election of 1976. Both President Ford and Congress, convening in its 94th session in 1975/76, were forced to propose still further bills and programs to deal with American exiles. However, what the exiles regarded as the political success of the boycott and the failure of the clemency program must be tempered by the fact that their assimilation into Canadian life was part of the channeling system to reintegrate them into North American capitalism dominated by American multinational corporations.

The Politics of Clemency and the Channeling System

One of the things that particularly annoyed American exiles in Canada was the juxtaposition of unconditional amnesty for former President Nixon's alleged criminality and only limited clemency for their own moral position in opposition to the Vietnam War. In this instance, President Ford's politics of granting half a loaf to both the Right and the Left did not serve his goals of national reconciliation and putting an end to the Nixon and exile problems as potential political issues in the 1976 presidential race that he had sought to achieve.

Amnesty is usually granted by a state after a period of conflict to bring the rebels back into the fold. The crimes against the state are overlooked in the greater purpose of political and social harmony. The implicit recognition is made that the crimes were essentially political and since the state had demonstrated its political mastery of the field, it could best display its newly regained power by generous acts of mercy. Thus amnesty has traditionally been used as a means of strengthening the power and legitimacy of authority after a period of bitter internal conflict. Less than general amnesty might suggest that the state is not nearly as tranquil in the knowledge of its authority as its leaders would wish to believe. In this sense, President Ford might have demonstrated that although the United States could assimilate a disgraced former president, it was in fact not yet ready to digest the opposition of many of its youth during the Vietnam War era. Hence the necessity to insist on an oath of repatriation and limited alternative service to bend the exiles to the "correctness" of the position of the government in pursuing the Vietnam War. The dilemma was a fine one for President Ford, as his amnesty for Nixon for alleged Watergate crimes implied that the position of the United States government during much of the Vietnam War era, at least during former President Nixon's tenure of office, had been an illegal one.

American refugees in Canada perceived not only the injustice of limited clemency for the powerless and unconditional amnesty with a pension thrown in for the former president and the injustice of continued exile for 40,000 American dissidents but also assimilation for 150,000 South Vietnamese refugees into American society. They also perceived the implicit uncertainty of the state and its insecurity in its own position. No wonder, then, that the usual response of the vanquished in recognizing the potency of authority if not its legitimacy was lost by President Ford in their eyes. Hence the lukewarm response that his stand generated in the American exile community in Canada and the continued persistence of the "exile problem" as a major issue in the Presidential campaign of 1976, dragging with it the "Nixon probelm," and the "South Vietnamese resettlement problem."

In addition, President Ford's 1974/75 program of conditional clemency proved to continue the same channeling system that had directed American dissidents to Canada during the Vietnam War era. First of all, the clemency program distinguished between dodgers and deserters. Under the program of earned reentry a good deal more was required of the working-class deserter than his middle-class compatriot, the draft dodger. Most individuals processed by the Defense Department were given close to two years alternative service.[59] At the completion of alternative service the deserter could at the most expect to have his less-than-honorable discharge converted into a clemency discharge. Even if he took advantage of the so-called "deserter's loophole" and did not actually put in his alternative service, the deserter would continue to be marked with his less-than-honorable discharge although he would be freed from jail time. In both instances, the economic consequences of living in the United States with a less-than-honorable discharge would be severe: greater unwillingness of employers to hire a "bad risk" veteran in a time of increasing unemployment due to both inflation and recession. The dodger could eventually return to the work force in the United States after his earned reentry; the deserter could not. Just as he had been channeled from high school into the military, so too he would be channeled into long-term unemployment by President Ford's "clemency" program. Clearly, the clemency being offered was merely a fine technicality that did not speak to the real needs of the deserter.

Once this is realized, we see that it is less of a coincidence than it might first appear that President Ford chose the Selective Service System to supervise the alternative service of both dodgers and deserters under his program. This bureaucracy was at a low ebb after the draft had been ended and was merely registering youth for future drafts in future wars. Little wonder then that he called upon the main bureaucracy of channeling to enforce the terms of a clemency program that represented a continuation of channeling. As it turned out, the recession in 1975 was so severe, even Selective Service could not locate sufficient jobs for the few exiles who chose to take up President Ford's offer.

In addition, clemency as proposed by the Ford administration did not speak to the main bulk of American youth really in need of amnesty; roughly half a million men and women veterans of the war who already had received less-than-honorable discharges. These were the men and women who had fought the war and had not gone into exile. They faced the same economic hardships as their exiled compatriots, the deserters who had fled to Canada. They numbered more than ten times those in exile. Yet there was little concern in America to reintegrate into American life even these youths who had fought rather than fled the war. American refugees in Canada saw the need for unconditional amnesty as a way of supporting their comrades in the United States who had fought the war but had nevertheless been victimized by it. They saw that the channeling system had worked in such a way as to make it easier for the working-class youth to get into the Army, easier for him to be ordered to the front lines where it was easier for him to be wounded or killed. They noted that the proportion of minority Americans among this group was higher than would be expected from a fair representation of the population. If the clemency program did not speak to the needs of this group, why respond to it in a positive way?

Americans in exile in Canada supported the fight for amnesty in order to assert the legal and moral rectitude of their opposition to the war. Most did not feel that they were guilty of any crimes; Presidents Kennedy, Johnson, Nixon and Ford, along with their advisors and officials were the ones who needed amnesties for their crimes in Vietnam. The exiles would have appreciated amnesty as an attempt by the United States government to rectify its own misdeeds. They would use amnesty in order to visit with friends and relatives in the United States and to travel there. But unconditional amnesty would not dislodge the American refugee from his position in Canadian society, often as a landed immigrant and, more frequently, as the five-year period for residency was satisfied, as a new Canadian citizen. For American refugees in Canada had made a fresh start toward a new life in a country where there was no draft and where the Army was not engaged in adventures abroad.

Conclusion: The Struggle for Self-Determination and Canadian Independence

Emigration reveals much about individuals, their societies and their heritage. We think of the United States as a country that welcomes the poor immigrants of foreign lands, that accepts the "huddled masses yearning to breathe free." Yet it has been Canada that has taken in quite a number of the masses since World War II. From 1964 through 1965 a large proportion of

Canada's immigrants were young refugees from the United States seeking to escape involvement in the Vietnam War.

These young men were not merely the flotsam and jetsam of yet another adventure by an imperialist nation. They were of pioneer stock, young men and women who chose to seek freedom rather than suffer the indignities of participating in an illegal, immoral war. They spanned the full range of the political spectrum but they were characterized above all by a desire to seek personal freedom from the repression of the state. To some of them this was perfectly natural, as they came from middle- and upper-class homes where they had been taught that the system existed to serve them and not vice versa. They were indignant at being asked to risk their lives in a foolish act of aggression. Self-centered, perhaps, but nonetheless courageous enough to act on their principles and go into exile. Others were idealists who had fought against the Vietnam War in the United States but who eventually decided they could no longer struggle in the belly of the monster. They sought the quietude and open spaces north of the border. Many of them had entered the Army with patriotic fervor or with doubts. They trusted their own senses and experiences better than anything else and so they had to see and feel the Vietnam War first hand before they recoiled from the horrors they were perpetrating. They turned to drugs and alcohol, but eventually they turned to themselves and decided to get out. Again in their sense of personal survival they recognized that opposition to the repression of the state was the only way to make a break from it. In this regard they were political refugees, motivated by self-interest, certainly, but perceiving that self-interest in the framework of a common good, in collective resistance to tyranny. They were individualists who saw the necessity for collective action, in the support groups of veterans, exiles, dodgers, deserters, in the movements that opposed the Vietnam War. Collective vigilance in the pursuit of liberty. They had learned well the lessons of Jefferson and Madison and the other Founding Fathers. They acted on this knowledge and imposed exile upon themselves, migrating to Canada to join the descendants of the Tories of an earlier age.

However, the young American refugees recognized that their flight to Canada had given them but a temporary retreat from the domination of America's multinational corporations and had not removed them from the grip of its channeling system. They knew that the "escape hatch" allowing them to emigrate to Canada could be closed by the United States, if it chose to barricade the world's longest undefended border with guards and FBI agents.

The United States tolerated this immigration to Canada because apparent freedom for the refugee from militarism in Canada provided a safety valve for America by removing its dissenters from the mother country.

What confronted the exiles in Canada was the fact that the American channeling system itself was continued in Canada in the form of the Canadian Immigration Act. Certainly the refugees had assumed that employment with multinational corporations in Canada that were run by their American head-quarters would not be accessible to them. But they had not anticipated that the Canadian economy would function as a resource-based branch plant for these American-controlled multinational corporations. The Immigration Act sought to serve these economic forces in Canada. Thus, educated dodgers were easily landed while unskilled deserters were channeled underground until a bureaucratic adjustment in 1973, itself designed to prevent masses of working-class men and women around the world from descending on Canada, temporarily suspended the North American channeling system for the sake of controlling world labor flow to Canada. Even the assimilation of the exiled deserter into Canada required that someone more unfortunate be excluded.

The continental system of channeling had allowed these young exiles a safety valve in immigration to Canada. North American capitalism sought to harness the life energies even of these dissident youth. Once assimilated into the mainstream of Canadian life, the exile would be reintegrated into North American capitalism, as had been the intent of the channeling system. The dissident would be incorporated into the multinational corporations' search for expanding production and profits in a competitive world economy. But could he be successfully integrated after this odyssey to Canada or had the channeling system inadvertently created a more formidable opponent?

Perhaps the strongest note of irony that indeed bespeaks some hope for the future is that the same rebellious young men that the channeling system sought to resettle so securely in Canada may yet prove to be among the very dissidents that successfully challenge American capitalism and the continental channeling system.

America fought the war in Vietnam to consolidate its economic empire built up over the past 30 years, fueled by the exploitation of cheap natural resources and labor in the Third World.[60] Yet the net result of the Vietnam War and America's efforts to spread the cost of the war to other nations led to international inflation and the consolidation by the resource nations of the world into a stronger union. Witness the rise of the economic power of the

oil-producing OPEC nations in the post-Vietnam War era. This rise of resource-based Third World nations implied that the United States was witness-
ing the beginning of the break-up of its world economic empire, an empire
based on an expansive military economy maintained by the multinational
corporations throughout the cold war period.

In Canada, similar forces of opposition to the further growth of American
multinational corporations in North America were manifesting themselves
in a national resurgence for an independent Canada, free of its economic and
cultural dependency on the United States. In early 1975, External Affairs
Minister Allen MacEachen, formerly minister of immigration, set out in a
speech on Canada—United States relations the present direction of Canadian
official policy toward political independence. He stated that the government
policy was one of a "strengthening of the economy and other aspects of
national life in order to secure our independence." Some of the most ardent
supporters of that Canadian independence were the very same nationalistic,
displaced American refugees that had fled to Canada in the Vietnam War era.
Roger Costain, a draft dodger who moved to Canada from Minneapolis in
1965 put it this way:

I believe my future and Canada's are interwoven. Day by day I continue
to identify more and more with Canada. As I must cast off my American
habits and reaction so must Canada....I sincerely hope that Canada
will pay attention to the situation in the United States and learn from the
obvious mistakes. Not being burdened with foreign and domestic problems
of the magnitude of the United States, we in Canada are in a position to
inaugurate a great social experiment.[61]

The very process of immigrating to another country had given these young
men a "critical detachment" that allowed them to perceive the effects of the
continental channeling system on their lives. According to Charles Campbell,
an American refugee living in Toronto: "As new Canadians who have gone
through the American experience, we are perhaps in a unique position to
comprehend the positive aspects of Canadian culture and to helpfully join the
new Canadian nationalist movement in affirming them."[62]

Similar sentiments were expressed by Rick Bebout, a former American
who moved to Toronto in 1969 but who was not involved with the politically
active exile community there.

I am not primarily an American exile from my point of view. I am a potential Canadian. I don't care about an amnesty, at least for my sake, because I came here with the intention of staying....There is a healthy form

of nationalism. It does not foster aggression or xenophobia, but it does make one aware of the occasional advantages of political separation. . . .Recent history has made the advantages of separation from the United States quite plain. . . .If Canada is not to become the fifty-first state (or the number one colony in every sense) then Canadians must regain control of their own destiny. . . .In Canadian politics and economic planning, therefore, a reasonable nationalism is a healthy and positive element.

A new sense of confidence is growing in this country, especially now that it is seen by itself and much of the world as the North American alternative to the many visible mistakes of America. . . .It is time to be confidently, openly, and humanly Canadian.[63]

Dee Knight summed up the position of the politically aware American exile in striving to:

> preserve Canada as an entity outside of the American empire and with the minimum of social justice; in which local, regional and national groups can manage their own lives and determine their own future. Furthermore, if we are to say in any seriousness that our flight here was based on opposition to the American military-industrial monster, we must acknowledge that the struggle for independence and socialism in Canada is the local fight against the same enemy.[64]

Thus, as the United States celebrated its 200th anniversary of the founding of the Republic in the wake of a severe military defeat abroad, America's multinational corporations were striving to maintain their control of the channeling system that regulated the economic and social lives of much of the population thoughout Nort America. Yet the call for an independent Canada both by Canadians and American refugees from militarism signified what could become the beginnings of serious opposition to that continental system in the decade approaching 1984.

NOTES

1.   Conrad, *Los Angeles Times*, September 1974, as cited in *AMEX* 5, (November—December 1974).
2.   The American government estimated that there were 3,000 Selective Service Act violators living in Canada and 2,100 deserters from the Armed Forces believed to be in foreign areas at the end of 1973. "Conditional Amnesty For Vietnam War Draft Evaders," *Congressional Digest,* October 1974, pp. 230—31. This is clearly at variance with our figure of 40,000 American exiles in Canada, both dodgers and deserters based on actual

and estimated data from Canadian immigration statistics discussed in chapter 4.

3.   *AMEX* 4 (July—August 1973):1
4.   Ibid., pp. 12, 21.
5.   John M. Swomley, Jr., "Memo to Nixon: Why Not an Amnesty?" originally printed in the *National Catholic Reporter,* January 1, 1969, and revised for Murray Polner, ed., *When Can I Come Home?* (Garden City, N.Y.: Doubleday-Anchor Original, 1972), pp. 131—41.
6.   Arlie Schardt, William Rusher, Mark Hatfield, *Amnesty? The Unsettled Question of Vietnam* (Croton-on-Hudson, N.Y.: Sun River Press, 1973), pp. 7, 8.
7.   Ibid.
8.   *Amnesty Hearings,* Subcommittee on Courts, Civil Liberties and the Administration of Justice, Committee on the Judiciary, 93rd Congress (Washington, D.C.: U.S. Government Printing Office, 1974). Testimony by Hon. Bella Abzug, a Representative in Congress, State of New York.
9..   Congressional Research Service, "Amnesty: A Brief Historical Overview," John Etridge, David Lockwood, Donald Alderson. Library of Congress, September 27, 1974. Also consult articles reprinted in *Amnesty Hearings.*
10.   *Amnesty Hearings,* testimony by Americans for Democratic Action, Joseph L. Rauh, Jr.
11.   John M. Swomley, Jr., in *When Can I Come Home?,* p. 131.
12.   *Amnesty Hearings,* testimony from Hon. Bella Abzug, a Representative in Congress, State of New York.
13.   Congressional Research Service, "Amnesty," p. 15.
14.   "Congressman Edward I. Koch Reports from Washington," *A Trip to Canada* 1 (February 1970).
15.   Ibid.
16.   Bill H.R. 831 and 832, *Congressional Record,* House of Representatives, March 1971.
17.   Kennedy Hearings on Amnesty, 1972 Senate Subcommittee on Administrative Practice and Procedure, Committee of the Judiciary.
18.   *Congressional Digest,* "Conditional Amnesty," p. 233.
19.   *AMEX* 2 (August—September 1970).
20.   Ibid.
21.   Pamphlets from Clergy and Laymen Concerned about Vietnam and from the Fellowship of Reconciliation Action, 1970.
22.   Press Release of Exiles, Canadian Coalition of U.S. War Resisters, Toronto, January 1972.
23.   Ibid.

24. *Amnesty Hearings,* 93rd Congress, 1974, pp. 345–380, 593–616.
25. *Amnesty Hearings,* pp. 594–604. Testimony of Hon. Bella Abzug, Representative from New York. H.R. 236 and H.R. 5191, pp. 2, 12. Testimony of Hon. Ronald Dellums, Representative from California, pp. 559–61, H.R. 3100, p. 8.
26. *Amnesty Hearings,* pp. 267–379, testimony by F.P. Jones, Director, National Security and Foreign Affairs, Veterans of the Foreign Wars of the United States.
27. *Amnesty Hearings.*
28. *Amnesty Hearings,* pp. 380–84. Churches of Christ Policy Statement on the Indochina War: "Healing the Divisions in the Nation," adopted by Board, December 2, 1972.
29. *Amnesty Hearings,* p. 43. American Civil Liberties Union, Policy Resolution of the Board of Directors, February 20, 1973, statement of Henry Schwarzschild.
30. *AMEX* 14 (March–April 1973): 46.
31. Jean Paul Sartre, open letter to the American press, reprinted in *AMEX* 14, no. 1: 51.
32. *AMEX* 14 (March–April 1973):45.
33. Original copy of Unity Statement adopted by Coalition of American War Resisters in Canada, Vancouver, B.C., December 13, 1973.
34. National Council for Universal Unconditional Amnesty (NCUUA) pamphlet, 1974.
35. *Amnesty Update,* issue no. 1, April 1974.
36. *AMEX* 4 (July–August, 1973): 30–33.
37. *AMEX* 5 (November–December 1974):32. These men disproportionately held the dishonorable discharges. Department of Army statistics reveal that in 1972, 17 percent of the Army were black and 32.6 percent of the dishonorable discharges were given to blacks; 20.7 percent of the bad conduct discharges; 19 percent of the undesirable discharges; and only 11.8 percent of honorable discharges.
38. Letter to editor, *Saturday Night,* December 1968.
39. *AMEX* 4, no. 6: 43.
40. *Vancouver Sun,* September 5, 1974.
41. Dave Smith, "Exiles' Story: Not Many Care About Amnesty," *Los Angeles Times,* March 4, 1973.
42. Ibid.
43. A Proclamation by the President of the United States, September 16, 1974, Washington, D.C.: United States Information Service. United States Embassy, Ottawa and American Civil Liberties Union, October 18, 1974, "The Clemency Program."

Amnesty And Exile

44.   *New York Times,* January 20, 1975.

45.   *New York Times,* December 22, 1974.

46.   John Liss, Earned Re-Entry and Canadian Status: Some Legal Advice," *AMEX* 5 (November—December, 1974): 118; and *New York Times,* February 18, 1975, p. 34.

47.   "The Clemency Program," American Civil Liberties Union, October 18, 1974.

48.   *New York Times,* December 22, 1974.

49.   "The Clemency Program," American Civil Liberties Union, October 18, 1974.

50.   *Los Angeles Times* article by Gerry Condon, reprinted in *Vancouver Sun,* September 28, 1974.

51.   *Toronto Globe and Mail,* August 20, 1974.

52.   Ibid.

53.   *New York Times,* January 7, 1974, and NCUUA *Amnesty Update,* April 1975.

54.   *Vancouver Sun,* January 22, 1975. The Selective Service System had problems finding enough alternative service jobs even for the small number of men who wanted them. See *New York Post,* November 25, 1975, and *New York Times,* September 28, 1974.

55.   Ibid.

56.   Ibid.

57.   *San Francisco Chronicle,* September 30, 1974.

58.   *The Courier-Journal and Times,* Louisville, Kentucky, November 17, 1974.

59.   *New York Times,* December 22, 1974.

60.   Noam Chomsky, *At War With Asia;* Gabriel Kolko, *The Roots of American Foreign Policy* (Boston, Mass.: Beacon Press, 1969), pp. 88—132.

61.   Jim Christy, ed., *The New Refugees: American Voices in Canada* (Toronto: Peter Martin Associates, 1972), p. 124.

62.   Ibid., p. 135.

63.   Ibid., p. 115.

64.   Ibid., pp. 133—34.

Appendices

APPENDIX A

QUESTIONNAIRE

Part I. *Background Questions*

1. Your age   Current marital status
2. How many people are in your family (immediate)?
3. Who do you live with in Canada? (give relationship only)
4. How long have you been in Canada?
5. Your hometown?   Where you lived before coming here?
6. Your occupation? Check one   Your parents' occupation?

Creative or artistic endeavor	Creative or artistic work
Student	Teacher
Farmer	Skilled tradesman
Skilled tradesman	Professional
Professional	Managerial, administrative
Semiskilled	Small business
Unskilled	Semiskilled
Unemployed temporarily (unemployment insurance)	
Unemployed, on welfare	Unemployed, on welfare
Other	Retired

7. What is the highest grade of school you have completed?
    Your parents' highest grade completed?
    Are you interested in more education?
8. Your nationality?   Ethnic background?

U.S. citizen	Anglo-Saxon
Canadian	Eastern European
U.S. alien	Italian
Other	Irish
	German
	Negro
	Asian
	Indian
	Latin
	Other

9. Your political orientation (such as radical, conservative, liberal, or other descriptive terms). Your parents' political orientation.

10. Your group affiliations
     Your parents'
11. Your religious affiliation   Your parents'
     Is religion important to your life?
12.* Your style of life:

Student	Easygoing
Traveling, moving	Up-tight
Middle-class	Straight
Lower-class	Hip (freaky)
	Other

Your parents' style of life:

Upper-class	Uptight
Traveling	Straight
Settled middle-class	Similar to mine
Lower-class	Different from mine
	Other

A. (Only fill out if you were in the Armed Forces)

1. Have your family members served in or been employed by the military?
      If yes, what is their relationship to you?
2. Were you ever in the ROTC?   Did you join to get a good
    position in the military?
3. Were you drafted, or did you enlist?   How old were you?
4. What was your rank?   Which service?
5. What were your work duties?
6. How did you find this training?

7. How many times have you been AWOL?   Why?

8. Generally, how do you feel you were treated in the military?

9. Have you spent time in a military stockade?   When?
    Alleged reason
10. Were you ever involved in antiwar or protest activities in the military?
      Briefly describe

*   These categories were derived from an open-ended question in earlier
     drafts.

11.   How long were you in the military before you decided to leave?
       How long were you AWOL in the U.S. before you came to Canada?
       Did you go underground?   What precautions if any did you take?

12.   Have your views toward the military changed since you first entered?
       What do you think is mainly responsible for this change (e.g., personal
       experiences, friends who influenced you, media information, etc.)?

       B. (Only fill out if the draft was a factor in your coming to Canada)
1.   What was your draft status when you came to Canada?
2.   What changes did you expect in your status?
3.   Have you had any correspondence with your draft board since leaving
       the country?
4.   Were you active in any antiwar or movement activities (e.g., civil
       rights, Vista, Peace Corps)?   Describe

5.   Have you been classified "delinquent" by your draft board as a re-
       sult of your activities?
6.   Have you ever initiated any law suits challenging draft laws?

7.   Have you ever been indicted on a draft violation charge?
8.   a. Have you renounced your U.S. citizenship?
       b. Have you ever considered renouncing your U.S. citizenship?

       Cite reason

Part II. *Coming to Canada*

1.   Was coming to Canada the only plan you considered?
2.   What alternatives, if any, to the draft/military did you consider?
       Check off all those items that apply to you.
              Resisting by going to jail
              Filling out an application for Conscientious Objector's status
              Active resistance activities in home community and/or military
              Leaving country and becoming an exile
              Others
3.   If there was a crucial event(s) before you left the country, briefly de-
       scribe it (such as seeking sanctuary, parental problems, etc.).

4.   What was your primary reason for coming to Canada?
          Moral opposition to all wars
          Opposition to the Vietnam war
          Opposition to the draft
          Opposition to U.S. imperialist system
          Specific order to report to Vietnam
          Treatment in the military
          Personal reasons (cite)

5.   Did you know anyone personally who had come to Canada as a war
      objector?   Was this person influential in your decision?
      Relationship to you

6.   In making your final decision to leave the country, which persons
      did you consult (such as wife, minister, etc.)?

7.   Did you correspond with an individual or Canadian support group
      before coming to Canada?   Which group?

8.   Think back to all the people you asked for information on immigrating
      and becoming landed in Canada. Without mentioning names, describe
      each person by their relationship to you, and what help each one gave
      you (such as sending you to another, addresses given, transportation,
      etc.).
      Relationship   Help or advice given

9.   Did you come to Canada by yourself, or were you with others?
      Relationship of others

10.   Did you make use of underground contacts in coming to Canada?
          Which contacts were the most helpful?

11.   How difficult was it for you to make the decision to leave the country
      and come to Canada?
          Most difficult thing I ever had to face
          Ranks among some of my difficult decisions
          Moderately difficult
          Not too difficult
          Relatively easy

12.   Did you receive counseling from the Vancouver Committee or other

Canadian groups to aid American exiles?   Were they helpful?

DO NOT USE NAMES TO ANSWER THE QUESTIONS (13–16), USE RELATIONSHIPS

13. Which significant persons have actively supported you?
    Initially supportive people
    Those I later won over
14. Which significant persons have opposed you?
15. Which significant persons have no knowledge that you are in Canada?
16. With whom do you maintain correspondence?
17. How do you consider yourself? Check all the items that fit.

Deserter	Draft dodger	Radical
AWOL soldier	Political resister	U.S. exile
War objector	Pacifist	U.S. expatriate
Other	None of these	New Canadian

18. Has your view of yourself changed since you came to Canada?
    If you answered "yes," please explain how

19. How do you feel about leaving the U.S. and coming to Canada?
    Best thing I ever did
    I'm glad I did it in retrospect
    Badly at first, but good now that I'm here
    I'm not sure; uncertain as to how it will turn out
    Negatively. I plan to return to the U.S.
20. How did other Americans refer to you in describing your actions (such as courts, friends, acquaintances, etc.)?
    Label(s) Used   Party Using Label

21. How much were you affected by what others thought of your actions?
    Very much affected
    Somewhat influenced
    Little influenced
    Ignored others opinions
22. What are your feelings regarding committing an act constituting a felony in the U.S.?
23. What were the immediate effects of leaving on your personal life?

24. Has coming to Canada altered your life goals or career goals?
Explain how

25. Do you feel that since you left the military/draft and came to Canada you have more control over your life?   Explain how

Part III. *Starting a New Life in Canada*

1. Are you in contact with other Americans who came to Canada because of the draft or military?   How many of your friends are Americans?   How many are Canadians?

2. a. Have you applied for landed immigrant status?
   Were you rejected?
   b. Are you a landed immigrant now?
   c. Where were you landed (at border, inside country)?
   d. Did you encounter any problems in this regard?

3. How have you supported yourself in Canada?
   By living in one of the hostels   How long?
   Money from family in U.S.
   Money from friends in U.S. or elsewhere
   Job in Canada
   Friend's or relative's job
   Other   Explain

4. Are you presently working?   Did you find it difficult to obtain work?

5. How did you find out about your job?

6. What type of work are you doing?
   Is it similar to what you were doing before coming here?
   Is it higher or lower status of work?
   Explain

7. What kinds of problems have you encountered looking for a job?

8. Have you helped other Americans in any way?
   Volunteer counseling or advice
   Housing other Americans, donating food to hostels
   Financial aid to Committee to Aid American Objectors
   To obtain jobs or job offers
   Other

9. What kind of hassles have you encountered since you've been in Can-

ada? Briefly explain

10. Have you had any encounters with the FBI?   RCMP?
    How often?   What was the nature of them?

11. Have the FBI or military personnel made any threats against your
    family?   Briefly describe

12. In your job hunting, did you usually mention your draft/military
    status?   Why or why not?
13. Did the employers you met ask you whether or not you were an
    American draft dodger or deserter?
14. How would you describe most Canadians' reaction when they find out
    you are an American dodger or deserter?

15. To which Canadians have you mentioned your draft/military status?
    (No names)   Relationship to you
16. When does your draft/military status seem to be an important consider-
    ation in an assessment of you?
                When I first crossed the border to Canada
                When I cross the border to the U.S.
                When seeking Canadian employment
                When seeking employment from an American subsidiary in Canada
                When I got landed
                When I got busted by the police
                In social situations of mixed company (Canadians and Americans)
17. Would you like to see amnesty granted for American exiles?
18. Would you consider returning to the States if amnesty were granted?
    Only for a visit(s)   Permanently to live
19. Do you feel pessimistic or optimistic about the future of the U.S.A.?
20. Do you feel pessimistic or optimistic about your own future?
21. Do you look more towards the U.S., Canada, or other countries in
    terms of your future life and plans?
22. What are your expectations regarding your life in Canada?

23. What are your plans for the immediate future?

24. From your experiences thus far, what do you like about Canada and

Canadians?

25. What do you dislike about Canada and Canadians?

26. Have you ever considered returning to the U.S. and turning yourself in?   What is mainly responsible for preventing you?

27. Have you returned to the U.S. since you've come to Canada?
     What was the purpose of your visit?
     How did you identify yourself at the border?
     Did you encounter any difficulties?   Explain

28. Do you have intentions of applying for Canadian citizenship?

29. What leisure time activities do you enjoy?

30. What people do you admire?

31. To your knowledge has any discrimination occurred due to your military or draft status to the following persons:
          My parents
          My relatives
          My friends
          My associates
          Others
     By whom?
     Explain the nature of this discrimination.

32. Have you ever been convicted of any criminal action(s) in the United States or Canada?
     If so, describe

33. Have you traveled through other parts of Canada?
     Which provinces?
     Which provinces do you prefer? Explain why.

     Do you plan to travel in other parts of Canada and other countries?
     Any additional comments will be welcome!

APPENDIX A (Continued)
VANCOUVER COMMITTEE QUESTIONNAIRE

Name:
Age:
City of residence (U.S.):
Note: The answers to all of the following questions are necessary in order to
help you get landed immigrant status. Your replies will be held in confidence.

1.   Have you ever applied for landed immigrant status before?
      If so, what was the result of your application and the date?
2.   Do you have a visitors pass?
      If so, until what date can you stay in Canada?
      At what border station did you enter?
      What means of transportation did you use?
      On what day and at what hour did you cross the border?
3.   Have you written to us?
4.   Do you plan to immigrate now or at some future date?
5.   What is your draft status?
      What changes do you expect in your status and when do you expect
      the changes to come?
      If you have an induction notice, give the date you are expected to
      report.
      If you are in the military, what service were you in and how long have
      you been gone?
6.   List all the jobs you have held (starting with present job), giving ap-
      proximate length of time you held each. Check those jobs which you
      think required skill or any time to learn to do.
7.   Have there been any time periods when you weren't working or going
      to school?
      If so, give approximate dates.
8.   Do you have a high school degree?
      If not, how much high school did you complete?
      Do you have a college degree?
      If not, how many years of college have you had?
      What was your major in college?
      Have you had any vocational training either in high school, vocational
      school, or as an apprentice? (Name kind of training and length of time
      you studied.)

9. Have you ever studied French?
   If so, give length of time you studied it.
10. Do you think you (or your wife) might fall into a prohibited class as considered by the Immigration Act?
11. Have you ever been convicted of anything?
   If so, name offense, date of conviction, and length of sentence.
12. Do you have any relatives in Canada?
13. Do you have any friends in Canada?
   If so, where do they live?
14. Are you married?
   Divorced?
   Separated?
15. Are you a U.S. citizen?
   If not, do you have permanent resident status in the U.S.?
16. Do you have with you in Canada
   a blank application for landed immigrant status?
   a birth certificate or passport?
   two passport-sized photos of yourself (and wife)?
   school transcripts?
   diploma or degree?
   court records (if applicable)?
   marriage licence?
   proof of any financial assets you left behind?
   employment credentials?
   money? How much do you have; or have access to?
17. Do you have a car?
18. How do your parents feel about your decision to come to Canada?
19. Would you approve of someone visiting your parents?

TABLE 1

EFFECT OF OTHER PEOPLE'S THOUGHTS UPON REFUGEES' DECISION TO LEAVE THE COUNTRY

	Draft Dodgers		Deserters	
	No.	%	No.	%
Very much affected	14	24	23	39
Little influenced	45	76	36	61
Total	59	100	59	100

TABLE 2
REFUGEES' TIME IN CANADA

	Draft Dodgers		Deserters	
	No.	%	No.	%
Few Weeks—11½ mos.	25	41	49	79
1—3 Years	36	59	13	21
Total	61	100	62	100

TABLE 3

AGE OF AMERICAN REFUGEES

	My Questionnaire				Vancouver Committee			
Years	Draft Dodgers		Deserters		Draft Dodgers		Deserters	
	No.	%	No.	%	No.	%	No.	%
17-18	0	0	6	10	34	11	13	12
19-20	1	2	12	19	93	30	37	34
21-23	25	41	33	53	115	37	39	35
24-26	27	44	11	18	53	17	19	17
27+	6	10	0	0	18	5	2	2
N/A	2	3	0	0				
Total	61	100	62	100	313	100	110	100

TABLE 4

EDUCATIONAL LEVEL OF PARENTS OF REFUGEES*

	Draft Dodgers		Deserters	
	No.	%	No.	%
High school dropouts	0	0	10	28
High school graduates	18	38	12	33
1—3 years college	7	15	4	11
BA, BS, professional	22	47	10	28
Total	47	100	36	100

*In families where the parents had different educational levels, I used the highest level attained by either one of them.

TABLE 5

OCCUPATIONAL LEVEL OF PARENTS OF REFUGEES

	Draft Dodgers No.	Draft Dodgers %	Deserters No.	Deserters %
Unskilled, unemployed	3	6	10	20
Semiskilled, small business	14	29	13	27
Skilled tradesman	2	4	8	16
Professional, managerial	29	61	18	37
Total	48	100	49	100

TABLE 6

REFUGEES' EDUCATIONAL LEVEL

	My Questionnaire Draft Dodgers No.	%	Deserters No.	%	Vancouver Committee Sample Draft Dodgers No.	%	Deserters No.	%
High school dropout	0	0	12	20	28	10	25	22
High school graduate	6	10	18	29	50	18	50	45
1–3 years college	16	26	25	41	126	45	27	24
BA, BS	24	39	5	8	72	25	10	9
MA, professional degree	15	25	1	2	6	2	0	0
Total	61	100	61	100	282	100	112	100

TABLE 7

REFUGEES' OCCUPATIONAL LEVEL

| | My Questionnaire | | | | Vancouver Committee Sample* | | | |
| | Draft Dodgers | | Deserters | | Draft Dodgers | | Deserters | |
	No.	%	No.	%	No.	%	No.	%
Unskilled, semiskilled	3	5	29	48	71	25	74	66
Skilled tradesmen	16	26	16	26	22	8	11	10
Professional	20	33	5	8	27	9	0	0
Students	22	36	11	18	168	58	26	24
Total	61	100	61	100	288	100	111	100

* The Vancouver Committee sample does not include those men above draftable age, veterans and women.

TABLE 8

REFUGEES' USE OF UNDERGROUND CONTACTS

| | Draft Dodger | | Deserters | |
	No.	%	No.	%
No underground contacts	51	85	38	61
Yes underground contacts	9	15	24	39
Total	60	100	62	100

TABLE 9

POLITICAL ORIENTATION OF DRAFT DODGERS

	Number of Earlier Dodgers (1966-67)	%	Number of Later Dodgers (1968-70)	%
Radical activists	26	72	9	36
Not Radical, inactive	10	28	16	64
Total	36	100	25	100

TABLE 10

RENUNCIATION OF CITIZENSHIP
BY AMERICAN DRAFT DODGERS (1965-70)

Time of Residence in Canada	Did not Renounce		Renounced		Considered Renouncing	
	No.	%	No.	%	No.	%
Less than 1 Year	9	41	0	0	13	52
1 to 2 Years	10	45	3	38	8	32
Over 2 Years	3	14	5	62	4	16
Total	22	100	8	100	25	100

TABLE 11

TYPE OF MILITARY SERVICE

	My Sample		Vancouver Committee	
	No.	%	No.	%
Army	45	75	63	57
Marines	6	10	20	18
Navy	4	7	18	16
Air Force	3	5	1	1
Reserves & National Guard	2	3	9	8
Total	60	100	111	100

TABLE 12

MILITARY RANK OF DESERTERS

	No.	%
Private	51	85
Noncommissioned officer	6	10
Commissioned officer	3	5
Total	60	100

TABLE 13

LENGTH OF TIME DESERTERS
SPENT IN THE MILITARY

	No.	%
1–3 months	12	20
4–11 months	24	40
1–3 years	25	40
Total	61	100

TABLE 14

LENGTH OF TIME DESERTERS SPENT IN THE MILITARY:
DRAFTEES VS. ENLISTEES

	Draftees		Enlistees	
	No.	%	No.	%
Short time (1–11 months)	16	94	20	46
Long time (1–3 years)	1	6	24	54
Total	17	100	44	100

TABLE 15

NUMBER OF AWOL ATTEMPTS BEFORE DESERTION

	No.	%
None	28	47
One	20	33
Two or more	12	20
Total	60	100

TABLE 16

AMOUNT OF MONEY BROUGHT TO CANADA BY REFUGEES

	Dodgers		Deserters	
	No.	%	No.	%
None	20	10	43	87
$50 or less	21	11	17	3
$100–200	62	32	28	5
$300–500	41	21	13	3
over $500	45	23	7	2
over $5,000	5	3	0	0
Total	194	100	108	100

TABLE 17

LANDED IMMIGRANT STATUS IN CANADA

	Draft Dodgers		Deserters	
	No.	%	No.	%
Landed status	50	82	29	47
Not landed	10	16	28	45
No response	1	2	5	8
Total	61	100	62	100

TABLE 18

AMERICAN REFUGEES' OCCUPATIONS IN CANADA

	Draft Dodgers		Deserters	
	No.	%	No.	%
Professional	20	33	5	8
Skilled tradesman	3	5	6	10
Semiskilled	3	5	14	23
Unskilled	0	0	16	26
Creative	13	11	10	16
Student	22	36	11	17
Total	61	100	62	100

TABLE 19
UNEMPLOYMENT RATE AMONG DESERTERS

| | Landed status | | Not Landed | | Overall Rate |
	No.	%	No.	%	
Unemployed	11	39	22	81	60%
Employed	17	61	5	19	40%
Total	28	100	27	100	

TABLE 20
UNEMPLOYMENT RATE AMONG DRAFT DODGERS

| | Landed status | | Not Landed | | Overall Rate |
	No.	%	No.	%	
Unemployed	6	13	6	60	37%
Employed	43	87	4	40	63%
Total	49	100	10	100	

TABLE 21
AMERICAN REFUGEES WHO RECEIVED VISITS FROM RCMP

Time in Canada	Draft Dodgers		Deserters	
	No.	%	No.	%
Later Refugees (1968—1970)	6	30	20	87
Earlier Refugees (1966—1967)	14	70	3	13
Total	20	100	23	100

APPENDIX C

American Immigration to Canada During the Vietnam War Era

Year	Number Admitted from U.S.* (Landed Status)	Total Number Admitted from Foreign Countries* (Landed Status)	Percent Admitted from U.S.**	Draft-Age Males (15–24) from U.S.△ (Landed Status)	Dodgers and Deserters from U.S. (estimated)△△ (Landed Status)
1960	11,247	104,111	10.8	1231	0
1961	11,516	71,689	16.1	1261	0
1962	11,643	71,586	15.6	1223	0
1963	11,736	93,151	12.6	1244	0
1964	12,565	112,606	11.2	1373	133
1965	15,143	146,758	10.3	1922	682
1966	17,514	194,743	8.99	2447	1207
1967	19,038	222,876	8.54	3032	1792
1968	20,422	183,974	11.1	4076	2836
1969	22,785	161,531	14.1	4405	3165
1970	24,424	147,713	16.5	5510	4270
1971	24,366	121,900	20.0	4778	3538
1972	22,618	122,006	18.5	3980	2740
1973	25,242	184,200	13.7	(6000,+est.)	4760++
1974	29,543	228,713	12.9	(3000,est.)	1760
1975	—	—	—	(1200,est.)	0
Total					
1965–1972	166,310	1,301,501	12.8	30,150	20,230
1965–1974	221,095	1,530,204	14.4	40,350	26,750

APPENDIX C (Continued)

*Freda Hawkins, p. 42, Table 4. From Immigration Statistics, Departments of Citizenship and Immigration and Manpower and Immigration.

**Calculated as follows:

$$\frac{\text{\# Admitted from U.S.}}{\text{Total \# Admitted from Foreign Countries}} \times 100 = \% \text{ Admitted from U.S.}$$

△ *Canadian Immigration Statistics*, 1960–1975, Queen's Printer, Ottawa.

△△ Draft-age males from U.S. minus 1240, the average number of draft-age Americans emigrating to Canada in pre-Vietnam War era during 1960–63 equals estimated number of exiles from U.S. in each year of the Vietnam War era.

+3,000 (estimated) due to 1973 Adjustment of Status Program and 3,000 (estimated) due to additional immigration.

++3,000 minus 1240 equals 1,760 + 3,000 (Adjustment) = 4,760

Index

Index